THE POWER OF LIVING BY DESIGN

TOM WARD

with

Paul Gustavson

and

Ed Foreman

Catherine
Really enjoy life. . .
. . . Living By Design!
Tom Ward

First Edition –May 2013

ISBN
978-1-4602-0832-8 (Hardcover)
978-1-4602-0830-4 (Paperback)
978-1-4602-0831-1 (eBook)

Limit of Liability/Disclaimer of Warranty: While the publisher and author have used their best efforts in preparing this book, they make no representations or warranties with respect to the accuracy or completeness of the contents of this book and specifically disclaim any implied warranties or fitness for a particular purpose. The advise and strategies contained herein may not be suitable for your situation. It is not the intention of the author to slight or offend any individuals, groups, or organizations by reference or implication. You should consult with a professional where appropriate. The reader should consult qualified professionals in holistic health care regarding individual conditions. Neither the publisher nor author shall be liable for any loss of profit or any other damages, including but not limited to special, incidental, consequential, or other damages.

Book cover photography image is from www.JohnHarveyPhoto.com.

Produced by:

FriesenPress
Suite 300 – 852 Fort Street
Victoria, BC, Canada V8W 1H8

www.friesenpress.com

Distributed to the trade by The Ingram Book Company

TABLE OF CONTENTS

Dedication vii
Preface ix
Introduction xiv

Part I 1
Chapter One
How do You Define "Successful Life?" 2
Chapter Two
Connect with Your Dreams 13
Chapter Three
Style and Character: The Way You Get There 25
Chapter Four
Those Nasty Old External Influencers 43
Chapter Five
Choices: You are Empowered 48
Chapter Six
Your Personal Mission Statement 55
Chapter Seven
Your Personal Guiding Principles 64
Chapter Eight
Strategies to Influence the Influencers 71
Chapter Nine
Your Personal Chief Aims and Goals 79
Chapter Ten
Your Personal Dream Mechanisms 87
Chapter Eleven
Your Personal Organization Processes 93
Chapter Twelve
Decision Making and Informating Processes 101

Chapter Thirteen
Your Personal Relationship Processes 110
Chapter Fourteen
Recognition Systems for You and Others 126
Chapter Fifteen
Your Personal Development Processes 132
Chapter Sixteen
Additional Tools and Thoughts 150
Invictus 161

Part II 163
Chapter Seventeen
A Design and Implementation Approach 164
Recommended References 209
Special Thanks 212
Appendix 215
About Tom Ward 218
About Paul Gustavson 220
About Ed Foreman 222
Notes 224

Dedication

THIS BOOK IS DEDICATED TO my wife, Emily, and daughters, Erin and Meg, who have traveled life's journey with me: the good, the bad, and the great, while I learned the importance of these lessons. It is also dedicated to my two mentors, Ed Foreman and Paul Gustavson, who openly and unselfishly shared their knowledge and insights with me. They encouraged me and helped me help others.

Preface

OVER MY THIRTY-FIVE YEAR CAREER in manufacturing and operations, I was blessed to attend dozens of terrific development seminars and classes. Reflecting over those thirty-five years, there were two seminars I attended that impacted my thinking more than all the rest put together.

The first of those impactful courses was *The Successful Life Course* from Executive Development Systems. I attended the course in 1985. The creator and leader of the seminar is Ed Foreman. Ed, in addition to being a very successful business leader and lecturer, is the only individual in the past one hundred years to be elected to the U.S. Congress from two different states. The *Successful Life Course* taught how to have a terrific day, every day, starting one day at a time. The course included classic lessons in goal setting, health maintenance, image projection, meeting management, and relationship development. Unlike many courses or seminars that promote the latest trend in business or personal development, *The Successful Life Course* taught time-proven principles of personal success. The principles held true for me when I learned them, and still hold true today. Over the years following my exposure to *The Successful Life Course*, I continued to remember many of the key concepts of the course and taught many of the principles over the final twenty-five years of my corporate career. I cannot say that about any other course I have ever attended.

In addition, I had the tremendous pleasure to meet and be exposed to Ed and his principles three times over the first two years after I attended *The Successful Life Course*. I'm sure repetition and frequency, coupled with listening to his cassette tapes dozens and dozens and dozens of times, locked in many of the lessons I gained from Ed and later taught my managers. Twenty-three years later, I was blessed to cross Ed's path again. Ed was still the same: energetic, enthusiastic, and loving life as he again shared his messages of success to an audience of fifteen hundred people that weekend. After I reintroduced myself to Ed, he asked me, "What's the best thing that has happened to you over the twenty-five years since you first attended *The Successful Life Course*?" My response didn't take me but a second to consider. Even though there were many personal successes I could have shared, like achieving my chief aim of being a plant manager by age thirty five, or being debt-free, or having paid cash for our "retirement" home in Tennessee, or even helping our children graduate from college debt-free. Instead, I told Ed the best thing was "being able to share many of the lessons I learned from *The Successful Life Course* with the people who worked for me." I really didn't know how important that statement would later become to me.

The second course with lasting impact that stands out in my career is *Organizational Systems Design,* created and led by Paul Gustavson. Paul is the owner and principle of *Organization Planning & Design Inc.*, a boutique consulting group located in San Jose, California. Paul is simply an amazing individual. Paul donates about twenty-five percent of his time to worthy organizations, communities, his college (Brigham Young University), and his church. I don't know any other individual who is so giving. Paul has recently co-authored a book entitled, Running into the Wind, Bronco Mendenhall—5 Strategies for Building a Successful Team, which describes the strategies and principles Paul shared with Brigham Young's head football coach Bronco Mendenhall as he took over the position. Paul teaches that "Organizations are perfectly designed to get the results that they get," and he helped develop and popularize a framework called the Organization Systems Design Model (OSD). OSD helps businesses separate the choices they have in order to achieve the objectives and the culture they desire. It is this model that made a huge impact on me and on my career.

I met Paul in 1996 in Philadelphia. Paul was teaching his course on Organization Systems Design to ten of my managers and ten managers from another company. When I first met Paul and saw his OSD Model, there was an immediate connection to both Paul and the model. We discussed the elements of the model that evening and I've used and referenced his model in business ever since. My career took me to three other companies. I invited Paul to consult with my teams and me at all of these companies. Both Paul and the OSD model helped me lead one of those companies through a massive reorganization. Paul spent every other week for six months with a special, in-house redesign team as he taught and led them through the principles and analyses of Organization Systems Design. The redesign was a huge success within my organization. The new design created a powerful culture of success that generated great results. My operations team became much better aligned with the rest of the organization, and individuals throughout the team grew in knowledge, position, and influence across the larger organization. Sixteen years later, the redesign concepts for the organization are still intact as designed and originally implemented. The redesign has also become the organizational template for all other functions across that business.

Like *The Successful Life Course*, the Organization Systems Design Model became a major tool for me to share with and teach to my managers at all of the other organizations I later served. (The model became a reference for me as I led change in several organizations.) Additionally, Paul has become a personal coach of mine as well as a trusted friend.

Later in my career I was considering the thought of making a personal change. I called Paul to bounce an idea off his creative mind. With sage wisdom, I didn't get a direct answer from Paul. Instead, he gave me a new model to guide me in my decision. Paul said to think of three overlapping circles. In the first circle, list the things you are passionate about. In the second circle, list the things at which you are very good. In the final circle, list the things that are "hot." The intersection will define your "sweet spot." Wow! His model was so simple, but so powerful. Over the next year or so, I consulted with people close to me that I trusted to help me define my first two circles. I learned from *The Successful Life Course* that my habits define my character. Instead of just letting my personal ego define my first two circles, I trusted more the "impressions" I had projected through my habits to define those first two circles. What other individuals saw as my passion and strength was that I am good at teaching. That may sound unusual considering the last twenty years of my career was at an executive level, but my trusted friends nailed it! I do love to teach, and I am thankful and grateful they also thought I did it well.

Frankly, the third circle was a little bit more difficult for me to define. What's "hot?" Does "hot" mean popular? Does "hot" mean trendy? Does "hot" mean in greater demand? What does "hot" mean to me? I finally guessed it could mean any of these. So I reflected on a personal mission I created ten years ago and recently updated. That mission, in short, is to help my family, myself, and others achieve their fullest potential. I realized it has always been my personal mission, or why else would I have developed a leadership style of teaching? So "hot" to me means aligned with my personal mission. It's kind of like the "hot" children tell each other when they play Marco Polo in the swimming pool. You're close; you're hot; you're on top of what you're trying to get. The third circle is doing those things that move me closer to my personal mission.

So why not take the thoughts and concepts from these two mentors who impacted me the most in my life and career and integrate them? Well, that might be good if my mission was to help companies and organizations, but my personal mission, my bliss if you will, is to help *people* achieve their fullest potential.

The result of merging these concepts is this book and the model defined within it. This book is the integration of several components. The model framework, including some of the specific categories, comes directly from the Organization Systems Design model. The OSD Model was the core framework used to reorganize a large organization to attain great results and a great culture. Altered for individuals, the framework could also help others lead themselves, moderated through their character and style, to achieve their personal dreams. Much of the content within the elements of the framework comes from *The Successful Life Course* and the additional knowledge and wisdom Ed's lessons led me toward. Add to these two cornerstones, additional knowledge, and insights discovered through research and my own personal experiences, and you get this book. It is an integration I have discovered of the best knowledge and the best model, and one that has truly helped me.

I hope you enjoy this book, but more importantly, my dream is that it leads you to live by design so you can achieve your dreams and your fullest potential.

Introduction

MOST PEOPLE DREAM WHEN THEY are young. They dream and aspire to be a teacher or a doctor, a sports hero or a policeman. They dream they can do something that makes the world a better place. I believe many of these dreams can come true. Unfortunately, along the way, many people find discouragement, barriers, and bad habits that rob them of achieving their dreams.

Now, don't get me wrong. I'm not saying that most people don't work hard. In many ways, I believe most people are very hard working. I've seen it in the factories and distribution centers in many of the companies where I've worked. The people work long, hard hours to put bread on the table and provide a few luxuries for their families. However, I question if they are working toward their dream. I question if they still have that child's voice inside their head whispering they can have, be, or do anything they want.

There can be distractions along the way toward achieving your dreams. Unfortunately, there are more people that will tell you why you shouldn't, can't, and won't achieve your dreams and goals than those who will help you achieve them. I heard that Ted Turner had a name plate on his desk that said, "Lead, follow, or get out of the way!" What he meant was that as a leader, if you brought him an idea or a dream, he should first try to lead you towards your success. If he didn't quite understand, then he should follow you as you took the initiative to achieve. And even if he didn't understand or believe in your dream, he should at least get out of your way and allow you to pursue your dream. Ted Turner is an unusual individual. He believed in his dreams and the dreams of others. Unfortunately, many people don't want you to achieve your dreams. Even worse, many of these people are very close to you. Why don't they want you to believe in and achieve your dreams? It may simply be because they haven't found the way to achieve their own dreams.

Why haven't they achieved their dreams? What were the potholes—the detours—that caused them to get distracted, drift away from their focus, or simply give up? Why do people seem to live by default?

Maybe you've made some really good decisions in the past, but the results coming from these actions seem less than you expected. The results might be muted or moderated for you when the same decisions seemed to work well for others. Why might this have happened?

The purpose of this book is to help answer some of these questions for you. The framework and the sequenced system provided here help individuals identify areas in their current habits, routines, and decisions that might not be aligned to a person's mission or the achievement of their dreams. Once the alignment issues are identified, they can be resolved. You *can* design your life and live by design instead of by default. Just as a builder follows the architect's plans to remodel an outdated house and turn it into a beautiful home, you can use the framework in Part I to identify the rooms in your life that merit remodeling and use the sequenced system in Part II to create a personal blueprint for reconstruction. You *can* have the success you yearn. For those who appreciate and desire a well-designed and organized house, just imagine the power of getting your habits, routines, and decisions just as organized and aligned toward your dreams. It will require action, but it can make a world of difference. The realignment or redesign of your personal choices and personal systems can enable more efficient ways for you to achieve your fullest potential and your highest aspirations.

This book can be used in several different ways depending on your preference and personal learning style. Part I of the book describes the framework: the Successful Life Systems Design Model (SLSD Model). Part II provides a 28-day methodology to redesign and align components of your life. Part II has several exercises you'll use to better understand where you are today in the various elements of the model and to help you make new choices.

Some people reading this book will choose to fully understand the SLSD Model before exploring any of the exercises. If you are one of these people, you will want to read all of Part I before reading any of Part II—just follow the sequence of the book.

Some people, however, will want to do some or all of the exercises related to each element of the model as they conclude each chapter relating to the model element. If this is your preferred approach, there is an exercise reference at the end of each chapter (beginning with Chapter 2). This reference will point you to the "day" of the exercise detailed in Part II and to the exercise sub-title. For you, much of the "discovery work" will already be complete when you begin reading Part II. You will then put the pieces together and align your choices to complete your redesign.

Either approach will work. It's my hope this book provides you the perspective and methodology to make new choices that align your thoughts, actions, and energies towards the accomplishment of your dreams as you achieve your full potential and live by design!

PART I

Chapter One

How do You Define "Successful Life?"

How does one define a "successful life?" To some, it's simply having more money than they can spend in a lifetime. Others may call it being in a state of love and happiness throughout their life journey. Still, others may say it is serving their Higher Power. In his book 5 Principles for a Successful Life, Newt Gingrich defines success as, "adding value to people's lives and making a difference to the world around us."[1] My mentor and friend Ed Foreman would say it's "laughing, loving, and living your way to the goood life!" (And yes, there are three Os in Ed's definition because goood is better than good!)

What makes a "successful life" is different for each individual. My definition is different from my wife's definition (though there are many overlapping components), different from my children's ideas, and different still from some of my closest friends. That's all right! More than all right, I truly believe it's healthy. There's an old saying: "The world would be a boring place if we were all alike." I agree.

My definition of a "successful life" is **the attainment of one's dreams in a style or with a personal character that creates self-pride**. This fits the discussion above relative to "all dreams don't need to be the same."

Examining my definition, there are two components to it. First, there is the "attainment of one's dreams"—the *where* you want to arrive. It can be something you want to *have*, something you want to *be*, or something you want to *do*. I believe it can be all three, but it needs to be defined. Why?

Yogi Berra, the legendary New York Yankee player and manager, once said: "You've got to be very careful if you don't know where you are going, because you might not get there."[2] I would add that you also have to be very careful if you don't know where you are going, because you might get where you *do not* want to be. Another way of saying the same thing is: "If you don't know where you're going, all roads lead there." There's also a corollary to this saying. "Even if you know your goal, the wrong road will take you longer to get there."

Do you want the destination—the dream of your life—to be defined, or do you want it to occur as a random walk through your time on this earth? I've heard it said that most people live their life as a matter of default instead of by design. How sad. I choose to create my direction through design.

The second component of my definition is "in a style or with a perceived character that creates self-pride." It is the "how will I get to my destination" portion. Betrand Russell describes the good life as being "inspired by love and guided by knowledge."[3] *Inspired* and *guided* are action verbs describing the "how" to achieve a good life. The point here is that not only does the dream destination matter, it is *how* one gets there that matters.

If you have started reading this book, then I must assume you want to achieve more success in your life. You might be doing well, but want more success. On the other hand, you might not like where you are in your life and want not just more, but a lot more. In either case, I want you to consider a quote I once saw on a poster:

> "If you want things to change in your life, you are going to have to change things in your life."[4]

Sorry—a successful life is not achieved by taking a magic pill or by following a simple three-step formula. I recognize that today's society wants to entice you to believe everything is easy, simple, and quick. I hate to tell you this, but that's marketing you are listening to, not reality!

If you are discouraged by this blunt statement, don't be. You *can* create your successful life. You can have your dreams and you can do it proudly. However, you cannot achieve your dreams by doing exactly what you are doing today. Believe it or not, *your life today is perfectly designed to get the results that you get.* If that's not okay with you, or if that's not what you really want, then you better redesign your life!

What's the alternative? You can complain about it. How has complaining about it worked for you in the past? You can cry about it. How has that worked for you in the past? You can argue and power over people to get things you want. Is that working for you? Or you can get depressed and feel sorry for yourself and continue to get what life gives you instead of what you want. All of these are examples of what I call living by default, *not* by design.

Life is about making choices. Interestingly, running a large organization was about making choices too. In order for the organization to be considered successful, we had to achieve results that in the future would create shareholder wealth, protect and develop employees, and satisfy customer needs and requirements. But that wasn't all we had to do. In today's business, those results had to be achieved according the values of the organization, as well. Hmm...doesn't that sound similar? The management team and leadership had to *create* future results and outcomes. These results were always compared to the business' strategic plan...something similar to a dream. Further, the management leaders today must do so by employing a set of values that create the culture of the organization. For an individual, this is analogous and comparable to the individual's personal style or character.

As mentioned in the Preface of this book, Paul Gustavson's Organization System Design Model[5] was the framework that helped and guided me when redesigning organizations. This model and the associated analyses led me to make choices to achieve the strategic plan. The choices included: reorganize an organization of close to two thousand people; achieve desired short term and long term outcomes;

and create a culture of results, growth, and development. With Paul's help, I've used the same concepts to create the Successful Life System Design Model (SLSD Model).

The SLSD Model represents a framework to make decisions about your life. It doesn't make the decisions for you. Those are your choices. Moderated by your style and character, your choices will create outcomes. Those outcomes then will be compared to your dreams. If your choices and moderated actions are moving you closer to your dreams, terrific! If you are not making progress, you must reconsider some of your past choices in life. You need to make new choices so your life activities and actions move you toward your dreams.

To develop a basic understanding of the SLSD Model, we'll start by defining the relationship of the major component areas. In this chapter, we'll also define subcomponents within each of the major component areas. This understanding will be at a very high conceptual level. Each of the following chapters will dig deeper into each subcomponent and provide additional thoughts and consideration for the particular subcomponent covered in that chapter.

So, let's begin....

There are four large components of the model as shown in the figure on the next page.

In the far right box of the model are results and outcomes. These are what we compare to our dreams. Our dreams could be a single destination, but I like to think of them as broken into six categories: Relationships, Spirituality, Environment, Passion-Time, Wealth, and Health. This part of the model will be discussed in detail in Chapter 2.

The second box from the right is Style or Character. This is the funnel our choices pass through to create the results. Our character and style moderates our choices either positively or negatively. Our character includes our habits, our emotions, and our skills. These are not the things we believe are our habits. Nor are they the things we think we are good at. These are only the things the outside world views or perceives as our habits, emotions, or skills.

Often people don't know what others' dreams are or what that other person is pursuing as dreams, but they can and do know what the person's style is. Does the person show anger quickly and power over others? Does the person smile at strangers regularly? Does the person condemn, criticize, and complain or does the person lift others up by providing positive recognition? Like it or not, we leave impressions with others. Some call it our "Personal Style." Another way of thinking about this area is that our personal character is defined by our habits, emotions, and skills. More will be discussed on this area in Chapter 3.

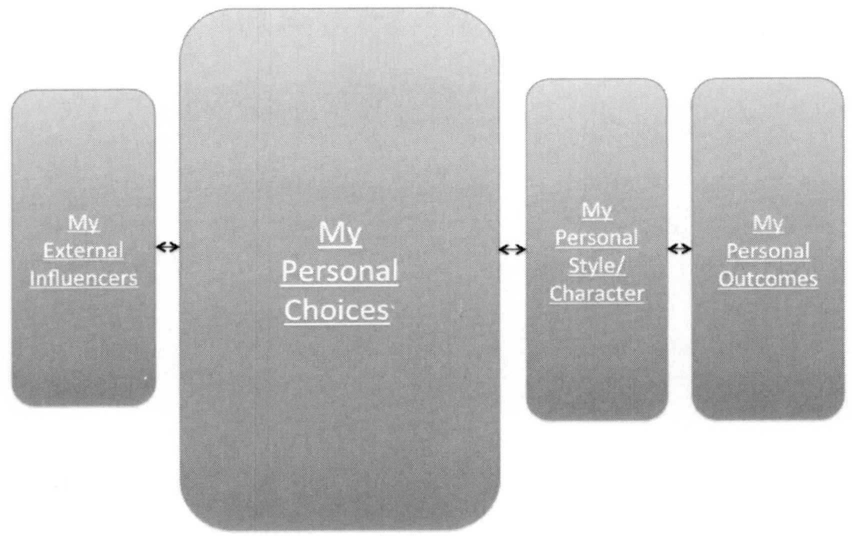

SLSD Model Basic

To the far left is a part of the model called "External Influencing Factors."Yes, we do live in a world of reality, a world of inclusion, not seclusion. Other individuals, both close and distant (our spouse, our boss, our children, our parents) have an impact on us. They can have an impact on whether we achieve our dreams, too, but only if we let them. Further discussion on this topic comes in Chapter 4.

The final main box in the model is Personal Choices. There are ten areas in which we have choices to make on our journey to success. Each of these will be the subject of a chapter. The choices you have include your Personal Mission (Chapter 6), your Personal Guiding Principles (Chapter 7), your Strategies to Influence (Chapter 8), your Goals and Chief Aims (Chapter 9), your Success Mechanisms (Chapter 10), your Personal Organization (Chapter 11), your Decisions—regarding how you get your needs met—and your Informating Systems (Chapter 12), your Relationship Processes (Chapter 13), your Recognition Systems of yourself and others (Chapter 14) and finally, your Personal Development and Renewal Systems (Chapter 15). Below is the SLSD Model with all the subcategories.

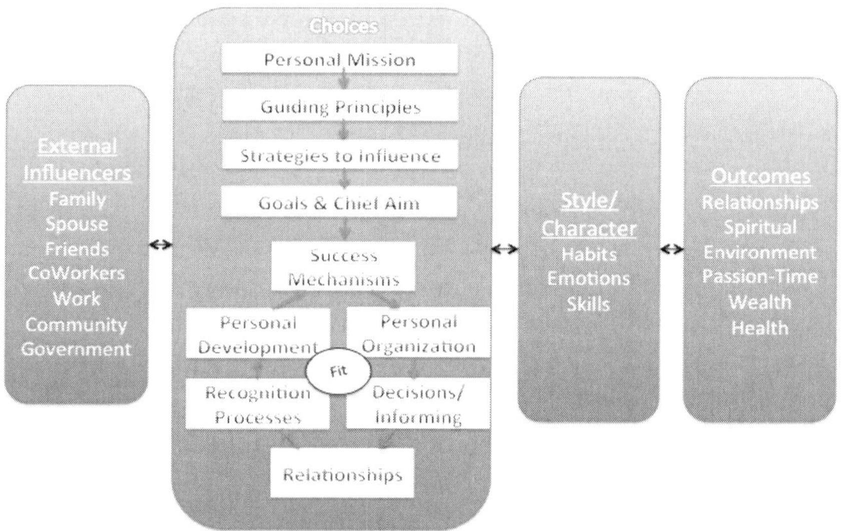

SLSD Model Complete

Notice that there are arrows. The arrows are pointing both ways from the Choices box to the Personal Style Box and then between the Personal Outcomes and Personal Style boxes. This shows that as you make choices among the subcategories your outcomes change. Both your Style/Character outcomes can change and your Personal Outcomes (or results) can change. As mentioned earlier, your Style/ Character outcomes moderate your Personal Outcomes.

Let's think about it. For a moment, let's say you make a change to your Recognition of Others process or system. Will it affect your Style? Probably, if it is repeated long enough to become a habit such that people notice you have a new style or habit for recognizing others. Will it affect your Personal Outcomes, specifically in the subcategory of Relationships? What if you create a strategy to influence your boss at work with regard to keeping him or her better informed (on daily or weekly results in your area), especially when things are a bit off course. Further, you then update him/her on your plans to get back on course. Will this new approach affect your Personal Style/Character? Absolutely it will, if the change becomes a habit that is noticed. Your manager will have improved impressions of your problem identification and solution creation skills. Will the improved perceptions of your new skills affect your Personal Outcome category of Wealth? I believe it can and will!

The arrow between External Influencers and the Choices box is also a two-way arrow. Clearly the external influencers have an impact on us (or they would not be an influencer). You, if you choose to, can also have an influence on the influencers. That is why the arrow is two-way. What if you don't make a conscious choice, should the arrow be only one-way? No, it should not be a one-way arrow because your lack of a conscious choice is actually a choice. It may or may not be the best choice, but it is a choice. We will get into that more deeply later.

I'd like to give you a personal example of how the model worked for me. By now, you know that twenty-five plus years ago, I attended a weekend seminar entitled *The Successful Life Course.*[6] Coming out of the course, many of my choices in life changed, especially in the personal development category. I decided to start running for my physical development. I chose to start reading non-fiction books from a book list that was provided, which changed some of my thinking. I chose to read before I went to bed and first thing after I awoke. I developed a collection of cassette tapes (now I've really dated myself) with great inspiration. I quit answering the question: "How are you?" with the normal response of: "Fine. How are you?" and started responding with a single word. "Terrific!" That one change was noticed everywhere, even at the grocery store. Responding to cashiers, I can't tell you how many times it was like the cashier suddenly woke up and would respond with a comment like: "Wow, I don't hear that very often!" or "Did you say perfect?" (Some times my enunciation needed a bit of improvement.) I went back to college to get my MBA (while maintaining a full-time managerial position leading 130 individuals). The point is I made a lot of development choices and thus my style and character changed. So did my outcomes. I achieved the major goal I had in my life at that time, which was to be a plant manager by age thirty-five. Other areas in my life improved, as well, including the relationship at the time with my child, my health, and frankly, over the next ten years my salary growth was beyond my expectations!

Unfortunately, I eventually drifted (unconsciously) away from some of the choices that had helped me succeed. My reading drifted to different topics, including a lot of fiction. My exercise program was inconsistent and eventually non-existent (even though I had great equipment and a dedicated room to work out in, in actuality, it just stored the equipment). My diet wasn't as rigorous either. To be very honest with myself, I started drifting away from my dreams. My thoughts changed. I quit thinking about how to achieve my goals for age fifty-five. I began rationalizing that my family and I were comfortable. Maybe those goals weren't all that important.

Though I maintained a very solid salary, my career trajectory flattened out and I was even fired! Though my history enabled me to quickly gain another executive position, I moved from growing and thriving to being stagnant developmentally. I was beginning to develop health issues and was holding on for survival. For the eighteen months prior, I wasn't enjoying my career.

The point is I made some unconscious choices that were not as positive and productive as the choices I made earlier. The model works in all directions. My habits and emotions moved in a direction opposite of my personal desired self-image. My outcomes were moving me away from my dreams because of all of the unconscious choices of what I read, what I ate, whether I exercised, and frankly, how I thought. Remember what I said earlier:

> *"Your life today is perfectly designed to get the results that you get."*

My life was perfectly designed to get the results I got. Both the good results from my conscious decisions and the disappointing results from my unconscious decisions occurred because of my choices! All of my choices can be found in one of the ten choice elements of the Successful Life Systems Design Model.

Then things changed. My wife called me while I was on a business trip. She told me she had an opportunity to attend a one-day Ed Foreman seminar. I wasn't sure where this had come from. Twenty-five years before, I had wished she could go to *The Successful Life Course*[6] with me. I was happy for her and supported her desire to go. We had made a prior family commitment the weekend of the course that had to be managed, but we made our choice and off to Dallas she went.

Of course, I knew what her going to the event meant. It meant she'd come back with Ed's Prescription Number One.[7]. (I'll share the prescription later.) In short, it meant I'd need to start getting up earlier and reading something inspirational first thing in the morning again. I'd need to take a walk with her before I went to work. You get the picture. I'd started doing much of what I did earlier in my life that had led to the success we now enjoyed.

She went to the course and we started doing all the good things I knew in my head I should have been doing all along. A couple of months later, we attended a convention where Ed was again speaking. By this time, my morning rituals were once again becoming habits. My attitude and thoughts were climbing the mountain of successful accomplishments, and I was beginning to set some new goals for myself.

It was great to meet Ed again and talk with him. As I mentioned in the Preface, Ed asked me that important question about what was the best thing that has happened to me since attending *The Successful Life Course*. I answered that it was sharing the lessons he had taught in the course with the managers that worked for me for the entire twenty-five years. Later that weekend, Ed handed me the microphone to relate my goals and story to fifteen hundred people! I thought I was just helping him and paying him back a bit to for the positive impact he had on my life and my family's well being over those twenty-five years. I didn't realize it at the time, but Ed was again helping me as I shared all the good things my *Successful Life Course* habits had created. In actuality, he was helping me once again to begin to sort out what I wanted to achieve next in my successful life journey!

Within three months from that event, I was able to change my life trajectory, change the state of my health, and become a much happier person and a better husband and father.

I had realized in those previous six months that I really wasn't happy in my career any more. My desired character and actual character didn't match. I had loved the career for thirty-four years, but I wasn't passionate about it any more. One of my personal beliefs is "there can be no excellence without passion." I wasn't passionate about my work anymore, and I wasn't excellent anymore either. It hurts to say, but it's the honest truth. I still may have been pretty good at my job, and I did care about the people I led, but passionate about my job? No. I really wasn't.

Fortunately, my previous success had placed us in a financial position where I could retire or, as I now tell others, "I kicked off my corporate boots." As a result, I was able to really enjoy my youngest daughter's wedding, and I was able to help her and her husband move to their new home in Florida. I was able to really enjoy my passion for golf, and I achieved my lifetime handicap goal.

More importantly, I looked back at those goals I set for myself when I turned fifty-five years old. I decided there was one I still wanted to achieve. That goal was to teach at a college level. In January, less than one year following my retirement, I began teaching at a local college. Now, I'm proud to say that I've set new goals as I enter the second phase of my successful life.

I've shared my story with you to point out a couple of things. First, making conscious (and unconscious) choices can have dramatic impacts on your personal success. It can have positive impacts and it can have undesired impacts. It certainly did on me.

Second, in order to view the choices we have made and their impact, having a framework to evaluate the relationship would have been extremely helpful. Since Paul Gustavson's *Organization Systems Design Model* worked so well to help me reorganize and make conscious choices that impacted positively the culture and outcomes of large companies, I've extrapolated that model to create the Successful Life Systems Design Model (SLSD model for short). It's not designed to make your choices for you. It's designed for you to compare your outcomes to your desires. The model is for you to compare your style as perceived by others to how you want to be perceived and how it might impact or moderate your outcomes. It's for you to compare the real status in six areas of your life to your dreams in those areas. Then, if you're not satisfied with the directions those areas are heading, it will help you look at the ten choice areas to see if you need to make some new conscious choices the same way I needed to make some new conscious choices.

As we begin to dive more deeply into each area of the model, I will integrate lessons and knowledge that have helped me over the years. I'm sure you too have had many great, positive experiences that have led to choices that helped you achieve success. Categorize those experiences into the model. Look at whether you can see your character or a result outcome that changed due to your choice and personal change. I'll bet you can, which validates the strength of the SLSD Model as a framework to look at what's working for your success and what might not be working. I'll then walk you through how to use the model. In addition to using the model to examine your current reality, you will be introduced to three different analyses to help you gather information to evaluate the implications of the data. You will then be able to decide if there might be a better "choice" for you. Putting in these new choices, and aligning them across the elements of the SLSD model, enables you to redesign your life. You can make your choices based on the analyses and live by design to create your successful life!

Chapter Two

Connect with Your Dreams

WHERE DO YOU WANT TO be twenty-five years from now? What do you want to have possessed in those twenty-five years? What do you want to have accomplished by then?

According to Ed Foreman's "Laughing, Loving and Living Your Way to the Goood Life" Success Guide, a goal is anything you can have, be, or do.[1] Examples of anything you can have would include a new home, car, boat, motorcycle, or maybe a cabin on the lake. Examples of anything you can be might include becoming a supervisor or officer of your company, working in real estate, authoring a book, becoming an inventor, or being a terrific parent. Finally, examples of anything you can do are improve your health and stamina, achieve your ideal body weight in 12 months, enjoy smoke-free lungs, play a musical instrument, or develop better family relationships.

Goals are important. They are footsteps to your dreams!

Now, don't tell me: "Man, I'm just trying to make ends meet today. I don't have time to waste thinking about those things!" Don't tell me that because if that's what you think, you are creating the reality that you'll never get any of those things. Napoleon Hill, in his classic book Think and Grow Rich, says that anything the mind of man can conceive and you bring yourself to believe, you will achieve.[2] So if you are thinking worrisome thoughts about just barely making ends meet, guess what you're going to continuously get? You're going to continue to barely make ends meet! Don't want that? Let's look further.

In the recording "The Strangest Secret," Earl Nightingale tells us: "You get what you think about most of the time."[3] He's saying the very same thing Napoleon Hill said. If you are thinking about barely surviving, then you're going to receive barely surviving. Napoleon Hill also said: "The starting point of all achievement is desire."[4] You have got to think bigger, desire bigger, and then act bigger.

In the previous chapter, I mentioned that I had a major goal to become a plant manager by the age of thirty-five. Calling it a major goal may have been an understatement. It was my focused goal…my burning desire. I made many decisions and worked hard to achieve the goal. At one point, I was confronted with two promotional opportunities at the same time. As my current boss was contemplating my next assignment, I was being recruited and interviewed by another company. Shortly after I arrived home after the final interview, the phone rang. It was the recruiter who had introduced me to the new opportunity. He presented an offer for the job we had been discussing. The salary increase was substantial and there was a bonus on top of the salary increase. I thanked him and told him I was very excited about the opportunity, but wanted to sleep on the decision. The very next morning, my old boss called me to his office. He said: "Tom, I need you to develop a training program for your replacement." He told me who was replacing me and when. I responded that I'd get it done, but didn't inquire about my next assignment. Fifteen minutes later, he called my office. He noted that I didn't seem overly excited and wondered if I was okay. I said sure and told him I assumed that if he could tell me where I was going next, he would have. He agreed he couldn't tell me, but said to go ahead and ask him some questions. I said, "Okay, am I being promoted?" He said, "Yes!" I asked, "Will I need to move?" He quickly responded, "No!" I said, "Okay, here's the sixty thousand dollar question. I'm thirty-one right now. I have a goal to be a plant manager by the age of thirty-five. Will this position get me there?" He hesitated and then said, "Uhhh, yes..." I said, " Sounds like maybe." He agreed, and then I added, "Which means probably, no." Hesitantly, he agreed it would be a long stretch, but it was a good job. I thanked him and knew what my decision was going to be. What you think about, you become. I joined the other company and became a plant manager when I was thirty-five, just as I had targeted.

So what's the difference between goals and dreams?

A dream is much bigger than a goal! A dream needs to be huge. It needs to be so big and so powerful it draws you toward it. It is very attractive to you and attracts you in its direction. Sometimes a dream is so big, it may take more than a single lifetime to achieve!

Does that mean we give up on our dreams because they might take longer than we are going to be around? Absolutely not! Why? In the movie *Flashdance*, Nick (the boyfriend and boss of the leading character, Alex Owens) confronts Alex in her loft when she seemingly has given up on trying out for ballet school by saying, "Don't you understand? When you give up your dreams, you die!"[5] It's true! This is one of my favorite quotes. When we give up on those things that pull us to be bigger and better than we are today, a part of us dies. Our drive dies. Our attitude dies. Our self-esteem dies. Our self-worth dies. Our spirit dies. We are all born for greatness and engineered for success, but sometimes we get in our own way. Loosing our dreams not only gets in our way, it creates detours and roadblocks that direct us where we are not happy and not our best selves.

Have I ever lost my dream? Sadly, I must admit I did for a while. That's why I can say those roadblocks and detours take you somewhere where you realize you're not happy. I realized I wasn't my authentic self either. I wasn't leading my organization by the design and by the principles in which I believed. I wasn't doing the things I should do to make positive changes in my life. Honestly, my health was deteriorating with high blood pressure from worrying about the wrong things. That's when I realized I had to change some things in my life. I don't blame anyone but myself for falling into that rut. I had to get out of the rut I was in! Dr. Ted Morter III, CEO of Morter HealthSystem, often tells us, "The difference between a rut and a grave is simply the depth."[6] I was digging my rut into a grave. It was only a matter of time, but I got out of my rut. I quit dying. How? By using the SLSD Model and creating new dreams! Never lose your dreams!

So how do dreams and goals relate to each other? Before we describe that relationship fully, I need to add another term. It's called your definite chief aim. Your definite chief aim[7] is best described in two of Napoleon Hill's classic books, Think and Grow Rich and The Law of Success in Sixteen Lessons. Your definite chief aim is smaller than your dreams, but bigger than your goals. A major difference is that you can believe you can achieve the chief aim, even if it is really big compared to where you are today. However, your goals, your definite chief aim, and your dreams need to be aligned with each other. In the discussion about becoming a plant manager by the age of thirty-five, that was a chief aim of mine. My dream is much larger. My wife-to-be, at the time, and I had selected our china based on what we wanted to serve the plant managers that would someday report to me. We were dreaming what felt like a huge dream at the time.

My chief aim was also huge to me, but I still believed I could achieve it and I did! To achieve my chief aim, there were several goals to achieve in between. In the figure on the next page you'll see that relationship.

Notice to the far left is a triangle representing your present reality. That is where you are today relative to your dreams. Your dreams are to the far right and are the largest ball. The ball is so much larger than even your definite chief aim. Your definite chief aim is still larger than your goals. Your goals are larger than your next step. The importance of this diagram is to show the relationships between all of the figures. First, as mentioned above, is the size relationship. The next is the alignment relationship. Your next step, your goals, your definite chief aim, and your dreams all lie perfectly centered on the same (dashed) line. They are not tangent or skewed off of the line. The most efficient route to your dreams is taking the next step directly toward your goals, which are directly in line with your definite chief aim, which is in perfect alignment with your dreams.

Relationship Between Your Present State and Your Dreams

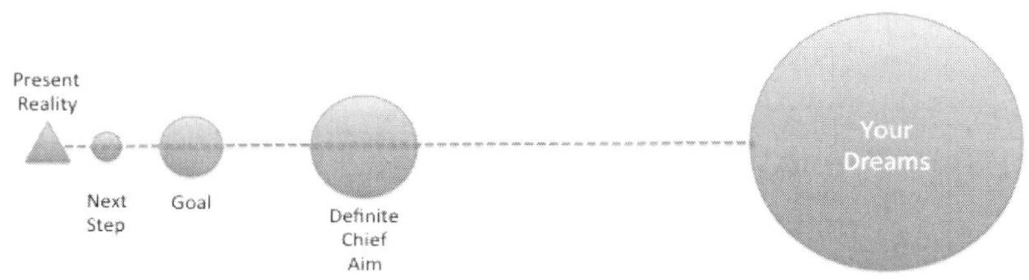

Present to Dream Diagram 1

So how do you know what your next step should be? First, you must define your dreams! I like to define my dreams in six different life areas: relationship dreams, spiritual dreams, environment dreams, passion-time dreams, wealth dreams, and health dreams. I do this to create balance. There was a time in my life when I focused almost exclusively on only one goal area. Focus did create success in that area, but in some other areas, I made no progress or even regressed. This experience has led me to believe in having goals and chief aims in all six categories that I keep in front of myself. Others believe you should put all your focus on the one chief aim. I recognize that there are times when you put more effort or focus on one or two of the categories for a short period of time, but I chose not to let myself completely ignore one of these areas for an extended period of time. You'll have to decide for yourself.

Relationship dreams deal with how you ideally see yourself relating to others. How do you want to invest your time each day with other people in your life? I often get amused with people who say, "I don't have time." As far as I know, there are still twenty-four hours in a day. No more and no less. Each of us gets to choose how we spend those twenty-four hours each day. One important way to invest the time is in developing our relationships. An example of a relationship dream is:

> *Spending two hours per day with my wife is my most essential objective followed by connecting with my daughters twice a week. Continuously reconnecting with distant acquaintances twice a week helps me stay connected with other people who are important to me.*

Can you imagine the positive relationships you would create if these were the continuous routine habits you developed? I can, because this is my relationship dream.

Spiritual dreams are how you ideally stay centered. For many it is service to their church or religion. For others, it is the habit of daily or many times a day prayer. For others, it is a life of spiritual role modeling how to best serve their Higher Power so that others may follow. My spiritual dream is:

> *I will assure daily that I am connected to God who provides me an inner peace and the ability to help others.*

Environment dreams speak to where we want to live and work. What is the environment we seek to have? It may be multiple environments. Maybe you want two or three homes: one close to where you grew up, one on the shore, and one in the mountains. Maybe it's a loft in your favorite city so you can enjoy the city environment and cultural attractions. For me, it's:

> *Enjoying our clutter free home on the golf course in Tennessee enables a calming retreat and a sense of freedom. Having an acreage close allows me an environment to find solitude and an opportunity to produce healthy food.*

Passion-time is how we invest our time to have fun. Enjoyment is such a vital part of our dreams. Ed Foreman says that: "Life is for laughing, loving, and living; not whining, worrying and working."[8] Life is for laughing, but you have to design that part of your life, too, by including passion-time as a part of your dreams. My passion-time dream is:

> *I will play two rounds of golf each week with friends, and practice twice a week.*

Some say: "Gee Tom, that's a frustrating game. Why spend all that time on a sport designed to turn men into boys—to turn the sane insane?" For me, golf has always been my escape. Even when I lost my dream for a while, I could escape to a golf course, enjoy my friends, and lose frustrations and worries. Now that my dreams are back on track and I'm happier than I've ever been with where I am, I don't want to forget the good golf has served me even in the darker days. You've got to have passion-time in your life. Without passion, there can be no excellence. In those twenty-four hours each day, make time for some passion-time.

Sometimes wealth dreams are the only things people seem to talk about regarding a successful life. "Money is not only a scorecard, it's the scorecard!" I've heard people say. I obviously don't believe that. I've made a lot of money in a single year and money alone doesn't make you happy or successful. There is, however, a level of income each year that is needed to support the rest of your dream areas. We do need to be aware of how much that is and build that income into our success design. It's also important that your wealth dreams and your other dreams are aligned. For instance, if you want more than one home, you'll need to have enough income to pay the taxes, insurance, maintenance, and upkeep for each residence. Maybe your environment dream is to have a large square footage home. Do you want to spend your passion-time cleaning it? Probably not, so you'll need enough income to have a maid service or, better yet, a full-time maid. Maybe your passion-time dream is extensive travel around the world. You might then need an income to support all those airline tickets! Are you going to travel first class when you travel? You better bump up the income some more. My wealth dream is:

> *Generating additional income each month above my current income level will enable me to secure our financial future, contribute toward important personal causes, and enjoy life more along the way.*

Finally, your health dream is a must. What good would any of the above dreams do you if you have bad health? You couldn't fully enjoy the great relationships you generate. Your spiritual dreams might be diminished by poor health. Your environment dreams would have to accommodate your health-state instead of being unlimited. Could you really enjoy your passion-time with poor health? I couldn't. So you've got to include a health dream. My health dream is:

> *I continuously improve the way I eat, drink, exercise, rest, breathe and think with the most important being to steadily improve how I think positively.*

So is it important to have your dreams written out? Absolutely! Even more than that, you really need to be able to see your dreams. See my dreams, you ask? Yes, see your dreams. Through seeing your dreams, you begin to *feel* what it would be like to reach them. So how do I see them? Through the beautiful glossy pictures I find and take, which I keep in a prominent place where I can see them.

There are several techniques to seeing your dreams. One of them is called a dream board. You can look up how to make and use a dream board on Google. Another technique is called a dream book. Once again, there are multiple ways to create a dream book that you can research. Although it has some similarities to a dream board, it is a scrapbook you fill with images of your dreams. I suggest you make a scrapbook from your images by covering both sides of an open page. You'll want to create a double page layout for each of your dream categories.

What's really important about using any of these tools is that you transform your thoughts into feelings. These feelings then help you move from conceiving the dreams to believing them. And remember what Napoleon Hill told us:

"Anything that the mind of man can conceive and you can bring yourself to believe, you will achieve."

Create your dreams. Make them visual for yourself to create connection. This is the first step in beginning to use the model. The box in the SLSD Model labeled Your Outcomes should measure where you are in each of your dream categories. You can then measure the direction your outcomes are headed relative to each of your dream categories relative to your specific, defined dreams.

After defining your dreams, you'll then want to define your definite chief aims. Remember: the same six life categories, but your definite chief aims are closer to where you are currently on your journey to success and believable to you.

For example, my dream may be to achieve an additional income each month. Each of us has an income or an amount of money that would secure our future. For some, it's $5,000 per month. For others, it's more. For some, it's a lot more. Your wealth dream is that figure. Your definite chief aim is a smaller amount, but a figure that stretches your thoughts and that you believe you can achieve. For instance, if your dream is to create $2,000 per month over where you are today, then your definite chief aim might be to earn an additional $1000 per month. Relative to my passion-time dream, if my dream is to play two rounds of golf with friends and practice two times each week, then my definite chief aim is to be sure to play four rounds per month each month for a year, and practice at least three times each month that year.

My goals should be even more short term than my definite chief aim, but they are leading me directly toward my definite chief aim and my dreams in each category. For my passion-time goal, if I'm only playing golf once a month with friends, then I want to play golf two times this month and three times next month. (Fortunately, I've already exceeded this goal, but I haven't achieved playing four times per month every month for a year yet!) For the wealth goal I described earlier, you would need to generate an additional $500 a month for a couple of months before achieving the definite chief aim of $1000 per month every month.

What happens when you achieve a goal or a definite chief aim? First, you celebrate! Pat yourself on the back. Go out to dinner with a loved one. Appreciate and enjoy your accomplishments. It's not bragging. Recognition of others and of your accomplishments is fundamental to being successful, so celebrate. Make your celebrations commensurate with your progress in all the categories. So if you are not making progress in the wealth area, a celebration might be taking time to visit an old friend or going to the library to read some inspiring literature, or something as simple as taking two hours to sit by a lake or a cozy fire while being thankful and grateful for your improved success!

Immediately after the celebration, it's time to set a new goal or definite chief aim. Why, you ask? Because we need to have some *tension* between our current reality and our desired future state as defined by our goals and definite chief aims. It's this tension that pulls us toward the goals and dreams. Think of it like two balls connected by a rubber band. One ball represents your current reality. The other ball represents your desired future state or your goals. With tension on the rubber bands, the current reality is pulled toward the goals. That tension is good for you.

Now I'm sure someone is thinking, but doesn't the tension pull the goals back to current reality? Actually, it could. It's bad tension that I call fear. The good tension is called desire. In order to be successful, you have to have a burning desire to achieve your goals. You have to have that tension of desire. If the desire is not there, then the goals or dreams probably aren't real. In his book Think and Grow Rich, Napoleon Hill talks about the need for that burning desire.[10] It is fundamental to success. It may define the difference between your own personal goals and dreams and what others think you should do to be successful. Make sure you really desire your dreams. Otherwise, you might be traveling someone else's dream journey and not your own. Again, make sure you are traveling your own journey to your dreams by feeling real desire.

There are some questions you can ask yourself to test your dreams reality. In their book Three Feet from Gold, Turn Your Obstacles into

Opportunities!, Sharon Lechter and Greg Reid share two key questions about testing your dreams.

The first question is really important. "If everything went bad, what is the real worst case scenario?"[11] The second part of the question is "Could you handle it if the worst case scenario happened?"[12] You have to confront the possibility to eliminate the invisible barrier that will stop you, but if the worst-case scenario happened, then could you live with it emotionally and financially? If the answer is no, then you will be thinking about the fear of the worst-case scenario. That thought will, by the Law of Attraction, attract the worst-case scenario. The fear will make the worst happen, and you've already said you couldn't handle it financially or even worse, emotionally. This key question "turns on the red light" before it happens. Be careful with this question. Be truthful to yourself. If the answer is *no*, then create a different dream where this critical answer can be *yes*.

For me, there is another equally important question that is also implied in Lechter and Reid's book. "Is it aligned with my mission, purpose or passion?"[13] It needs to be aligned. Later in this book we'll discuss extensively your personal mission. For now, does the feeling you get when you think about your dream give you chills of joy? Does thinking about it make you smile as you imagine achieving it? Does thinking about it give you a boost of energy because of how exciting it is to think about fulfilling the dream? If not, frankly, start over because the dream isn't aligned with your passion.

Another question to consider is: "How many resources is it going to take?" What resources, you ask? Specifically, the resources called your time and your money. Now don't fool yourself by being overly optimistic. Get an estimate on each that is realistic. Once you think you have an answer, add at least 50% more time because there are always unforeseen delays and holdups. Are you okay with investing the amount of time it will take? How much money is it going to take to accomplish the dream? Did you think of all the costs? Did you even include the costs at times to invest more money to create your wealth stream? Did you look at the costs associated with non-wealth dreams while you're getting there? Now add 50% to the total! How do you feel about the amount? It's probably pretty big. What's important about this process is that by going through the questions, you once again eliminate the next invisible barrier that comes from thinking about how much money and time you're investing. When you already know you are going to spend that amount, there is no surprise. It's the surprises that stop us. Figure it out in advance and decide that it's *worth what paid* to you.

These questions eliminate the subconscious blocks, those invisible barriers you would hold if you didn't ask the questions. These subconscious blocks could hold you back and work counter to your success. We want to create dreams, definite chief aims, and goals that pull you toward your success, not wishes that have no energy. People live their commitments to their dreams; wishes have no commitments!

Understand dreams. Create and connect with your dreams. Commit to your dreams. Achieve your dreams. Having defined dreams that you are fully connected with is a very important part of living by design.

Reference Link to Part II

For those wanting to immediately begin the Dream Exercises in Part II of this book, you should first complete the "What Needs Changing Questionnaire." Further, I strongly suggest that you then read Chapter Six called Your Personal Mission. Read that chapter and do the exercises associated with developing your Personal Mission. This way, you will assure the dream exercises and dreams you create are aligned with your Personal Mission.

======================================

The Dream Exercises associated with this chapter are:

- Prescription Number Three (Day 1)
- Dream Board Exercise (Day 7)

======================================

Chapter Three

Style and Character: The Way You Get There

THERE'S A SECOND FORM OF outcome you create with your choices. It might be described as the perception you leave with others as you are achieving your dream outcomes. It is sometimes considered your personal style. If you really want to get up close and personal, it's your character.

One of the key lessons and illustrations I learned from Ed's *Successful Life Course* is shown in the diagram[1] on the next page.

What this little diagram represents first is that thoughts create actions. Don't believe it? Just read the following and let's see what happens.

Imagine you are opening your refrigerator. (Now don't just read this, really imagine you are doing this exercise.) You reach in and pick up a lemon. As you close the refrigerator door, you look closely at the lemon. Notice the texture and the dimply little spots on the skin of the lemon. Notice the two pointy little ends. Now take a knife and cut the lemon in half, right in the middle between the two pointy ends. Look at the distinct sections in the lemon. A little of the juice is trickling on your fingers. Now bring the lemon up to your nose and smell the citrus aroma. Now bite the lemon!

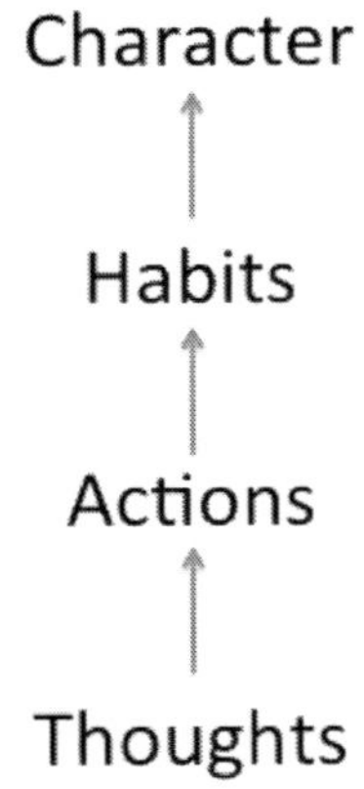

Thoughts to Character Diagram

Did you notice what happened when I told you to bite into the lemon? Extra saliva secreted into your mouth to wash away the acid juice of the lemon. You didn't really bite the lemon, but just the thought caused your body to perform the function as if it were real. I once did this exercise verbally with an associate and even before I told him to bite the lemon, he said: "My mouth is filling up with saliva!" Thoughts create actions.

Next in the diagram: actions repeated twenty-one days in a row create habits. Where did the twenty-one days come from? I've heard about the twenty-one day rule from several sources, but one of the best-documented sources is from Dr. Maxwell Maltz in his book Psycho-Cybernetics.[2] Dr. Maltz was originally a plastic surgeon when he noticed it took twenty-one days for amputees to cease feeling phantom sensations from the amputated limb. From further observations, he noticed the twenty-one day rule for creating new habits. Further science has revealed that engrams (memory traces) repeated in a brain twenty-one days in a row can produce neuro-connections and new neuro-pathways to change your habits, but only if they are repeated for twenty-one days in a row. Notice the "in a row" phrase.

You can't miss a day or the engram neuro-pathway won't be produced. So just try it. Start a new action you want to become a habit and repeat it twenty-one days in a row. At that point, it will become very natural to repeat the action. Further, something will feel missing if you don't do the action after the twenty-one days.

Why are habits so important? Because people measure our character not by the action we take one time, but the repeated same action they observe us take. Our habits define our character. That's the symbolism for the third arrow on the diagram. If people continuously see a person be overly aggressive at getting what they want or at trying to point out a slight that might have occurred, then that's what they come to expect every single time the least little slight occurs. The person's character might be considered aggressive, intimidating, or impatient. It could even be called being a bully.

How do I know about this particular example? This was me, for a time. If I went to a restaurant and the waitress didn't bring the food in a reasonable time, or if the check didn't come in a timely fashion, I would start getting fidgety and start looking around for the waitress. My daughters cringed at what might happen. Today I've changed the habit.

In the SLSD Model this section of the model is entitled Style/Character. The sub-categories are Habits, Emotions, and Skills. These categories are analogous or comparable to the subcategories in Paul Gustavson's Organization Systems Design Model.[3] In his business version, he terms it the BFA's for organizations. BFA stands for behaviors, feelings, and attributes. As I have taught the OSD Model over the years, I've also termed it as the culture of the organization. Below are the diagram from above and the analogous diagram for businesses.

I share this analogy to demonstrate the commonality between the OSD Model for organizational improvement and success and the SLSD Model for individual improvement and success.

So what are some of the habits that lead to success? Obviously, there are many. One of the keys before sharing some basic habits comes from my favorite Ed Foreman quote:

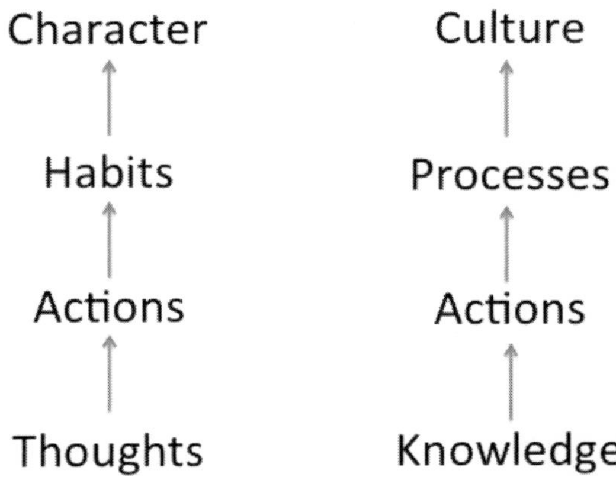

Knowledge to Culture Diagram

> *"Winners develop the habits of doing the things that losers don't like to do."*[4]

Notice the quote carefully. Did it say anything about skills? No. You see, it's not that winners have more natural skill or ability. It's not about their initial skill. It's about their attitude. Winners do the things that losers are capable of doing but don't do. They rationalize or make excuses because they don't like the particular action. It's not as cool or not as much fun.

Ben Hogan, the great golfer, was known to have less initial skill than many of the golfers he later beat. The difference was his habit of "digging it out of the dirt" and practicing "until his hands bled."[5] He practiced more than his peers. Don Mattingly, captain of the New York Yankees from 1991 – 1995 was the same way. He had great skills, but he was also out hitting balls and fielding grounders sometimes two hours before practice. It led to Don becoming a Yankee great.[6]

Another extremely important habit is making a choice about what kind of day you're going to have each day. I learned this from two people who are very special to me: my dad and Ed Foreman. Dad once shared with me that the thing he hoped I'd learned from him was that each day we have a choice to make on whether to be happy or not, and that he chose to be happy every day. We show it in how we walk, how we talk, and how we behave. I had never thought about it before, but he's right. We can make a choice if we live our lives by design instead of by default. Unfortunately, many people live by default and we can see it in their whole demeanor. They either project happiness and enthusiasm, or lethargy and apathy, or sometimes even anger. It's the regularity of these projections that come out as the individual's style or character.

Ed Foreman put it a different way. He said that each day we should wake up and think about which side of the menu[7] (shown below) we are going to choose.

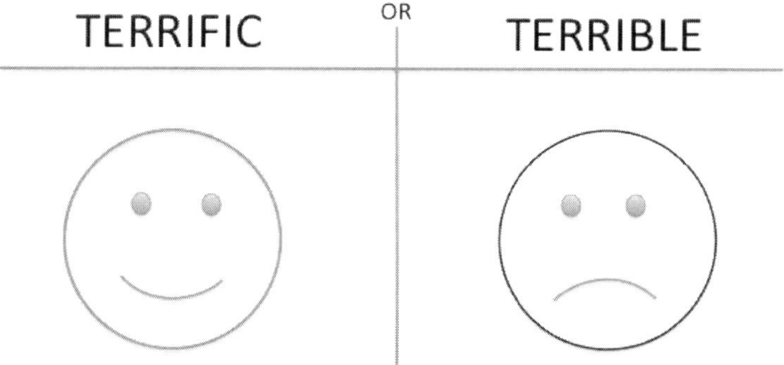
Life's Daily Menu
WHICH DO YOU CHOOSE TODAY?
TERRIFIC
OR
TERRIBLE

Life's Daily Menu

Which side are you going to choose? Better choose one consciously, because every one around you recognizes which side you've chosen.

My oldest daughter, who teaches third grade, puts this on the door entering her room for the students to see every day. She helps them make the conscious choice each day. It has dramatically helped with the attitudes in her classroom and encourages the students to make a positive choice. It probably helps some of the other teachers as they walk past her room, too!

So what are some of the other habits we should develop to live by design and achieve a successful life? There are twelve I'd like to share with you that have been very meaningful to me. No surprise, they all come from my experience with Ed's *Successful Life Course.* They are called the Basic Habit Patterns of a Winner.

The first habit is **winners don't condemn, criticize, or complain.**[8] They think of ways to improve a situation. As I mentioned earlier, I was once too well known by my daughters for being way too aggressive complaining about poor service to waiters and waitresses that waited on us. It got so bad my children and wife really would cringe when I would gesture for the waitress to come over after dinner or if the check took too long to be delivered.

About two months ago, I attended a seminar in Charleston, SC with my wife, oldest daughter, and several friends from our area. We were given an hour and a half for lunch, so we decided to have lunch at the hotel restaurant. We had eleven in our party, so as you might imagine, service would be a little bit slow. In this case, service was extremely slow. After an hour of waiting for our lunch, all of us were beginning to be concerned about returning to the seminar on time. Fifteen minutes later and still no food, one member of our party had started to look for a manager. Ten minutes later and still no food, we now had only five minutes to get back to the seminar on time, so I motioned to the waitress to come speak with me. My wife and daughter cringed. My wife told me she could feel her blood pressure starting to rise, just as she had so many times over the years. I said to the waitress, "I know you don't control the kitchen, but with our need to get back to the seminar, you might consider handing out the checks even before the kitchen finishes with the food. That way we can already be paid up when the food arrives. I just thought you might want to have a way to speed the process up." The waitress smiled. Both my wife and daughter were shocked that instead of complaining and criticizing, I helped the waitress relieve some of the pressure she was feeling. My daughter texted her younger sister: "You wouldn't believe how good Dad was today in the restaurant. I like the new Dad much better." In the end, everyone was given fifty percent off of our lunch bill. I like the new Dad better, too!

Ed Foreman tells a story about an individual named Tom who had fallen into a rut. Day after day he would come home from work always complaining. His constant complaining caused him to overlook all the good things in his life for which he should be thankful. After attending an Ed Foreman lecture about these twelve habits of winners, he caught himself. This night he came home with a changed outlook and changed behavior. Not only was he not complaining, he was being thankful and grateful for several small things in his life. The change was so dramatic, his wife asked if there was another woman in his life. He responded: "No, dear. There's a new husband."[9]

This story is not about me, even though the name is the same, but it could have been. As I went through my days of not enjoying my work and not growing toward my dreams, there were many nights I came home, ate dinner watching Fox News, complained about all sorts of stuff, and fell asleep on the couch. Thank goodness I *changed the channel.* Not on the TV, but on the station I was playing in my head. My relationships with my wife and my daughters became so much better. Get yourself out of the habit of condemning, criticizing, and complaining, and think of ways of to improve the situation. The big rewards are paid for finding the solutions, not the difficulty.

Too many of my managers over the years were great at finding the problems. Many of them wanted to condemn, criticize, or complain about their employees, the company, or their peers. You recognize very quickly that you don't need them and their attitudes on your team. You need them on the competition's team because otherwise they will suck the life out of your organization and out of you. Find the winners who come to you with solutions. Be the one who brings solutions with every problem to your manager, spouse, and friends.

The second basic habit is to **show real, honest, and hearty appreciation for others.**[10] Let them know they are loved. Unfortunately, that's not what most of us talk about first, is it? If we see someone (our children at home or our employees at work, for example) do one thing wrong and five things right, what do we talk about? It's the one thing wrong, isn't it? If we recognize the things they do right before we comment on the opportunity to improve on the thing done wrong, we'll get more response from others to improve.

My oldest daughter teaches third grade in a socially and economically stressed area of her school district. The children come from broken homes and tough neighborhoods where the teachers are cautioned not to travel far from the school area. She continuously shows these children appreciation and respect. One of her students had a problem with his personal discipline until she started working with him, talking about the good things he'd been doing and the progress he'd made. She raised his conduct score to the point where he became eligible for school field trips. Well, the young boy had a problem away from her class where the environment wasn't as supportive. He got into a pushing match on the bus on the way to school. The Christmas field trip was coming up, and the assistant principle was going to restrict him from the trip as punishment. My daughter stood up for the little boy who had the problem on the bus. She pointed out: "if we don't recognize and appreciate the improvements he's made in my class, he'll never believe having good conduct is worth the effort." The assistant principle trusted my daughter's judgment and permitted the student on the trip. When my daughter told the student he was allowed to go on the trip, his face looked up in amazement that someone of authority had appreciated the improvement he had made even though he did have the one breakdown.

There are countless examples of how letting people know you appreciate them can change people's view of themselves. My newest habit is to sincerely thank every person in the Armed Services I come across in my travels. I thank them for the freedom they provide us and for the service they are providing to our country and the world. No matter what your politics are, the courageous men and women of our Armed Services deserve to know we truly appreciate the sacrifices they make for you and me.

The third basic habit is to **think good thoughts about other people and yourself.**[11] What we dwell upon—whether it is worry, anxiety, fear or courage, or enthusiasm and vitality—will manifest itself into reality. I remember well a time just after I finished *The Successful Life Course* when I was asked to move to a new position and a new city by my employer. It wasn't a plum assignment. The plant I was asked to join had one of the worst reputations in the system. Just prior to the request, I had been to the plant with a team to teach the managers how to improve their packaging labor productivity, so I knew the challenge going into the potential new position. On my pre-acceptance orientation visit, two product managers hosted my tour of their respective areas. At the end of the first tour, the young manager expressed his delight at my joining and leading the team. He believed in his people and believed that with some help and leadership, they could dramatically improve results. The second product manager talked about all the problems in his area. He did not display confidence in his team of supervisors or the people running the production lines. At the end of the tour, he said: "Now Tom, I know we need to improve, and I know you bring a lot of knowledge to the plant, but I just want you to have realistic expectations. This plant will never perform as good as the best plant in the system." (He actually used the other plant's name.) Guess what happened. You got it. After I relocated to the plant and started working with each product manager, the first product manager's team results started soaring. Shortly, they were consistently in the top quartile of performance across the entire company. The second product manager's performance continued to lag. Within a few months, the individual's performance and attitude was so bad he had to leave the company. The first product manager was asked to take over the team that was lagging in performance. You guessed it again. He helped lead that team to success and was rewarded with a promotion within a year.

Each of the product managers had thoughts about the people working for them, and each of them got exactly what they thought they would out of their people. The product manager that looked for and found the good in his team got good results. The product manager that looked for and found the bad got the bad results. But when the person looking for the good in people took over leadership of the same people, he got good results.

Always look for the good, and think good thoughts about other people and about yourself.

The fourth basic habit is to **give before you get.**[12] Always give others a reason to agree with you before asking anything of them. Use the phrase "If there were a way that you could…"[13] as a lead in to the benefits others may receive before asking something of them. For instance, if you are asking an employee to do something, you might point out the benefit to the team or to them personally before asking them to complete the task. Too many supervisors think they can tell employees what to do and that the employees have to take it. Not so. The employees can eventually figure out a way to get back at an arrogant, demanding supervisor.

Today, most managers understand this concept, but the same thing occurs at home. For instance, say you need some clothes picked up at the cleaner and you tell your spouse not to forget to pick them up for you. Uh-oh. Here comes the argument. "Why should I be your personal valet?" Instead, what if you reminded them you knew they would really like to be on time when the two of you attend the party scheduled for tonight? If you then said, "With my late client in the office this evening, it would help the two of us be on time if you would be so kind as to drop by the cleaners and pick up my suit for tonight's party." There's a benefit before the request. What you're doing is thinking about the other person's benefit first. When people benefit, they are glad to help you benefit them.

The fifth basic habit is to **smile often.**[14] It generates enthusiasm, friendliness, and goodwill. This is a habit I really had to work on. I remember when, as a plant manager in a pretzel plant, I was simply walking through the facility when I got an idea about how to improve an administrative process in the office. As I was walking from the back of the plant to the front office, I was concentrating so much on sorting through the idea that I was frowning. About ten minutes after I got back to the office, the plant supervisor came to me and asked what was wrong in the plant. I said: "Nothing, why?" He said the people were all upset because of my frown as I walked through the facility. My frown had disrupted the entire operation. Not only can a smile generate enthusiasm, friendliness, and goodwill; a frown can create worry, doubt, and fear in those around you, especially when you are the leader of the organization.

Since I've been consciously keeping a smile on my face, I notice the tremendous number of smiles I get back. So many people may not have a smile on their face when I smile at them, but immediately they smile back. I get better service and, frankly, it makes me feel better to think I might have brightened someone's day. Give it a try!

The sixth basic habit is to **remember names.**[15] A person's name is the sweetest, most important sound they hear. It immediately captures their attention each time it is used. My wife is remarkable at remembering names. When we were getting married, my mom's best friend and next-door neighbor gave a bridal shower for my wife. There were almost fifty ladies that attended the shower. My soon-to-be wife met each of them as they arrived. A year later, my younger brother was getting married. The same sweet neighbor gave another bridal shower for my brother's soon-to-be wife. My wife was invited and asked to be in the receiving line. Mom told me that all the guests were amazed my wife had remembered every single person's name even though she had only met most of them the one time at her own bridal shower a year before. It sent the message to each of them that they were important and she cared about them.

What's my wife's secret to remembering names? She uses multiple techniques, but always repeats the individual's name she is meeting at least three times before she allows that first conversation to end. Try it. It may work for you too!

The seventh basic habit is to **be an effective communicator by listening.**[16] Encourage others to talk about themselves by asking questions. Remember we have two ears and one mouth, and that's the ratio we ought to use for listening to others speak. The questions when, where, who, what, how, and why serve as the "six honest serving men of clear communication." Ed Foreman told a story about how his business partner used the questions to make a point.

> *"Earlene Vining, a talented, dynamic speaker and business partner of Executive Development Systems in Dallas, Texas was once being interviewed in Houston, Texas on a noontime television program. Earlene arrived at the last moment and she was to be interview by an overly aggressive guy. Immediately as the cameras came on he said, "So, you're the great salesperson type, let's see you sell me something!" Wham! He hit her with a question just like that. Earlene smiled pleasantly and leaned forward and asked, "What do you want me to sell you?" Wham, back at him! She hit him with a question. He said, "Oh, I don't know. Sell me this ashtray." Earlene asked, "Well, why would you be interested in buying this ashtray?" She hit him with another question. He said, "Oh, I don't know it's big. It's beautiful. It's colorful and blends into the set." Earlene then asked, "Why would you be interested in buying an ashtray like that one?" She hit him with still another question! "Well," he said, "We want to keep the set clean and with some guests smoking, we need a place to have them put their ashes." Earlene then said, "Well what would you be willing to pay for an ashtray like this one?" Wham, another question! He said, "Oh, I don't know, I guess about $30." Earlene said, "Sold!" It took Earlene twenty-seven seconds to make the sale. She found out what he wanted, why he wanted it and what he'd pay for it.*
>
> *That's really the secret of selling. It's not trying to sell something to someone that they don't want. It's finding out what people want and helping them get it. If you help people*

get what they want, then people will be grateful. You do that by asking questions and finding out what they don't have that they need and getting it for them."[17]

The eighth basic habit pattern is **think, act, and look happy and successful, and you will begin to think, act, and be successful.**[18] Some people will say: "Come on now, if I'm not actually feeling happy and successful, I'm not going to put on any false front and act like I'm happy and successful. Here's my feeling and response (and Ed's too) to that statement, and I've checked with dozens of people and they agree. I'd much rather deal with and be around someone who is acting happy and successful, than spend a minute with someone who is a sincere sour puss! I don't want to invest a single minute of my precious twenty-four hours each day listening to people who are sincerely negative and letting everyone know about their issues with the world. So you can be a sincere sorehead and have people try to avoid spending any time with you, or you can act enthusiastic and happy and attract enthusiastic and happy people into your life.

Several years ago, I went through an exercise to ferret out some of my beliefs. One of my personal beliefs is: Enthusiasm is contagious. If you are enthusiastic and negative, you will attract more enthusiastically negative people into your life. I choose to be enthusiastic and positive, so I will have more enthusiastic and positive people in my life. If you don't like the word "act," then use the word "practice." Practice being positive and enthusiastic. Winners practice doing the things they don't like to do until they become comfortable with the new habit.

Ed Foreman says: "Dance like nobody's watching, love like you've never been hurt, sing like no one is listening, and work like you don't need the money. When you do that, you'll find little difference between your work and your play."[18] You'll actually find, and people will see, that your work and your play are the same.

The ninth basic habit pattern is to **never engage in worry conversations or participate in gossip sessions.**[19] You can always get out of a worry conversation you don't want to be in. You dismiss yourself with a statement like: "I apologize, but I have a client waiting for me to call right now. I'll have to get back to you." If people start coming to you with gossip or worry, you turn it around to the wholesome, the positive, or the pure.

Ed Foreman tells the story about a man that had a lot of worries on his mind one night as he went to bed. He kept tossing and turning and tossing and turning. Finally, after waking his wife up for the fourth time she said, "Honey, what is the matter?" The man said, "Dear, you know that note that we have at the bank for $500,000 that's due tomorrow?" She said, "Yes." "Well," he said, "we don't have the money to pay that note tomorrow." She said, surprised, "We're not going to be able to pay it?" He said, "We're not going to be able to pay it." The wife asked, "Can't you factor some receivables?" He said, "Honey, I've already factored the receivables." She asked several other questions, all of them leading to the same negative response of "No." So, she reached over to the bed stand, picked up the telephone, and called the bank president at his home. The sleepy banker picks up the phone and the wife says, "You know that $500,000 note that we have at your bank. It's due tomorrow and we're not going to be able to pay it, but my husband will be in at the bank tomorrow at 10:00 and will talk to you about it. Good night." She hung up the phone and turned to her husband and said, "Go to sleep, Sweetheart. Now, he's got it!"[20]

As silly as it sounds, it was as though his wife grabbed this big bunch of worry-worms out of his head and hurled them through the telephone line right across town to the bank president. As the husband lay there, he began to think about things he could do. He had some big contracts coming up. He came up with some good ideas of how he might handle that loan, or, at a minimum, he might be able to pay the interest. The next morning, he met up with a sleepy-eyed bank president who was more than willing to jump on any proposal to keep him from foreclosing on the business. The ideas had come because he had gotten away from the worrying and instead started thinking about the ways to make things work.

Worry is defined in two ways. First, it's negative goal setting. I believe in goal setting, which is thinking about what you want and developing plans and taking actions to achieve them. Worry is nothing, more or less, than negative goal setting. Unfortunately, it works extremely well at getting you what you are thinking (or worrying) about as well. Another way to look at worry is that it is the misuse of your imagination. Use your imagination to create solutions, not to create negative potential events.

The tenth basic habit pattern is to **always greet people with a positive, cheerful statement, not the typical question: "How are you?"**[21] Why not? You don't want to offer any "negaholic" a chance to complain, so replace that question with: "Good Morning, you're looking great today!" or "Good Morning, I like that bright smile on your face! It cheers me up as we start the day! Thanks."

You see the difference? Most of the time you have passed on a compliment to people and they appreciate it. There is little room this way to allow negative people to start complaining.

Now, if you see someone who's not looking so good, don't lie and tell them how great they look. They will know it's insincere. You can, however, tell them you're glad to see them. And you know what? They'll be glad to see you, too.

The eleventh basic habit pattern is to **respond to another's question of "How are you?" with an enthusiastic, meaningful "Terrific!"**[22] This was the first habit pattern I went to work on following my weekend at *The Successful Life Course*. As I mentioned in the preface, I get incredible reactions to my "Terrific!" Just the other day, I got the response: "Oh, I was about to answer "Fine," but you didn't ask that question did you?" People are in such a habit of answering and asking that there is no real sincerity. Be sincere with people. Don't say "fine" and tell your subconscious mind you're just barely okay. You're not just okay. You're a special, terrific person and you need to be telling yourself and your subconscious mind just that!

Interestingly, as I reflect back on those couple of darker years, I didn't respond "Terrific!" as often. It should have been a real clue to me that I wasn't thinking positive thoughts like I should have been. As Zig Ziglar would say, I had "'Stinkin' Thinking!"[23] It was a clue. Today, my response is immediate and without restraint: "I'm TERRIFIC!" You are too!

The final basic habit pattern is to **look for and expect "Goood" things to happen to you, and to inquire of others: "What 'Goood' Things are happening with you today?"**[24] When you look for good things, you find good things. One way I have used this habit was by beginning each staff meeting with the agenda topic of "Tell about a good thing that happened in your department last week." It was so much fun. In fact, it became a positive feeding frenzy. Each staff member would share something positive from his or her department that was better than the last member's offering. It started the meeting off on not just a positive note, but on thinking about accomplishments. As we planned for the upcoming week, it was with thoughts of what we were going to accomplish! These staff meetings were fun and helped the business we were leading to move forward.

These are twelve basic habits winners develop. Frankly, all of them are simple, but many are not easy because of our current habits. Are these some habits you would wish to be yours? Would they make your life's journey more efficient and help make your results outcomes accelerate toward your definite chief aims and your dreams? As you make changes in the "choices" areas of the SLSD Model, see what happens to your habits, but here's a tip: Don't try to create these habits all at once. It's too much. Select one habit a week to begin. In roughly four months (after you do each for twenty-one days), you'll have all twelve habits! Good luck.

Below is a summary of the twelve habits:[25]

1. Don't condemn, criticize, or complain. Think of ways to improve the situation.
2. Show real, honest, and sincere appreciation.
3. Think good thoughts about other people and yourself.
4. Give before you get. Always give others a reason to agree with you before asking anything of them.
5. Smile often to generate enthusiasm, friendliness, and goodwill.
6. Remember people's names.
7. Be an effective communicator. Encourage others to talk about themselves by asking questions (remember the six honest serving men of communica-

tion: when, where, who, what, how, and why?)

8. Think, act, and look happy and successful.
9. Never engage in worry conversations or participate in gossip sessions.
10. Always greet others with a positive, cheerful statement instead of the question, "How are you?"
11. Respond to the question: "How are you?" with an enthusiastic: "Terrific!"
12. Look for and expect goood things to happen to you.

I've spoken extensively about habits and really haven't discussed emotions and life skills. We've touched on the emotions of happiness, feeling positive, or feeling negative. Again, people key off of our emotions and how they are expressed as they determine their perception of our character. How many times have you referenced a person as happy or bitter or angry or upbeat or fun? Those emotions that are regularly displayed are what we use to describe them. It's a part of who they are.

How do you want to be described emotionally? I've heard people say they can't control their emotions. I disagree. They've developed the habit of not controlling their emotions for various reasons. Sometimes the role modeling from their parents, friends, or managers allows them to rationalize their emotions. Sometimes it is part of how they decide to get their needs met. Many of these will be discussed in later chapters, but realize right now: we can make choices that lead to how we react or respond emotionally to situations or circumstances we are faced with. Then, believe it or not, however you typically react emotionally is noticed and noted by people who are around you. Like it or not, they describe you that way. You can control how you are described by controlling your emotions.

Finally, our style or character is linked to our skills. My youngest daughter describes herself as the mathematical type. My oldest daughter is an organizer. My wife has great fine motor skills and is an excellent seamstress. I was always proud of my problem solving and conceptual skills. These become significant because they become some of our competencies that people recognize and draw upon when they think of us.

If my manager had an extremely conceptual problem to deal with, he would assign me the task or problem. Why is this significant? Because the skills we develop either open doors of opportunity toward our success or they close them down. We need to make choices on the skills that will propel us toward our dreams.

Habits, emotions, and skills are attributes of your personality that people can and do observe. For people, these repetitive observations define your style and your character. Your character is the outcome of your choices that we will explore in further chapters. Your character also moderates these choices to improve or dampen the outcomes leading toward your dreams.

If your style and character are what you want others to perceive, if they are enablers of your dreams, and you feel good about them, then you are right on! If not, then new choices can help you move closer toward how you want to be perceived, what will enable your dreams, and what will create personal pride.

Chapter Four

Those Nasty Old External Influencers

We live in a real world, not in a vacuum or life-long seminar where the environment is totally controlled and all the negative influences are buffered from impacting us. The reality of life is we are most often in an environment where other individuals or other organizations try, can, and do have an influence on us. Their influence can be small or great depending on many factors including the amount of exposure we have with the influence, the frequency or how often we have exposure with the influence, and how we allow the influence to impact us (but more on that later).

In the operations management business, whether it was actually said or not, planning would be easy if it weren't for the customers. They always seemed to want what we didn't have enough of and didn't want what we had too much of! Clearly, the customer's decisions on what to buy from our companies have a huge impact and influence on the choices the companies we work for need to make.

There are other external influencers in business as well. They include competitors, shareholders, stakeholders, employees, suppliers, unions, the community we operate in, and government regulations around the world. Any and all of these can impact and influence the decisions a company needs to make to be successful in achieving their long term desired outcomes and their desired culture.

It's true with each of us as well. There are many, and I mean many, external influencers in our lives. It's important to identify what and who those influencers are as we leverage the SLSD Model.

Begin with those closest to you. Your spouse, your children, and your best friends are some of them. You will later need to identify as many of these external influencers or influences as possible. Mine influence list begins below:

- My wife
- My children
- My father
- My brother
- My brother-in-law Tom
- My mentors: Ed Foreman and Paul Gustavson
- My spiritual advisors
- My wife's mother and other family members
- My friends at Tennessee National Golf Club
- My friends through other clubs
- My manager*
- The people I work with*
- The company I work for*
- My financial advisor
- The students I teach
- Some of my former employees
- My close neighbors
- My health advisors
- The authors of books I read
- The Internet
- Newspapers
- What I watch on television
- Golfers I compete against
- My community
- The stock market
- My state and national government

* denotes key individuals or groups that used to have a large influence on me.

Like it or not, all of these people, groups of people, and organizations have an influence on me. Many of the influences are good and positive; some are less so.

It's been said that your income is the average of your five best friends. Wow! Is that an influence? You bet it is! It's also been said that your closest friends and associates influence how you think. That's even more powerful!

We've all had both the good influences and some that are less favorable. Paul Gustavson and Ed Foreman have both always been great influences on me. They provide positive encouragement and support every time I'm associated with them. Paul has always challenged my thinking and helped me look at things from different perspectives. He's a teacher and a coach while being a true friend. Ed's words to me are always so encouraging, but I also learn from his actions. His actions are so consistent with what he teaches from the lecture platform. He inspires me to be a better person and to always improve on how I lead others.

Unfortunately, we have times when we follow or are influenced in the wrong direction. With a bit of a chuckle, I can remember learning to curse while playing playground football in fifth grade. I heard others cursing and believed I needed to curse to either be accepted by the group or maybe to be a better football player. It wasn't very appropriate to be influenced that way.

Neither was it good or appropriate to later in life drift in my management style to fit the style of the manager I worked for. I never completely adopted his style, but I moved far enough that I wasn't authentic in my behavior. Only after I recognized the drift and brought myself back to center did I feel good about myself and start making a better difference for my team.

What I'm trying to say is we all are influenced, both positively and negatively. We need to surround ourselves with more of those positive influences and less of the negative influences.

What other influences are there in your life in addition to people? Have you ever thought about it? Let's see, how about what you listen to, what you watch, and what you read?

Do you listen to the radio when you are driving to and from work? If so, what's on the radio? If it's the news, how positive and uplifting is that? If it is music, is it baroque classical music that stimulates your thinking or a country-western station with songs about the spouse that did you wrong? You have a choice. My favorite thing to listen to in the car while commuting is recorded audios from great speakers like Earl Nightingale, Denis Waitley, or Ed Foreman. Even when my commute was only ten minutes, I would walk into the office uplifted from the audios, ready to go instead of worrying about the latest murders, wars, and rapes discussed on the news station of the radio.

What do you watch on television? Again, it's your choice. Do you think watching violence or arguing political adversaries benefits you? Probably not. Again, there are uplifting movies you can watch and educational DVD series you can view.

The same is true with what you read. Reading the front page of most newspapers is only slightly better than watching the news on TV. It's filled with last night's murders, disasters, and political arguments. You can make other choices for your reading pleasure, if you choose. Books to inspire, teach, and develop would have a better influence than the front page of the newspaper each morning, or better than a fiction novel filled with violence or less than positive stories.

I'm not saying you should never read the front page of the newspaper, watch a TV political news station, or listen to rock or country-western music. What I am suggesting is you should know and understand the influence they are having on you. Then, if there's something to be gained by adding some variety beyond your current influences, consider trying the alternatives and measure the effect (influence) on how your feel and how you think.

So understand the influencers in your world and the type of influence they are having on you. Later we'll discuss some strategies you might be using on your influencers today and some strategies you might want to use on your influencers in the future. For now, just recognize you are influenced by the people around you and the other things that are picked up by your senses, like television, movies, radio, books, magazines, and newspapers.

======================================

The exercise associated with this chapter is:

- Key Influencer Identification Exercise (Day 9)

======================================

Chapter Five

Choices: You are Empowered

THE NEXT PART OF THE model contains your choices. There are four categories of strategic choices and six categories of what I call life choices. This is the area where the "rubber meets the road." It's a tough area because we have to make conscious choices, otherwise we choose to live by default by not making a choice.

Over the next ten chapters, we will review and provide thoughts for each of the ten mentioned categories, but before we get into those thoughts, I need to discuss some key concepts to help you accelerate your path toward your dreams.

Do I mean you really have a choice in how your life flights? Absolutely, but often it might be easier or a more convenient approach to just "fly by the seat of your pants." Or even easier, let's just do what our friends do. By choosing something different, we might make waves. It might offend our friends if we don't agree with what they have chosen (or defaulted).

Sometimes it is tough making a choice. Could you make a wrong choice? Yes, as a matter of fact, you could.

Earlier I mentioned a corollary to the saying "if you don't know where you are going, then any road will get you there." The corollary is: "Even if you know what your dream is, the wrong path or road will be inefficient in getting you the success you want."

I recently lived out this corollary. Let me explain.

Shortly after I began this book, my wife and I were in Dallas, Texas to attend a seminar. Our daughter was flying into Dallas to meet us for the course. Her flight was delayed for a couple of hours due to weather in Dallas, so we went back to the hotel instead of waiting two hours longer at the airport. As we headed back to pick her up, there were two parallel freeways within two blocks of each other that crossed the road our hotel was on. Unfortunately, I didn't notice the second freeway as we had come back to the hotel earlier. As you might guess by now, we (or should I say I) took the wrong freeway and shortly started heading north instead of west.

Trying not to backtrack, I began taking back roads trying to find the westbound freeway. It was dark that night due to the rain as we traveled through an industrial area, when suddenly I hit the pothole of all potholes! Immediately, the low air pressure warning light came on. I was able to quickly get the car to a well-lit filling station. As I went inside to find out whether they had an air pump station, I could tell the front passenger tire was completely flat. As I pumped the tire with air, I heard the sickening sound of escaping air. As I located and felt the leak with my hand and told my wife the tire would not inflate, a kind man parked his truck behind us and got out to ask if we needed any help. He also informed us we were definitely in a bad part of town. It was then that I noticed the strip joints and liquor stores across the highway. I told him I could use some help and he graciously proceeded to help me change the tire and provided directions to get us quickly back on course. He was a guardian angel for us that night.

As we headed toward the airport, things seemed to be going fine until the low air pressure light lit up on the dashboard again. We cautiously made it to the terminal and pulled over to wait for our daughter. I checked the doughnut tire to see if it was going flat, and though it was a bit low, it seemed okay. It was when my wife walked back to the car from checking on our daughter's new arrival time that she noticed the rear passenger tire was now completely flat.

Unfortunately, cars don't come with two spare tires, so AAA became our next best friend. While I waited for the tow truck, my wife and daughter took a shuttle to pick up a rental car. An hour or so later, our car was ready to be towed. The AAA tow truck driver landed us safely to a tire store and we arrived back at our hotel well over two hours later than the time we would have arrived had I taken the right road in the first place.

There were some lessons for me to learn through this experience. The first was mentioned earlier. Even when you know what your goal is (ours being the DFW airport, Terminal B), if you take the wrong road, then it takes longer to reach your goal. There were a couple of other interesting lessons as well. There were people trying to help us reach our goal safely even though we got on the wrong road. It would have taken me longer to change the tire without the kind gentleman that took the time and effort to help. I probably wouldn't have gotten back on the right path without his coaching and guidance.

In life, it's the same way. You can end up on the wrong pathway even if you know what your goals and dreams are. The wrong road will cause you to be less efficient in attaining your goals. It may even cost you more. (Two new tires and a new alignment at the cost $588 in my case.) The good news is there are people to help you, but who do you listen to? There are two criteria. Listen to the people who have been where you are and who have achieved or gotten to where you want to go. The gentleman who helped me—my guardian angel that night—worked close to where we were and was filling his truck up when he saw us limp the car to the air pump. Second, he had been where we were trying to go, which in this case was out of the bad part of town and headed to the DFW airport. We listened and followed his sage advice. As you find yourself on a road that isn't moving you toward your goals and dreams, find someone who has been where you are and is now living your dreams and goals. They are the best source of sage advice.

The next concept before we get into the various categories is called the Teach-ability Index.[1] The Teach-ability Index is simply this: your willingness to learn and your willingness to change. Each of the components is measured on a one to ten scale and then multiplied together. Let's look at a few examples.

George is a very smart individual. He reads books and magazines regularly, especially magazines about his goal to achieve his ideal weight of 175 pounds. Today, however, George weighs 253 pounds. George has read and learned he needs to reduce his caloric intake, consume a lot less processed sugar and processed flour products, and he should be drinking half his pound weight in ounces of water each day. Let's say that with this knowledge, George's willingness to learn is an 8.

But what does George eat? Well, he doesn't enjoy breakfast very much, so often he skips it, which he knows isn't right. When he does take time for breakfast, he eats corn flakes with two scoops of white sugar on it. He doesn't like the taste of the corn flakes without the sugar and he has reduced the sugar from four scoops to two. At lunch he eats a peanut butter sandwich with grape jelly and drinks a soda he brings from home. He saves a lot of money this way. For dinner, George often eats pizza.

So what is George's Teach-ability Index? Well, as we said, his willingness to learn is high. He scored 8 in that category. However, his willingness to change—to eat as he has learned—is low. Maybe a 1 or a 2. So two times eight is 16 versus a maximum score of 100. His unwillingness to *do* what he has learned is better for him dramatically lowers his index. But he's teachable, right? Well, if you know better, but don't do it, then is there really any value in knowing what to do? I think not. One might even say you've wasted your time learning if you're not going to take action and make the changes necessary to improve yourself. It almost sounds like an oxymoron.

This leads to the second concept I'd like to share with you before we move on. The concept is pretty simple: You are 100% responsible for your success and your current situation.

Some people will not take this statement very well. They prefer to blame it on others and actually suffer from a form of *excusitis*.[2] My parents didn't teach me so and so… I have a boss who doesn't respect and appreciate me… John got the good assignment and I got stuck in this crummy job. Yeah, yeah, yeah. It's always someone else's fault. I've heard it before. I've even done some of the same rationalization myself, but when I'm truly honest with myself, I am 100% responsible for my successes, my failures, my happiness, and my disappointments. I'll bet you've heard the phrase: "If it's going to be, then it's up to me!" Have you ever really, really thought about the phase? Isn't it really saying, "I'm 100% responsible for my outcomes"? Sure it is, and sure you are!

Andy Andrews wrote a terrific book entitled The Traveler's Gift. The traveler, an individual at the crossroads of his life, receives letters that are gifts as he meets some incredible historic individuals. The first gift, the first decision for success, is entitled "The buck stops here!" and is captured as an excerpt below:

> *"From this moment forward I will accept responsibility for my past. I understand that the beginning of wisdom is to accept the responsibility for my own problems and that by accepting responsibility for my past, I free myself to move into a bigger, brighter future of my own choosing.*
>
> *Never again will I blame my parents, my spouse, my boss, or other employees for my present situation. Neither my education nor lack of one, my genetics, or the circumstantial ebb and flow of everyday life will affect my future in a negative way. If I allow myself to blame these uncontrollable forces for my lack of success, I will be forever caught in a web of the past. I will look forward. I will not let my history control my destiny.*
>
> *The buck stops here. I accept responsibility for my past. I am responsible for my success.*
>
> *I am where I am today—mentally, physically, spiritually, emotionally, and financially—because of decisions I have made. My decisions have always been governed by my thinking. Therefore, I am where I am today—mentally, physically,*

spiritually, emotionally, and financially—because of how I think. Today I will begin the process of changing where I am—mentally, physically, spiritually, emotionally, and financially—by changing the way I think.

My thoughts will be constructive, never destructive. My mind will live in the solutions of the future. It will not dwell in the problems of the past. I will seek the association of those who are working and striving to bring about positive changes in the world. I will never seek comfort by associating with those who have decided to be comfortable.

When faced with the opportunity to make a decision, I will make one. I understand that God did not put in me the ability to always make right decisions. He did, however, put in me the ability to make a decision and then make it right. The rise and fall of my emotional tide will not deter me from my course. When I make a decision, I will stand behind it. My energy will go into making the decision. I will waste none on second thoughts. My life will not be an apology. It will be a statement.

The buck stops here. I control my thoughts. I control my emotions.

In the future, when I am tempted to ask the question, "Why me?" I will immediately counter the answer: "Why not me?" Challenges are gifts, opportunities to learn. Problems are the common thread running through the lives of great men and women. In times of adversity, I will not have a problem to deal with; I will have a choice to make. My thoughts will be clear. I will make the right choice. Adversity is preparation for greatness. I will accept this preparation. Why me? Why not me? I will be prepared for something great!

I accept responsibility for my past. I control my thoughts. I control my emotions. I am responsible for my success.

The buck stops here."[3]

Will you take this affirmation and make it your own? Will you take 100% responsibility for your thoughts, for your life and for your success? Will you begin asking, "Why not me?" in place of "Why me?" Will you use your ability to make decisions and then, if need be, make them right? This is the section of the SLSD Model where you start taking 100% responsibility and start learning more about the choice categories we have in our life. The buck actually starts here for your choices.

The SLSD Model has ten subcategories of choices. Four of those categories are more strategic, meaning they are usually a bit more long range or look at the bigger picture. These choices generally don't change very much over the short term. These four choices are:

- Your personal mission
- Your personal guiding principles
- Your strategies to influence your external influencers
- Your chief aims and goals.

The other six subcategories in the SLSD Model are called Life Choices. They are a bit more tactical. Often times when your personal style/character or your personal results are not where you wish them to be, changes in these areas can be made to make course corrections.

As a friendly reminder:

If you want things to change in your life, you're going to have to make changes in your life.[4]

So, get ready, let's start looking at the choice categories, so you can start making changes to start living by design.

Chapter Six

Your Personal Mission Statement

WE NOW BEGIN BY DEFINING your first strategic choice: your personal mission statement.

It seems for the past twenty years or so, every business I have worked for has developed a mission statement for the company. Mission statements for companies are designed to provide direction and clarity to the employees about what business they are in. It should help guide them with decisions they need to make. The mission statement often is inspiring to employees and customers as well. At Bristol-Myers Squibb, the mission was to "extend and enhance human life."[1] Wow, talk about inspiring! It really was. It brought energy and passion to employees as they went about their jobs.

I came to realize that individuals needed a personal mission statement several years ago as I read the book by Jim Loehr and Tony Schwartz entitled The Power of Full Engagement. Further, I realized I needed my own personal mission statement. Through their book, I realized there is a purpose within me that "lights me up." When I am "on mission" or "on purpose," I feel better about myself and what I'm doing than when I'm not "on purpose." The authors go on to explain, "Purpose creates a destination. It drives full engagement by prompting our desire to invest focused energy in a particular activity or goal. We become fully engaged only when we care deeply, when we feel that what we are doing really matters."[2]

When you are fully engaged, time doesn't matter. Spending an hour "on purpose" seems like but a few minutes. In his book The Success Principles, Jack Canfield writes: "Identifying, acknowledging, and honoring this purpose is perhaps the most important action successful people take. They take time to understand what they're here to do—and then they pursue it with passion and enthusiasm."[3] He continues, "But with a purpose, everything in life seems to fall into place. To be 'on purpose' means you are doing what you love to do, what you're good at doing, and accomplishing what's important to you."[4]

Most people don't take the time to understand their mission or purpose. So caught up in the activities of the day, they often begrudgingly float from one activity to the next, from one meeting to the next, from one purposeless task to the next. It's living by default, not by design. Without mission or purpose, others seem to direct your activities instead of you deciding if the activity is aligned with your mission.

We've all known someone who pursued one direction in life only to discover that though the direction might create a terrific income, they were not happy or content with how they were spending their life. They may have been successful by other people's definition, but they were not following their own mission or purpose. They were spending the majority of their awakened hours "off purpose" and the results were characteristics such as disengagement, lethargy, and sometimes anger or hostility. Yet those same people, once they start doing things that are "on mission," seem to light up. They're engaged and contributing at a very, very high level.

I know an individual who seemed to really enjoy golf as we were growing up. He was good at it too. He was captain of his high school golf team and went to the state championships regularly. He thought he wanted to become a golf professional so began studying agronomy in college. During his fourth year in college, he realized that becoming a golf professional was really not his passion any more. He changed his major to engineering (how different is that!), graduated, and went to work in that field. Later he went back to college to get his masters and continued on to receive his doctorate. Today, he plays very little golf, but listening to him speak on the different engineering features of his own home, or the project he is leading at work to reduce home energy consumption by fifty percent, I know he is "on purpose" because of the passion and energy he exudes as he tells me about these things.

Are you "on mission?" Have you defined your mission? According to the Power of Full Engagement, the book which really caused me to define my mission, "Purpose becomes a more powerful and enduring source of energy in our lives in three ways: when its source moves from negative to positive, external to internal, and self to others."[5]

When your purpose is negative, or fueled by a feeling of deficit, your possibilities to fulfilling the mission become more limited. A negative purpose creates negative emotions such as fear, disgust, anger, or even hatred. Some of these emotions can create strong (negative) energy, but at a great cost. Eventually these emotions drain your energy. They also prompt toxic hormones in our bodies that eventually create exhaustion and disease. Therefore, your source of purpose needs to come from positive desires and emotions such as love, passion, fulfillment, gratification, tranquility, or enjoyment. These emotions create positive energy, and being "on mission" helps to renew the energy instead of drain it.

Your mission becomes more powerful also when it becomes intrinsically motivated. Intrinsic motives are those we desire to engage in because of the value we receive just for the satisfaction the action provides. You may say the only motive in intrinsic motivation is the joy received by doing what we believe is the right thing to do. The opposite, extrinsic motivation, is the desire to get more of something we feel we don't have enough of (the desire to do something we may or may not like to do because of external rewards). A prime example would be money. It's true that people are motivated by money, but there is no correlation between the amount of money people have and happiness. There is a base level of money needed to meet our survival needs, but beyond that level, as they say: "Money can't buy happiness." The point is that by doing activities by which we are intrinsically motivated, the more likely our purpose or mission will be enduring and will provide us needed energy.

Finally, our mission should move beyond ourselves in order to provide even more energy and strength. According to Joanne Ciulla, author of The Working Life, "Work makes life better if it helps others; alleviates suffering; eliminates difficult or tedious toil; makes someone healthier and happier; or aesthetically or intellectually enriches people and improves the environment in which we live."[6] When we help or serve others, we receive great satisfaction. In Sonja Lyubomirsky's book, The How of Happiness, one of the twelve happiness activities is "Practicing Acts of Kindness."[7] Developing a personal mission that moves you to help others helps you stay happy.

Another reason to have your mission statement is shared on the Nightingale Conant website. Their definition of a personal mission statement is "a purposeful promise that carries you toward your goals."[8] It provides you focus and direction. Think about some of the people you know who do not have a mission statement. Are their activities scattered or focused? Are they clear about the next decision they need to make and how it will move them closer to their dreams and goals, or do their decisions seem to come from different directions? Are they likely to achieve success? You can only do it by random chance, but certainly this approach is not by design.

It may seem too simple that you need to start your choices with your mission statement. Why? It's because all other choices need to be in alignment with your mission.

As I came to understand my personal need for a mission statement, I reflected back upon times when I was completely happy and satisfied. It turned out those times were often when I did things that caused others to grow even though they may not realize or recognize what I might have done to help them. I characterized these times as when I was helping others achieve more of their full potential. Those times included both personal and professional experiences. They included times when I saw my daughter's face light up as she conquered a perceived hurdle growing up, or times when one of my managers received a promotion as their skills and knowledge grew, or a time when I helped a friend improve their golf game, or a time when a friend came over for career advice. I really, really enjoyed helping others grow and become able to do the things in their life or with their career that, at one time, they didn't believe they would achieve. Even as I am writing this, these memories have brought a smile to my face. So for me, that's the center point of my mission statement—to help others achieve their fullest potential.

So what's my full mission statement and how did I develop it?

A few years ago, I went to a class about management and leading others and participated in an exercise to create my personal brand story. It ends with my personal mission statement. The exercise caused me to reflect on my past and consider key moments, key influences in my life which caused me to develop certain beliefs. Fortunately over the years, I had developed a set of beliefs I could examine as I wrote my story. The process we did in class that day is very similar to the process[9] shared in Jon Gordon's terrific little book entitled The Seed. (It's a book I highly recommend as you are considering your purpose or personal mission.) At the end of the exercise, each participant wrote their personal brand story and shared it with the others. It was an emotional exercise. I cried as I developed and wrote the essay and my voice cracked with emotion as I read my story aloud. After I returned home from the exercise, I shared my story with my wife. I also shared my story with the managers that worked for me. It truly became my story and my personal mission. Below is the personal brand story I wrote that day and my personal mission at the end of the story.

Tom Ward's Personal Brand Story

I grew up in Tullahoma, Tennessee, a small town in the middle of the state. I was actively supported in sports and there were always high expectations of me academically and morally from my two terrific parents.

Dad was an engineer's engineer who read business literature on his own and to this day, at 83, works harder than most people.

Mom was a coal miner's daughter from a family of nine brothers and sisters. She was a stay-at-home mom for my younger brother, Bob, and me. As we left for college, she began her career becoming the most successful realtor in town selling "homes, instead of houses."

Mom and Dad were an incredible team, providing Bob and me opportunities to grow in many directions and along the way set a high expectation that we grow.

I attended the University of Tennessee where I learned to enjoy learning. There, I also learned I had much more capability than I thought I had entering college. UT was an environment that opened the boundaries of my world.

My career began at the Proctor & Gamble Jackson, TN Plant, home of Pringles New Fangled Potato Chips. P&G Jackson was another unusual and mind-stretching environment for a new engineer just out of college. The plant had a non-traditional social structure where technicians were encouraged to grow through a skill based pay system and received two growth appraisals and two merit appraisals each year. As a team manager, most of my time was spent developing growth plans for each individual on the team and providing feedback for their growth instead of the traditional supervisor roles of "filling out timecards" and "chasing flashlight batteries" for people. It was a special environment of empowering employees and managers. It taught me to set high expectations for people that stretch them beyond their comfort zones at times.

I was then transferred to the Ivorydale (Cincinnati) Food Plant. Ivorydale was at the opposite end of the social spectrum, a 100-year-old union plant with many, many classifications and boundaries. It put me in a situation where I had to choose to conform to the status quo or become a change agent and bring the concepts from Jackson to Ivorydale.

P&G helped me shape two of my core beliefs:

1. *Status Quo kills.*
2. *People make the difference (not a difference, THE difference).*

At P&G I also set a riveting goal to become a plant manager by the age of 35. Why 35? It was because I learned that was the youngest age anyone had ever achieved the position at P&G, and the competitive nature from my early days in sports came out. In order to achieve that goal I was recruited and accepted a role with Frito-Lay. I achieved the goal and in so doing, it cemented a third basic belief:

3. *Persistence pays.*

Upon achieving the plant manager role, I had a short period of joy and satisfaction, but then began feeling lost without that strong goal to pull me forward, so I set a direction for age 45 and age 55. Notice I said "direction" versus specific goal. This time, I identified three options at each age target. Analyzing the age 45 direction, the step that would support any of the three was to get my MBA.

I entered the Washington University Executive MBA program and met a soul mate and great friend, Dean Kropp. Dean was my Management Science professor and my advisor. Through Dean, I learned the joy of helping others achieve their goals and dreams.

I learned in a book called The Power of Full Engagement that we have to manage our energy: our physical, mental, emotional, and spiritual energy. Spiritual energy is not just about religion—it's your personal mission that motivates you and gives you energy. So my personal mission became:

"For my family, my friends, and my associates, to help them achieve their fullest potential."

This became my spirit within. This internal spirit is energized when I'm helping others grow and similarly saddened and de-energized when I do things that slow others' progress to their full potential.

I'd like to add that this spirit has been recently re-energized. Re-energized, it is helping me have fun at work, at home, and at play.

This reinforces three of my other beliefs and values:

4. *You have to be passionate to be excellent.*
5. *Enthusiasm and belief are contagious.*
6. *Extraordinary people create extraordinary outcomes.*

Finally, there is an extraordinary person in my life: my wife, Emily. She is not only my wife, she is my best friend, my greatest supporter, and my angel on earth. From her I've learned that:

7. *Alone I am less and together we are more.*

So my personal (mission) is:

To be the teacher and coach who helps others achieve their fullest potential to become extraordinary, enthusiastic, passionate achievers.

Don't believe it's important to have a personal mission? At the time I wrote this mission, I was leading a large operations organization and, as is mentioned in the story, my spirit was re-energized in that role. However, I began to dream about other ways to teach and coach others to achieve their fullest potential. Over the six months that followed, my life and engagement in this mission completely changed. I moved on from the corporate world and moved into my next phase of contribution, including sharing this book. Has really understanding what my mission, my internal spirit, been important to me? As Robert Frost shares with us in his poem, The Road Not Taken:

> *"…and I,*
>
> *I took the one less traveled by,*
>
> *And that has made all the difference."*[10]

======================================

The exercises associated with this chapter are:

- Personal Mission Statement Exercise (Day 5)
- Personal Mission Survey (Day 6)
- Personal Mission Statement Test (Day 6)

======================================

Chapter Seven

Your Personal Guiding Principles

ON BUSINESSDICTIONARY.COM, GUIDING PRINCIPLES ARE defined as "any principles or precepts that guide an organization throughout its life in all circumstances, irrespective of changes in its goals, strategies, type of work or the top management."[1]

Defining your guiding principles or personal values is important to creating your success. In their book The Leadership Challenge, James Kouzes and Barry Posner share: "We are much more in control of our own lives when we're clear about our personal values. When values are clear, we don't have to rely upon direction from someone in authority."[2] Sadly, if *you* don't define your beliefs, others will do it for you. It could be your parents, your boss, other family members, or your friends. By developing your own guiding principles, you define what's important to you. You are building a foundation that will withstand and hold strong through the storms of life. These principles give us a basis from which to make decisions and take actions in our life. This is why developing your personal guiding principles is a strategic choice for you.

In essence, guiding principles become the "compass" for you to follow as you design and live a successful life. Another analogy is that guiding principles are the roadmap for action. Why? Again from

Kouzes and Posner: "Values influence every aspect of our lives: our moral judgments, our responses to others, our commitments to personal goals. Values set the parameters for the hundreds of decisions we make every day. Options that run counter to our value systems are seldom acted upon and if they are, it's done with a sense of compliance rather than commitment."[3]

Who wants to live a life of compliance? Not me, but we've all been there. It's not fun. You *have* to go to work instead of wanting to get started each day. You do things because you are *told to* instead of because you believe the directive is right. I remember vividly a conversation I had with my manager once about one of my beliefs at work. It wasn't a major principle, but it was the belief that people earn their vacation, and by not disrupting their (and their family's) plans, it created loyalty to the company and a willingness to go beyond the call of duty during their non-vacation days. My manager believed there would be no vacation if it weren't for the business, so why the (expletive deleted) did I allow (my subordinate) to take vacation one particular week. (It was actually two weeks.) I didn't change my subordinate's vacation, but without my value of integrity, it would have been much easier to force the individual to change their vacation than deal with the tension I felt for standing on my belief. I was committed to my belief. My value of integrity drove my decision not to interrupt the individual's vacation. In the end, I felt better for standing up for my belief than I would have felt if I had caved in to the pressure and complied with my manager's wish.

According to Jim Loehr: "Across cultures, religions, and time itself, people have admired and aspired to the same universal values—among them integrity, generosity, courage, humility, compassion, loyalty, perseverance—while rejecting their opposites—deceit, greed, cowardice, arrogance, callousness, disloyalty and sloth."[4]

Further from Kouzes and Pozner: "Values also motivate. They keep us focused on why we're doing what we're doing and the ends towards which we are striving. Values are the banners that we fly as we persist, as we struggle, as we toil. We refer to them when we need to replenish our energy."[5]

Values and guiding principles are individual, though. Some are more compelling than others to different people. Some hold a higher degree of importance to one person than they do others. Below is a list of some of the Deepest Values[6] listed in The Power of Full Engagement

• Authenticity	• Health
• Balance	• Honesty
• Commitment	• Humor
• Compassion	• Integrity
• Concern for others	• Kindness
• Courage	• Knowledge
• Creativity	• Loyalty
• Empathy	• Openness
• Excellence	• Perseverance
• Fairness	• Respect for others
• Faith	• Responsibility
• Family	• Security
• Freedom	• Serenity
• Friendship	• Service to others
• Generosity	
• Genuineness	
• Happiness	
• Harmony	

Each value has meaning that is personal to you. I know what integrity means to me, but it may be slightly different for you. Integrity may mean being honest in words and deed to you. To me, integrity means having the strength of character not to give way to dishonesty or deceit during times of stress. As you identify the key principles and key values to develop your principles, you need to define what those values mean to you.

Below are examples of two different guiding principles so you can see how they have defined an action roadmap. First, take a look at Ben Franklin's guiding principles or governing values.[7]

Temperance: Eat not to dullness. Drink not to elevation.

Silence: Speak not but what may benefit others or yourself. Avoid trifling conversation.

Order: Let all your things have their places. Let each part of your business have its time.

Resolution: Resolve to perform what you ought. Perform without fail what you resolve.

Frugality: Make no expense but to do good to others or yourself: i.e. Waste nothing.

Industry: Lose no time. Be always employed in something useful. Cut off all unnecessary actions.

Sincerity: Use no hurtful deceit. Think innocently and justly and, if you speak, speak accordingly.

Justice: Wrong none by doing injuries or omitting the benefits that are your duty.

Moderation: Avoid extremes. Forbear resenting injuries so much as you think they deserve.

Tranquility: Be not disturbed at trifles, or at accidents common or unavoidable.

Chastity: Rarely use venery but for health or offspring, never to dullness, weakness, or the injury of your own or another's peace or reputation.

Humility: Imitate Jesus and Socrates.

(Ben Franklin's words may be slightly, shall we say, old fashioned, but most of his principles are on the earlier list just called by a different name.)

I found another great example of personal principles on the Internet at www.paradox1x.org. These are the principles of Karl Martino.[8]

People shine when given the chance to create, express, and grow. *Empower.*

People feel the need to be understood just as or even more strongly than the need to be loved. *Listen.*

People don't need more opinions; we already drown in data. People need clarity. *Drill down.*

People learn from example, not only from words. *Exemplify.*

People are attracted to honesty and have bullshit detectors. *Be true.*

People need new experiences to expand their knowledge or reality. *Adventure.*

People can learn from mistakes. *Recognize, don't fear, failure.*

People search for simple solutions to problems when they are rarely simple. *Dig.*

People shine when they believe they can make a lasting impact; this may be the core of everything we do. *Inspire.*

People and companies are driven by visions, not ideologies. *Lead.*

Ignorance is the fear of truth. Truth is more important than pride. *Learn.*

A life without passion is a life not lived. *Live.*

Faith is the cure of doubt. *Have faith.*

When you forgive, you are forgiven. *Forgive.*

Love is stronger than death. *Love.*

Do you see how principles can help each of these individuals guide their actions? Not knowing Karl Martino yourself, would you like to know him based on his personal guiding principles? I would. I envision him as a positive, energetic, caring, action-oriented, successful leader. Once your guiding principles are developed and used as your roadmap, would others want to get to know you better? Would the principles guide your decisions toward your defined success? Your principles hold you to a different standard for managing your life and living your success.

I have been blessed to be involved in several classes over the years that helped me examine my beliefs, form some of my principles, and identify many of my values. They have been worded differently from time to time. Sometimes I used a sentence; sometimes just a single word I valued. I've chosen to create consistency for myself by tying them together as directives to me. Below are my personal guiding principles by which I want to live my life.

Grow Continuously
Be ***Passionate*** to Be ***Excellent***
Practice ***Persistence*** with ***Discipline***
Create Contagious ***Enthusiasm***
Unleash ***Talent***
Earn ***Trust*** with ***Competency***, ***Integrity,*** and ***Intimacy***
Embrace and Share ***Wisdom***
Promote ***Creativity***
Spread ***Love*** and ***Happiness*** for No Reason
Exercise ***Health***
Dignify ***People*** with ***Respect***
Develop and Honor ***Family***
...and above all Connect with my ***Spirituality***

The bolded words are my values of growth, passion, excellence, persistence, discipline, enthusiasm, talent, trust, competency, integrity, intimacy, wisdom, creativity, love, happiness, health, people, respect, family, and spirituality. They are put together as my personal guiding principles. These guiding principles are personal to me. They may not—and probably don't—mean as much to others, but they create a strategic guidance for me. They guide me in how I should behave. They guide my decisions. They guide my choices.

Have or do I ever drift from these principles? Honestly, I must admit I do, occasionally. "Practice Persistence with Discipline" is the most challenging for me. It's not the persistence with which I have trouble. It's the discipline side of the guiding principle on which I still need some work. Discipline, to me, means well controlled and without being offensive to anyone. When I confront a situation where I believe there is an issue with principle (like honesty or fairness), I still have a tendency, although not near as frequently, to go into a stronger style. Often when I do, the other party gets defensive. By not being disciplined, I am lowering the chance to obtain an optimum outcome (i.e. what I want). I'm a whole lot better than I used to be, and the fact that I catch myself now—either during or right after an episode—to reflect upon it, is a step in the right direction. As I get better and better, I'll get more "optimum outcomes" and feel better about myself, as well. It's a win-win when you truly live by your guiding principles!

Create your guiding principles and then live by them. The difference will be huge!

======================================

The exercise associated with this chapter is:

- Personal Guiding Principles Exercise (Day 8)

======================================

Chapter Eight

Strategies to Influence the Influencers

THE NEXT ELEMENT IN THE SLSD Model is to examine your personal strategies relative to your external influencers. We discussed and I shared a list of some of my external influencers in Chapter 4. Before we look at that group for you, let's discuss what is strategy, really? Michael Porter states, "Competitive strategy is about being different. It means deliberately choosing a different set of activities to deliver a unique mix of value."[1] Porter is speaking about competitive business strategy. Does this definition have meaning for individual success? I believe it does.

First, consider the word *competitive*. We as individuals have to consider ourselves competing as we progress toward our dreams and goals. You might say we are competing against our current self, especially if we are not satisfied with the current progress of results we are attaining. Remember the saying quoted earlier in the book: "If you want things to change in your life, you're going to have to change some things in your life." Therefore, as Porter points out, we are going to have to be different. Different, in some cases, as it relates to our external influencers.

Porter continues to say that we must choose "a different set of activities to deliver a unique mix of value."[2] This means we must change our activities relative to some or most of our key external influencers in order to change our current reality of outcomes: both character and results toward our dreams.

What are the typical choices made regarding external influencers? There are four choices about how to respond to the demands from external influencers:[3]

- Cope with the external influence
- React to the external influence
- Adapt to the external influence
- Influence the external influence

Let me give you a real example to further explain what each of these mean. When I was a freshman in college, an upper classman in the dorm developed a fever and was feeling pretty bad one Saturday night. In addition to the fever, he had a really bad tooth ache. His mother was a nurse, but lived a hundred miles away from campus. My friend called his mom to get her thoughts and advice. She asked him several questions and deducted that flu had settled in a cavity in his tooth. Aspirin gave him no relief, so late that night (around midnight), since he did not have a car, I was asked to take him to the hospital.

Upon our arrival at the hospital, we met the admitting nurse. Being a busy Saturday night, I guess she wasn't having a terrific night because as my friend explained what his mother had deducted, the nurse curtly replied, "This is a hospital. We don't have any dentists here!" It was obvious she just wanted us to leave.

At this point we had a choice on what strategy to use with this obstacle (and influencer). We could cope with her curt style and continue to tell the story about how the mother had diagnosed the issue. My friend tried that strategy next, and it didn't work any better than the first time he told her. We could react and start shouting and arguing with her. I really don't think that strategy would have done anything but push her to call for assistance, maybe even the police, so we didn't try that strategy. We could have adapted to her wishes for us to leave and just go to another hospital. My friend, by this time, was sweating profusely under the pressure and duress of the admitting nurse. He needed help, so my strategy was to try to influence the admitting nurse. I pointed to my friend and said: "Ms., please look at my friend. He's sweating, shaking, and obviously not well. I believe you do have doctors here who might be able to deal with the flu and the fever. Can he please see a doctor?" The admitting nurse looked at my friend and asked if that was what he wanted. To wit, he vigorously responded, "Yes, please." The nurse then admitted him and the doctor treated his symptoms.

The point of the story is we had choices on which strategy to deploy toward this influence. You have those choices, too. Our problem lies in often not recognizing influencers and not making conscious decisions on which strategy to use.

You need to look at your external influencers and honestly evaluate what your choice has been with each influencer. For those who are a negative influence on your dreams (or your character/style), which strategy have you employed? Is the choice getting you the success you desire? We examine this more in Part II of the book.

In an ideal world, all of our key external influencers would have a positive impact on all dream categories, but that's not real or feasible. But what is possible? What is required for you to have the character you desire and the results toward the dreams you deserve? You have to move to influence the influencers.

A way to begin might be to consider the set of actions to move all of the negative influences to, at minimum, neutral. Sometimes an influencer will create a positive influence on one of your dream categories, but will negatively influence one or more other categories. Will your action to influence the negative influences also have a desired impact on the neutral and positive influences for this influencer? If so, great! If there is a consequence in the first chosen strategy, consider another strategy until you eliminate the negative impact and hold other categories in the same or better positions. When you do this, you then influence the influencer. What might some of those strategic activities be?

Let's begin with an influence that touches most of us: television. Each of us has to determine the influence television has on each of our own dream categories. My personal assessment and logic of each category follows.

Relationships: Having a television on when I'm trying to develop relations is a distraction. It can distract me from listening to others, and if I'm trying to lead a conversation, it can distract the person with whom I want to develop the relationship. Depending on the program on the television, the low negative impact turn into a high negative impact.

Environment: Generally, having television in my environment does not have a high impact on my dream category, either positive or negative. Even the presence is low impact. My wife might disagree. She might rate the noise from the television as being clutter to her thoughts at times, and therefore would rate it slightly negative.

Spiritual: At first thought, I rated this category as a low, positive impact, because I thought of being able to use the television with a DVD player to view tools and techniques I use to stay connected with my Creative Intelligence: God. Then I considered whether I was using the term television to mean the physical electronic instrument, or whether it was the content and programming coming through the satellite system that had the influence. My rating is about the latter. As I reflected on how much the television used to be on in our home, and the programming we used to have on (which for a long time was one of the political news stations) I dramatically changed my rating. During that period of my life, little of the programming we watched created positive emotions or helped me stay connected to God.

Passion-Time: So much of my passion-time dreams surround golf, and my television viewing often surrounds the Golf Channel and major golf tournaments. This viewing helps enhance the time I spend directly on my passion-time dreams. It's not a big impact, but there is some enhancement there. One could argue it has a low negative impact because I could be actually spending that same time playing or practicing. I chose the low impact positive because when practicing, you need perfect practice to improve, not just time practicing. A low, positive rating shows that what I watch helps improve my mental image and practice drills.

Wealth: We do spend money to receive satellite programming for our viewing pleasure, so that is money we are not saving or investing. Therefore, it is a slight negative. It's not a very big impact, but in all honesty, there is a slight negative impact.

Health: I'm again referring to the time when we had the political news station on every night. In reflection, this programming did nothing to create positive emotions. Instead, it created worry, fear, hostility to the party I didn't support, and sometimes even anger. As will be discussed in the chapter on personal development, all of these emotions are harmful to one's health.

In review, the ratings were four negative impacts ranging from low to relatively high, one neutral impact and one slightly positive impact. Put it all together, television was clearly a negative external influence to me achieving my dreams. What strategic actions could I take or did I take to change the impact television had on me?

First, I have quit watching the fairly large, negatively impactful political news station. Information I need to determine how I will responsibly vote, I can get through other sources and with much less time consumed.

Next, I don't have the television on as much. Our total television time is down probably 80%, and almost never is it on as background noise as it was it the past.

Finally, I make a conscious choice on what we watch. If I believe there will be a negative impact, or if I am surprised when a program begins to create negative emotions, I change the channel or turn the darn thing off.

The only slight negative impact for me is in the wealth dream category, and there are choices I could make to deal with that: eliminate satellite programming, reduce the size of the satellite-programming package, or switch to basic cable or basic satellite programming. I have made one of these choices, but I know I could go further, if I so choose.

Quickly, let's look at another external influence category that might be more sensitive: People. I'm blessed with a wonderful spouse that is a very high positive influence in my life. So first, let's look at those positive or neutral external influencers in our lives.

I have a brother-in-law that, for many years of our marriage, I seldom saw. After Emily and I moved from our first home together, my brother-in-law and I have never lived in the same town. Each of us was focused on our careers, so it was easy to rationalize why we didn't make time to spend with each other. For over thirty years, his influence on my dreams was very low impact and neutral. Then, a bit over a year ago, we attended a seminar together with our wives. It gave me more real exposure with him than I'd probably had over the entire thirty years before. I realized we had more in common than we had in difference. Over the next year, we became much closer. Now, we talk with each other regularly and encourage each other toward our dreams. The strategic step I took with him was inclusion. We have attended other development seminars together. We speak with each other often. We bounce ideas off of each other and share revenue generating ideas with each other. Even though we couldn't reduce the geographical distance between each other, we have reduced the intellectual distance and have increased the frequency of exposure to each other: both physically being together and using phone calls, emails, and texts as a way to stay closer. He moved from being a neutral influencer to a strong positive influencer on my dreams.

Like everyone else, however, I've had people in my life that did not help me move toward some of my dream categories. Being totally honest as I look back, some influencers actually influenced me away from some of my dreams. As I look at the type of negative influences, there were those who elicited negative emotions including anger, fear, judgment, and other negative responses. There were those who demanded an undue amount of my time away from family. There were those who would tempt me away from my beliefs or guiding principles. There were those who tempted me to spend extravagantly or needlessly. First, let me say that I am 100% responsible for how I reacted to any of these influences. Not the other person, me! I could have taken many, many actions that would have neutralized or minimized the impact, so for any loss of momentum, I take full accountability!

What are some of the different strategic actions with other people I could have taken and that I now take? Where possible, I simply eliminate the exposure to those people in my life. Like a bad employee that continuously breaks the rules or causes loss or damage at work, I *fire* people from my life. You try not to make it totally obvious. It's not like you play Donald Trump and go up to them and announce: "You're fired!" First, however, you do tell yourself you are firing them. You need to know in your mind that you are taking action and making a change. The easiest way has come through times when I've moved and you just never reach back to stay connected. There have been other times when I discussed the problem with the individual and we mutually agreed that continuing the relationship and the exposure made no sense. When benefits of the termination significantly outweigh the consequences of continuance, you create ways to eliminate exposure.

Those are the easy ones. The tougher ones are where you can't eliminate the exposure. An example might be a negaholic at work who is not helping you achieve your dreams. You know what a negaholic is, don't you? They are like an alcoholic that can't drink without becoming intoxicated. A negaholic can't seem to speak without griping and complaining. What do you do? What actions do you take? First, if you can reduce the exposure without consequences, reduce it. When you can reduce the frequency of exposure, reduce it. When you still have the exposure, you have to take control of your reactions and create positive responses! Many times what impacts our dreams are our reactions to the individual. We get angry or sad or fearful. Those are reactions. You can create responses. Instead of getting angry, you can control your emotions and think to yourself: "I wouldn't behave or speak the way that individual does!" One response I enjoy when someone is attempting to make me angry is to simply smile back. Just smile. No confrontation, no argument. Simply smile and as you do, plan your next positive response to the situation. Keep your thoughts, emotions, and responses positive.

For every type of influencer, you can create a strategic action or series of actions to eliminate, reduce, or change the impact on you and your dreams. Too often we fool ourselves into believing we have to take the negative impact and we do nothing differently. That's living by default instead of living by design. Might there be some consequences by the action(s) you take? Yes, but usually only in the short term. Your dream is in the long term. Not taking some of the actions might block you from ever reaching your dreams and goals. Which is worse: the impact of short term consequences in order to achieve long term gain, or living with your current reality and achieving long term failure? Only you can make the choice, just make it a conscious choice!

Design your strategies so the majority of the impacts are positive. Influence the influencers that need to become more positive as you begin living by design and moving toward the achievement of your dreams!

====================================

The exercise associated with this chapter is:

- Key Influencer Strategy Exercise (Day 10)

====================================

Chapter Nine

Your Personal Chief Aims and Goals

According to Andrew Carnegie, the richest man in America in the early 1900s, "If you want to be happy, set a goal that commands your energy and inspires your hopes."[1] Why should we set goals? What's different between a personal chief aim and personal goals? What do I do to achieve my personal chief aim and my personal goals? Let's begin with the first question.

Why should we set goals? Zig Ziglar, a wonderful success teacher, speaker, and motivator, wrote in his landmark book See You At the Top, "It's just as difficult to reach a destination you don't have as it is to come back from a place you've never seen. Unless you have definite, precise, clearly set goals, you are not going to realize the maximum potential that lies within you."[2] The reason you are reading this book is to improve yourself. My hope is that you *want* to achieve your maximum potential—your fullest potential. To do so, you need not only to set goals, but to set them clearly and to create your goal process to achieve them.

Said another way, it's documented on Goalmaker.com that Harvard Business School researchers studied what creates the difference between successful and unsuccessful people. Through their research, they discovered three categories of individuals with similar background and educational standards. Three percent of the individuals were categorized as successful. Thirty percent of the people were categorized as moderately successful. The remaining sixty-seven percent of the individuals were "happy to watch the world go by."[3] That remaining sixty-seven percent of people were clearly living their lives by default. The significant difference between the group of successful people and the group of moderately successful people was that the successful group had written, specific goals. The moderately successful group had a general idea of their direction, but did not have any formalized goals!

So how does one make sure their goals are good, effective goals? The answer is to create S.M.A.R.T. goals.[4] S.M.A.R.T. is an acronym for:

- Specific
- Measurable
- Attainable
- Relevant
- Timely

Let's go through each of the characteristics of a properly created goal.

Specific

Your goals need to be specific. Vague goals will allow you to drift from your intended target. Specific goals provide the direction you need to stay on the right track toward achievement of the goals.

Measurable

Your goals need to be measurable. You need to include precise dates and quantities of improvement in your goals. An example of this poorly done might be "to lose weight this year." A better way of setting the goal is to weigh 175 pounds by a specific date. See the difference? I can get on the scale and know if I've achieved the goal.

Attainable

Your goals need to be attainable. If you set goals your subconscious mind knows you can't achieve, you will only de-moralize yourself and quit. On the other hand, you can't set goals that are too easy or too low either. Your objective is to set a goal that is challenging, but not set so easy that there's no intrinsic reward in achieving the goal. You need the goals to have balance. They need to be challenging, yet realistic.

Relevant

Your goals need to be relevant. Your goals should be relevant to the categories you set for your dreams. Remember the diagram in Chapter Two that showed the relationship between dreams, chief aims, and goals? Your goals are set on the line that leads directly to your dreams. If you set goals unrelated to those dreams, you will lose focus. You will be spending time and effort on areas of your life that are not moving you toward your dreams.

Timely

Finally, your goals need to be timely, meaning they need to have an end date. You need to have a deadline on your goals. Having deadlines creates a sense of urgency to achieving the goal. Unbounded goals tend to let you drift, and even if you achieve the goal, it may be achieved much later than if you had set your goal deadline.

That's how you set S.M.A.R.T. goals, but I need to add one additional characteristic. Your goals need to be aligned with each other. I guess you might say you need A-S.M.A.R.T goals, where the first A stands for Aligned. Since you are setting goals in up to six dream categories, the goals you set for each of the categories need to align with each other so they can compliment and not conflict with each other. I first learned this concept in business when different functions would set their annual goals and plans that actually conflicted with each other. There's enough tension in setting proper goals to move you toward your dreams. You don't need to create additional tension by creating goals that conflict. Since all of your goals are moving you toward your dreams, the conflict generated is seldom direction. Usually the conflict is a timing issue. You could have all the goals due or timed on the same exact date. Sometimes it has to do with managing your budget. Two goals may need investment in the same month causing a tension. Keep the goals aligned and, where possible, complimentary.

Be sure, as pointed out by the Harvard Business School scholars, to have your goals written out. When you write out your goals they become more real to you. You increase the tangibility because the paper they are written on has a physicality or mass to it. Though this may sound a bit overboard, write the goals in your own handwriting. Write it out; don't print it. There are more neuro-pathways used in your brain when you write in cursive versus print, and there are significantly more used when you write versus type them out. So, be sure to write out your goals.

As you are writing out your goals, do so in a positive statement. The use of positive statements is more appealing than negative ones. As an example, which sounds better to you? I will lose ten pounds or I will weigh 175 pounds. The first statement is telling your subconscious mind you are overweight. The second statement says I will weigh my ideal body weight of 175 pounds. So be positive in your goal statements!

Keep your goals in front of you. There are many techniques to do this. One of my favorite techniques is a slight modification to a technique[5] described in Stephen Covey's book <u>The 7 Habits of Highly Effective People</u>. He has you list your goals (for the week) next to the role to which it applies. I use a slight modification to this system. I list my dream categories and have the current goals I am working on written and categorized for each dream category. This keeps my goals in front of me every day as I review my priority-planning system. Other techniques include posting your goals (and a picture of the achieved goal, if possible) in a place where you see it often, or keeping a copy of your written goals in your pocket or purse. This last technique causes you to think about the goal every time you bump into it as you put your hand into your pocket or purse.

After you create your goals, I'd suggest you sit back and review them. Why? Because you need to be able to really commit to them. You'll be committing your time, your energy, and often times some of your money to achieving your goals. Are you really willing to commit to them? How will you know? One big question you can ask is: "In order to achieve these dreams, what must I give up or quit doing, and am I willing and really going to give these things up?" This is a big step toward achieving your goals. I assume you are already consuming your twenty-four hours each day in some fashion. Are you willing to change some of the things you are doing with your time today in order to spend time to achieve your goals? If not, then you are not committed to the goal, and it probably won't be achieved. At one time in my life, one of my goals was to obtain an MBA because the MBA would advance me toward one of my chief aims. (More on chief aims later in this chapter.) In order to create the time to go back to school, my calendar had to change radically. The way I was using my twenty-four hours each day dramatically changed. Much of my off-purpose leisure time was eliminated. Watching golf tournaments on Saturday and Sunday afternoons on television—boom, gone! Instead of reading adventure novels, I spent the time reading textbooks and doing research. No regrets! I loved the experience of going back to college after being away from the campus for thirteen years. I was committed and committed to use my time (and my money, since my employer tuition reimbursement only covered twenty percent of the tuition) toward this goal. Had I not been committed, there would have been times it would have been easier to quit than to stay on course. Make sure you are really committed to the goals you've set.

Next you must create an action plan to achieve your goal. This step is often overlooked or missed in the goal setting process. Without creating an action plan, a goal becomes simply a *wished-for* or a *hoped-for*. Remember again, "Individuals are perfectly designed to get the results they get." Therefore, if you want your goals to come true, you have to create a plan to get there. They don't happen just because you've set an A-S.M.A.R.T goal. You have to also create an action plan. As you create your action plan, be sure to list the specific steps to achieve your goal. That's the *how*. You also need to plan the *what* needed to achieve your goal. This means what resources are needed. Remember that I mentioned your money a couple of times. Sometimes there are resources required to achieve the goal. I needed some significant financial resources to achieve my MBA goal and had to plan how to obtain the funds. Finally, your action plan needs to identify the *when*. Some action steps need to occur before other action steps. In order to begin MBA classes, I first had to be accepted by the university, which also meant my employer had to approve the time away from work. There was a deadline in getting my application turned in, so the written approval had to be received prior to the submission deadline. Know the action steps required, the resources needed, the timing, and the time relationships among the action steps. Finally, there's the *who* for each of these action steps. Who is going to assure these things get done? There's really only one answer—you! You are 100% accountable. Only your goal suffers if these things don't happen, so *you* are the person that has to make sure each step happens.

You'll also need to track the progress you make toward your goals. To accomplish this, you need to build a system that helps remind you of your progress. You can track the percent of goal completed versus percent of time allocated. You can track your action steps by crossing them off and dating them next to the planned completion date. There are numerous ways to track the progress of your goals. Be sure to find a technique that works for you, and as Nike says: "Just do it!"

Remember, there might be and probably will be some barriers, roadblocks, or setbacks which occur. You need to maintain some flexibility in your planning. One technique is to maintain some slack resources in your action plans. This is a cushion of resources you can use if need be when a plan gets off track. It might be a cushion of time or a cushion of money. If every penny you have is needed to complete each action step of the plan on time, then the plan is probably unrealistic because things happen. Inflation or a price increase in a particular resource needed would throw off the plan. You need to create flexibility in your plan.

I have mentioned chief aim and goals as being different. In the Management Theory course I teach, the textbook calls them distal and proximal goals[6]. Proximal goals, which I am terming *goals*, are short term or sub-goals. Distal goals, which I am terming *chief aim*, are the longer term or primary goals of your life. Napoleon Hill, in his classic success book Think and Grow Rich, refers to these distal goals as a definite chief aim[7]. So think of goals as a series of sub-steps or sub-goals that lead you to your chief aim. Refer to the diagram. This is the diagram from Chapter 2 now expanded to show how a series of goals leads to the chief aim.

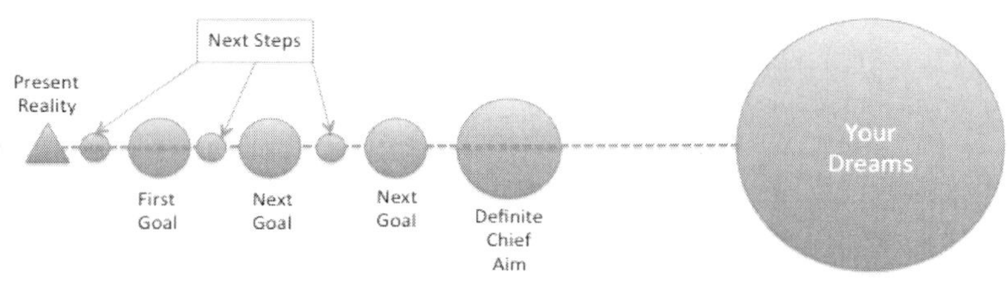

Present to Dreams with Next Steps

The accomplishment of your series of goals, each with their own plans, each with their own next steps, lead you toward the achievement of your chief aim, which leads toward your dream.

Why do you need a series of goals instead of just one chief aim? Remember that your goals need to be attainable to be S.M.A.R.T goals, but there's another reason. Earlier, I shared that I set what was a very big goal to be a plant manager by the age of 35. I accomplished that by becoming the Frito-Lay St. Louis plant manager in 1988 when I was 35 years old. Within a month following the achievement of the goal, I felt something was lacking. I was proud of the accomplishment, but there was something missing. I needed that next milestone, that next goal to move me toward my next chief aim and dream. The next goal, mentioned above, was to obtain an MBA. As soon as I set that goal, which was the next goal in then a series of goals, my energy and enthusiasm was restored. So, in addition to assuring my goals were reasonable, I needed and enjoyed the energy and drive that comes with setting the next goal toward my chief aim in life.

So, set your goals properly. Keep your goals in front of you. Commit to the goals. Create action plans. Monitor your progress toward your goals. Let the goal achievements lead you to your chief aim and the achievement of your dreams. That's the next step in living by design!

======================================

The exercise associated with this chapter is:

- Chief Aim Exercise (Day 11)

======================================

Chapter Ten

Your Personal Dream Mechanisms

Over the past three chapters, you have learned about strategic choices that are the first elements of living by design. Those included your personal mission, your personal guiding principles, your strategies to influence the external environment, and your personal goals and chief aims. Now is the point where we begin to make tactical life choices.

The first life choice is your personal dream mechanisms. What are mechanisms? Webster's New Collegiate dictionary defines mechanisms as "a process or technique for achieving a result."[1] The results we desire to achieve are the goals that lead to our chief aims that are perfectly aligned and lead us to our dreams.

Each day we use many techniques and processes. Some of these are moving us toward our dreams and, frankly, some are not. We need to make conscious choices on which techniques or processes we put into action.

Let me provide you some examples of potential techniques or processes. With the aspiration of our wealth dream, we could choose several processes or techniques. One technique would be to graduate from high school, attend college, earn a degree, and then obtain a position leveraging the knowledge gained from our degree. This technique might create a revenue stream that contributes toward our wealth dream.

That's not the only technique we might choose. Some may choose to enter the military to develop skills they can leverage toward their dream; others may go to a technical college to obtain the knowledge and skills to begin moving toward their dream. There is no one technique to achieve success.

What we are looking for are techniques that are efficient and effective in leading us toward the achievement of our dreams. What does that mean?

In the Management Theory course I teach, we learn that efficiency is "getting work done with minimal effort, expense, or waste."[2] Effectiveness is "accomplishing tasks that help fulfill the organization's objectives."[3] Said another way, effectiveness is doing the right things to achieve our dreams. Efficiency is doing those things right so as to employ the best use of our available resources.

I teach that managers are responsible for both being effective and efficient. The same is true for each of us as we manage our journey toward our dreams.

Let's look at what this really means to each of us. Our techniques—our mechanisms—to achieve our dreams are the vehicles that move us to those dreams. Some of the vehicles we use are slower than others. A bicycle is slower than a car. A car is slower than an airplane. Some vehicles or mechanisms we choose are just slower than others.

Even after we make an initial choice of vehicle, we may need to make more choices along the way. I chose to obtain a mechanical engineering degree and enter the workforce out of college with my BSME degree. It was a great start, but along the way I chose to change companies as new opportunities were presented to me. Each time I changed companies, my salary or my salary ceiling (or both) increased, moving me toward my dream to exit the corporate world early. (Some people call that *retirement*. I think of it as my next phase of contribution.) Those choices moved me in the right direction, but they weren't the only choices I needed to make to achieve the dream. I chose to make investments in real estate and the stock market to create cash flow and cash reserves to support our lifestyle in our next phase.

I wish I could say that every decision was perfect and moved me in the right direction. They weren't always perfect. Sometimes the decision moved me in the opposite direction. The good news is, in most cases, I learned quickly that the mechanisms were not effective and that I could make another decision to change the momentum.

Not all the mechanisms we use are equal contributors toward our dreams. As a matter of fact, not all of the mechanisms we have in our lives move us directly toward our dreams. Some don't move us toward them at all, but have to be done. I look at the mechanisms, processes, or vehicles and categorize them in one of five categories:

- Contributors
- Contributor-Enablers
- Life Essential
- Compliance
- Waste

Contributors

Contributors are vehicles or techniques that directly move us toward our dreams while being perfectly aligned with our mission and within the boundaries of our guiding principles. An example for me would be the authoring of this book. The book is perfectly aligned with my mission—to help others achieve their fullest potential—and within all the boundaries of my guiding principles. The sales of the book and any stipends received for lectures will contribute toward my wealth dream above my current residual income. The book also contributes to my health goal of how I think. Reflecting upon my personal life lessons, as I have pulled together the many thoughts and tidbits of knowledge and experience that have helped me, has contributed positively to the way I think.

Contributor-Enablers

Contributor-Enablers are the techniques or processes in our lives that enable the contributors to be effective and efficient while in alignment with our mission and guiding principles. An example is some of the research I've done in writing this book. The research itself doesn't contribute to my wealth dream, but enables the writing to be more effective in contributing toward the wealth dream.

Life Essential

The next category is Life Essential techniques. There are certain things that don't move us toward our dreams, but certainly have to be done in life. No matter how efficient we are at doing these tasks, we will not move closer to our dream by doing them. An example might be paying bills. Though paying my bills might not move me toward my goals and dreams, it must be done to keep playing in life. Even if I chose to use electronic banking, which may be more efficient, I'm not getting any closer to my dreams, but I still must do it. For some, preparing a meal and eating is the same. Without nourishment we cannot sustain life, but just eating won't move us closer to many of our dreams. If we eat out instead of taking the time to cook, we may be more efficient, but we are no closer to dream attainment.

Compliance

Compliance techniques are those things that must be done, move us no closer to our dreams, and add no value toward our dreams. Paying taxes is a great example. Spending money on taxes does not contribute to our dreams. In paying the taxes, we are being compliant toward our state and national laws, but we do have to spend the resources (time and money) to pay them.

Waste

Finally, there are techniques and mechanisms that are categorized purely as waste. These mechanisms or techniques in our lives are not mandated by regulation or law, don't contribute toward our dreams either directly or indirectly, and are purely optional for our existence. Watching television might be an example. No law requires us to spend time watching television. Much of the programming on my satellite feed would not contribute toward my dreams, and I certainly don't have to watch television to be able to wake up tomorrow morning. When I watch television, much of that time is wasted in regard to the achievement of my dreams.

What's important about these categorizations is the tactics we choose to use regarding each of the processes or techniques. There is a definite strategy for the categories that will accelerate us toward our dreams.

Let's begin with the waste category. Since techniques and processes you categorize as waste add no value to our dream journey, aren't mandated by law and aren't necessary for life, the most effective strategy is to eliminate these techniques. Wow, am I saying that I should eliminate television in my life? To be totally focused on my dreams, then yes, I should eliminate all television, especially the mindless surfing I used to do.

The optimal strategy for life essential and compliance mechanisms is to improve efficiency. How do you reduce the time or expense required to get something done? Sometimes your time is more precious than the expense, so these are perfect categories for outsourcing. Some people call these "minimum wage activities." These activities are not contributing toward your success, so hiring someone else to do them might be more efficient than doing them yourself. If you can make more money with the time gained than the cost to get them done, make the money instead of doing the activity yourself. Examples in my life have been mowing grass, cleaning the house, doing my taxes, and sometimes doing the cooking (that's also called eating out). Are there mechanisms or processes you are doing today which are keeping you from doing the things that will move you toward your dreams? If so, you should look for ways to make them more efficient.

Finally, the two categories of contributor and contributor-essential techniques have two strategies to deploy. Because the first strategy is so important, I'm discussing it first. These are the areas in your life you need to invest in to accelerate the progress toward your goals and dreams. Investing means spending resources. Those resources include your time and your money. How do you spend your time? Have you really looked at it? If you looked at it over the past week, how much time was spent on mechanisms or processes that were contributors or contributor-enabling mechanisms? If you spent half of your wasted time on contributor or contributor-enabling techniques, how much closer to your dreams would you be this week? How much did you waste over the past month or the last year? It adds up. Invest your precious resource of time in the mechanisms that will move you closer to your dreams whenever you can.

The second strategy for contributing and contributing enabling works the same as for life essential and compliance techniques. Make them more efficient. This frees up more of your resources for the mechanisms and processes that do move you toward your dreams.

So what are the mechanisms, vehicles, or processes you are using in your life? Categorize them into one of the five categories. Eliminate the waste. Gain efficiency in the life essential and compliance techniques. Gain efficiency and, more importantly, invest in the contributor and contributor-enabling techniques. You'll move faster toward your dreams when you are living by design.

====================================

The exercise associated with this chapter is:

- Dream Mechanism Identification Exercise (Day 12)

====================================

Chapter Eleven

Your Personal Organization Processes

How do you organize yourself? I mean, how well are the multiple dimensions of your life organized? When asked the first question, most people simply think about their time organization. Time organization is important, but that's not the only dimension of your life you have to assure is organized.

Your organization creates structure in your life that helps you in your pursuit of your goals and dreams. A lack of structure can create or accentuate drifting off-purpose and getting off-track. Managing your life, as in managing a business, needs to be structured consciously. You need to consciously make decisions about your personal organization.

Rather than starting with time organization, which, as I mentioned is where most people go to first, let's begin with the organization of our environment. It's our home, our office, and even our car. It's important that your environment be organized. It needs to be free of clutter. Clutter causes you to have lower energy levels or stuck energy. Karen Kingston has written a terrific little book entitled Clear Your Clutter with Feng Shui. According to Ms. Kingston, there are three causes of stuck energy levels. The three causes are physical grime, predecessor energy, and clutter.[1]

Clearly, a dirty environment lowers energy and reduces your ability to get as much done. Dirt, grime, filth, dust, and general grunge always lower energy levels. Think about it. Sometimes just the thought of needing to clean up can lower energy. Imagine the impact if you live in that type of environment all of the time.

Predecessor energy is energy recorded due to everything that happens in an environment.[2] It may sound a bit extreme, but think about it. Haven't you walked into an environment where there is tension and felt it? I once visited the museum in Deerfield Village in Dearborn, Michigan and stood next to the chair Abraham Lincoln was sitting in when he was shot. I felt really strange standing there, really strange! It was the predecessor energy from the chair. Environments can pick up stuck energy, too.

The third cause is clutter. According to Ms. Kingston, "Any kind of clutter creates an obstacle to the smooth flow of energy around a space."[3] We all know what clutter is. You can walk into a space, see it, and feel the lack of organization. I once worked with an individual whose office was truly clutter-free—spotless! The habits of the person who replaced him were the opposite of his habits. Soon there were papers on every table surface. They weren't even neatly stacked. They seemed to be placed everywhere haphazardly. You'd walk into the very same four walls and get a completely different impression. Interestingly, the first individual seemed to get more done. Hmmm?

You have control over your clutter and your physical grime. You can make the conscious choice to clean up and de-clutter your environment. Finally, according to Ms. Kingston: "Every aspect of your life is anchored energetically to your living space, so clearing your clutter can completely transform your entire existence."[4] It can provide you additional energy to get more things done, which will move you faster toward your goals and dreams.

Until recently, I had never really thought about the impact of clutter. Since I started my career in a clean desk office environment (which was almost sterile it was so clutter-free), I've always had pretty good habits about keeping my office de-cluttered. At home, we always had the space to store our possessions so we seldom felt cluttered there. Then, it happened. When I left the corporate world and began this new phase of my life (as I said, some call retirement), we needed to consolidate two homes of equal size into one of the spaces. That meant giving away a lot of furniture to family and friends, but the rest of the stuff was brought with us to our Tennessee home. Suddenly, we had clutter. Half the garage was filled with boxes; the closets were filled with boxes; some rooms initially had more boxes than empty floor space. We had clutter! I had done the best job I could before my wife arrived by sticking the boxes in every closet or on shelves in the master bedroom closet, but still there was clutter, even if we didn't trip over it. It took a while for us to really understand the impact it was having on us. Two things happened that helped us rethink and learn the impact it was having on our lives.

First was a brief conversation with Katrina Mayer in an airport in the Bahamas. Ms. Mayer is an expert in financial planning and wealth accumulation. She made an interesting comment that the biggest obstacle to increasing your abundance is clutter.[5] She said that sometimes you must get rid of some stuff in your life to make room for the new. I shared the conversation with my wife and it really made us think about the clutter still in those closets. Second, we bought and read Ms. Kingston's book.

That was it. We had to find out for ourselves. We started with the garage. We had much earlier dealt with the mass of boxes from the move and could get both cars in the garage, but there was still opportunity for improved organization. We both felt it. Every time we'd walk into the garage, it felt good. It was more relaxing—the tension was reduced. Next, we attacked the master bedroom closet. Believe it or not, this was a much bigger project. We were amazed at all that was in those boxes overhead. Much we didn't need and gave away to charity, but some of the items were long lost friends! We reorganized the whole space front to back and you can't imagine the freedom we felt. We were able to move on to other tasks with more energy every morning because that space was no longer lowering our energies.

Think about your environments and whether they are clutter-free or cluttered. If you need more energy in your life to accomplish your dreams and goals, start de-cluttering and de-griming your environment. You'll find a sense of relaxation and freedom as you live and work in a cleared space that is both pleasing and rewarding.

What other areas of your life need structure to be clutter-free? What about your time? Do you schedule your time, or does your time schedule you? Wow. That's an interesting question, isn't it? There are thousands of calendars and organizers on the market to help you schedule your time, but before we get into scheduling your time, let's look at how you are investing your time.

Is that a term you've heard before—investing your time? It's true. We each choose how to use our time, either consciously or unconsciously. One of my pet-peeves is hearing people say, "I don't have time." Excuse me. I believe that unless something has changed, there are still twenty-four hours a day, each and every day of the year (with the two exceptions of changing to and from daylight savings time, but you get the drift). We all have the same amount of time every day, so it's not that you don't have the time. It's just that you choose not to spend it in a particular manner. Spending time is like spending money. Some of our money is spent on investments, some is spent on necessities, and some is spent on luxuries or frivolities. We either consciously invest or unconsciously spend, sometimes even wasting our precious time.

We can make conscious choices on how we spend or invest our time. If we really look at how our time is spent, we might find that some of the time spent is really clutter. In his classic book The 7 Habits of Highly Effective People, Stephen Covey introduced a different way to categorize our time.[6] His method created a two-by-two matrix. The vertical axis is relative importance from low to high. The horizontal axis is relative urgency from high to low. There's much more to learn and study about this method of looking at your time, but Covey pointed out several interesting points. First, as long as you keep focusing on the high importance and high urgency activities, that quadrant keeps getting bigger and bigger until it dominates you. People like this, who are beaten up by problems all day, seek relief by moving to activities in the low importance and low urgency area. What are low importance and low urgency activities? They are activities like trivia, Facebook, some mail, some phone calls, busy work, gossip, and pleasant activities, often like random television surfing at home. I would define these activities as time clutter. Covey also points out that effective people stay out of either quadrant that is low importance.[7] Therefore, much of the things people bring to you with high urgency, but low importance is a type of time clutter, too. Spending your time in high importance, low-urgency activity (for example, in planning) is where you're investing. According to Covey, "Quadrant II (Low Urgency, High Importance) is the heart of effective personal management."[8] Earlier we defined *effective* as "accomplishing tasks that help accomplish organizational (personal) objectives." Covey was saying the very same thing. Your objectives are your goals, chief aim, and eventually your dreams. Effective personal management is investing your time in the activities that help accomplish those objectives.

Interestingly, the cause of many people's time crunch is because the highly important, low urgency activities are not urgent. They get put off for any number of reasons. It's the proverbial "I don't have time" or "I'm tired" or any other number of rationalizations. As pointed out, much of the time it's because we seek (stress) relief by doing something of low urgency and low importance as a recovery technique. However, it is this same habit of putting off the high importance, low urgency activities that allows the high importance, high urgency activities to grow and grow. Highly important and highly urgent activities can often be termed problem solving. The problems continue to build until we eliminate them before they occur. That work is usually highly important, but not urgent because the problem hasn't surfaced yet.

The other thing Covey points out is the only place to get time to accomplish high importance, low urgency activities is from the low importance activities in your life today.[9] This really hits home for many of us. As I mentioned earlier, there are only twenty-four hours in a day. If you are doing activities that aren't very important, then you're losing time to accomplish low urgency, highly important activities. You must do the highly important, highly urgent activities. You can't just not do them. So to get to the highly important, low urgency activities you have to get the time back from the low importance tasks. It comes down to saying no to low importance activities and saying yes to the low urgency, high importance activities.

So, how do you get around to doing the low urgency, highly important activities? You start with them. As you sit down each week to plan your week's activities, start with scheduling the low urgency, highly important activities first. If you have your personal mission and personal guiding principles defined, this task will seem quite natural to you. Much of highly important, low urgency activities are principle centered, so the activities will seem quite natural to schedule. What are some of these things in our lives? These are activities like relationship building, longer range planning, exercising, preparing or writing your personal mission statement (if you haven't done it). In the corporate world, one of those highly important, low urgency items is organizational development—developing the individuals that work in your organization. It's so easy to put off succession planning and other activities that help provide new opportunities and new growth for a team. In order to make sure my staff and I would get this work done, I would schedule it in advance. The other rule I had relative to this work was when doing the succession planning (high importance, low urgency), we focused only on that work. In one company, I scheduled a minimum of four hours per month. My team would isolate themselves from the problems of the minute for highly important, low urgency work. Those four hours created the need for each of us to spend more time than just the meeting time for pre-work and follow-up from the meeting. But the low urgency, highly important work got done because it was scheduled.

This is such a critical step. If you want your goals and dreams to happen, you have to create the time for the low urgency, highly important activities to get done. If you don't, the urgency of the minute, whether high importance or low, will consume your time, your schedule, and your life. What do you want? It's your choice.

Are there other areas of organization where we need to eliminate clutter? Obvious from the question, my answer is yes. How about organizing your thinking. Is there clutter, at times, in our thinking? There must be or Zig Ziglar wouldn't be famous for his expression: "Stinkin' Thinking."[10] There can be clutter in our thoughts just as much as in our environment and in our time. One common form of clutter is worry. Ed Foreman taught me that "worry is nothing more or less than the misuse of your imagination. It's negative goal setting!"[11] That really hit me. As you can tell from the chapter on strategic choices, I believe in the power of goal setting. So, if worrying about the things I don't want to happen can actually aid in their accomplishment, why would I do it? What do we accomplish in worrying anyway? We create toxins in our body when we worry, but we don't really change a thing about the subject we are worrying about, do we? Worrying can become a habit—a deeply ingrained habit. According to Charles Duhigg, author of The Power of Habit, in order to break a habit, we have to understand what cues the habit, the routine we go through, and the reward we are seeking by doing the habit.[12] Habits can be reshaped. We have to identify the routine, experiment with rewards, isolate the cue, and have a plan or a substitute routine to replace the habit.[13] I would suggest a routine to experiment with to break the habit of worry is to begin thinking about what you do want instead of what you don't want. Consider, what are the rewards you can receive by that thought routine. Clearly, worry is a waste of your time. It is thought clutter that needs to be eliminated.

Another common form of thought clutter is criticism or judgment. Criticism, I was once told, was feedback that is given to hurt or harm an individual. According to Webster's New Collegiate dictionary, "to criticize is to stress the faults of."[14] Synonyms are: reprehend, blame, censure, condemn, or denounce. None of these words do anything to help build a person up, do they? None of the words are constructive; they are all destructive. Therefore, the term *constructive criticism* is totally counter-intuitive. How can you constructively destruct someone? You can't, so it's a waste of your thoughts. It's clutter.

Can you provide someone critique that is constructive? I used to say yes, but since critique is the act of criticizing, the answer must be no. Clearly, at times, you must provide your observation of a situation or event. Be sure to provide your observations about the event or behavior, *not* about the person. A child might make a careless mistake, but the child is not careless. It is an important distinction. Remember that the first habit of a winner is to never "criticize, condemn, or complain."[15] It's thought clutter.

A final area of thought clutter I'll mention is gossip. One could say that if you have time to gossip, then you must not have much going on in your life. Gossip serves no purpose. Be sure you use what I've heard referred to as the "Wall Street Journal" rule. Never say anything about anyone or anything you wouldn't want published on the front page of the Wall Street Journal. From an integrity standpoint, never say anything about anyone you wouldn't say directly to them. Doing otherwise is off-purpose and, most likely, outside of your guiding principles, so it is wasteful. It is clutter.

Make conscious choices about your personal organization. Assure your environment is clutter-free. Design your time to be clutter-free. Assure your thoughts are clutter-free. Clutter only reduces your energy and distracts you from achieving your goals and dreams. Reduce the clutter in your life as you live by design!

======================================

The exercise associated with this chapter is:

- Personal Clutter Identification (Day 13)

======================================

Chapter Twelve

Decision Making and Informating Processes

In addition to making choices through the use of the SLSD Model framework, you will be faced with making decisions on a daily and an hourly basis, as well. These many decisions you make can advance you toward your goals, aims, and dreams, or they can hold you back. In preparation for making decisions, you will have to choose what information you feed yourself.

First, let's look at your decision making process.

Several years ago, I was introduced to a very different model that caused me to seriously reconsider the decisions I made. The model, created by Dr. Gary Applegate, is shown on a separate page. According to Dr. Applegate: "All thoughts and actions are purposeful, directed to meet our internal needs."[1] Dr. Applegate taught us that we each have eight fundamental, internal needs. Those needs are:

- Security
- Faith
- Worth
- Freedom
- Belonging/Love
- Fun/Entertainment
- Knowledge

- Health[2]

Dr. Applegate defines these needs in his book Happiness, It's Your Choice and are discussed below.

Security

Security is present when one has a sense of personal strength, when one has control over his or her life, and when one realizes he/she can't control what anyone else does or thinks. It's when we have the skills to meet all of our needs.[3]

Faith

Faith is a belief in our selves to meet our needs to be happy and a belief in a greater power. It is a positive attitude about our selves and about life in general.[4]

Worth

Worth is the feeling we receive when we sense a positive value about ourselves and when we see that we have gone a step beyond where we were. Through our decisions that lead to our action, we feel good because we are achieving our goals that move us toward our dreams.[5]

Freedom

Freedom is a state of mind, not a condition of our environment. It comes when we realize we have choices over our thoughts and actions. We feel free when we think and respond instead of reacting without conscious decision. Freedom is the exhilarating feeling that comes from responsible decisions and actions.[6]

Belonging/Love

Belonging/love is when we have friends, when we're involved with community activities, and when we care for others. We demonstrate love when we put others first. The first step to love is commitment to others.[7]

Fun/Enjoyment

Fun/enjoyment is when we experience laughter, excitement, and humor at work, home, or anywhere. When we make fun happen, we feel a special joy that only a sense of humor brings.[8]

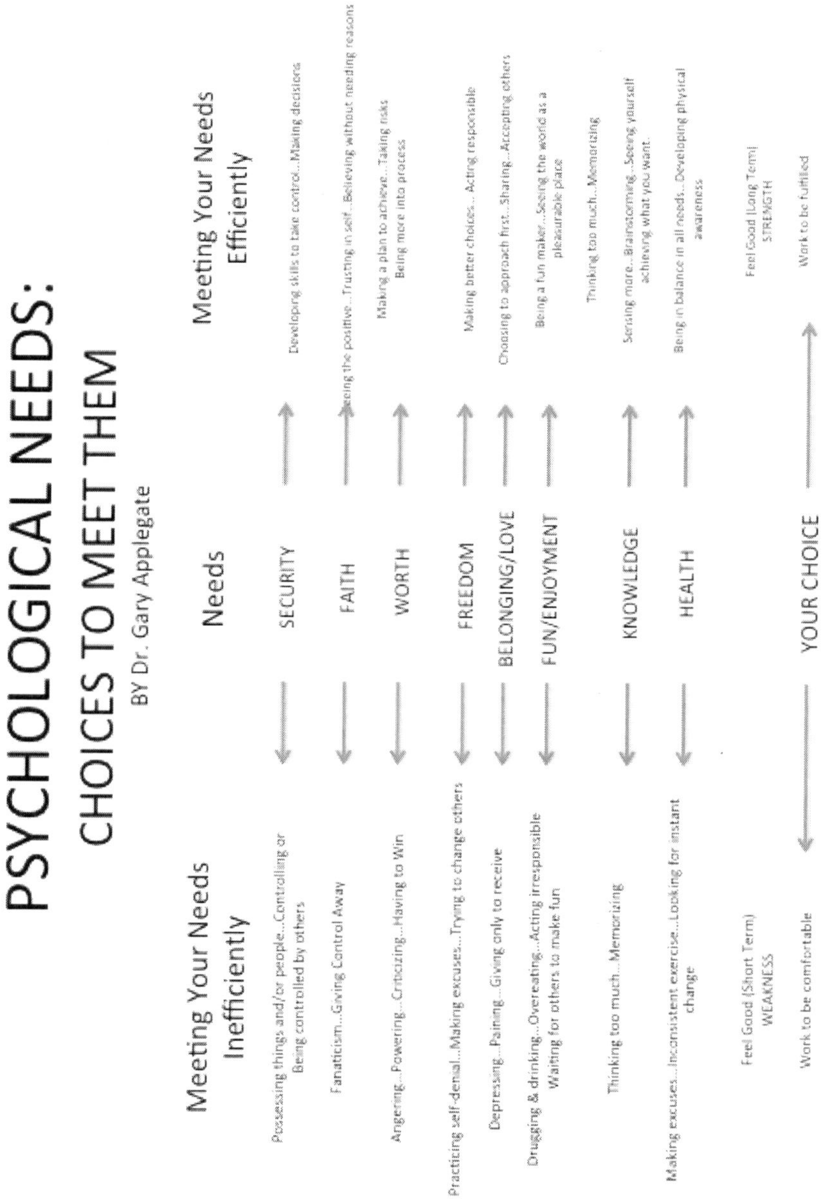

PSYCHOLOGICAL NEEDS:
CHOICES TO MEET THEM

BY Dr. Gary Applegate

Meeting Your Needs Inefficiently		Needs		Meeting Your Needs Efficiently
Possessing things and/or people...Controlling or Being controlled by others	←	SECURITY	→	Developing skills to take control...Making decisions
Fanaticism...Giving Control Away	←	FAITH	→	eeing the positive...Trusting in self...Believing without needing reasons
Angering...Powering...Criticizing...Having to Win	←	WORTH	→	Making a plan to achieve...Taking risks Being more into process
Practicing self-denial...Making excuses...Trying to change others	←	FREEDOM	→	Making better choices... Acting responsible
Depressing...Paining...Giving only to receive	←	BELONGING/LOVE	→	Choosing to approach first...Sharing...Accepting others
Drugging & drinking...Overeating...Acting irresponsible Waiting for others to make fun	←	FUN/ENJOYMENT	→	Being a fun maker...Seeing the world as a pleasurable place
Thinking too much...Memorizing	←	KNOWLEDGE	→	Thinking too much...Memorizing Sensing more...Brainstorming...Seeing yourself achieving what you want.
Making excuses...Inconsistent exercise...Looking for instant change	←	HEALTH	→	Being in balance in all needs...Developing physical awareness
Feel Good (Short Term) WEAKNESS				Feel Good (Long Term) STRENGTH
Work to be comfortable	←	YOUR CHOICE	→	Work to be fulfilled

Psychological Needs Chart

Knowledge

Knowledge is gaining and having more information, thus giving us more alternatives in our decision-making.[9]

Health

Health is when we have a balance between our physiological and our psychological needs. Feeling unhealthy is a clear signal to make decisions to change what we are thinking about the world around us.[10]

We all make decisions to take action on how to get our internal needs fulfilled. There are various alternatives to getting our needs met, as we have learned. Dr. Applegate calls these wants. There are efficient decisions on how to get the needs fulfilled. There are also inefficient decisions on how to get the needs fulfilled.

An efficient decision on how to get the needs fulfilled is defined as a decision that fulfills at least one of the needs with no loss of fulfillment of the other seven needs.[11] An inefficient decision also fulfills at least one of the needs, but reduces or frustrates the fulfillment of other needs.[12] An efficient decision allows us to feel in control because we are changing ourselves, whereas an inefficient decision tries to change others, things, or situations, and causes us to feel out of control. An efficient decision focuses on the present or planning for the future, thus creating options. An inefficient decision tries to change the past or control the future. The immediate payoff from an efficient decision is power, mastery, and control of your life. You receive a feeling of fulfillment. An inefficient decision goes for immediate payoff and seeks a feeling of comfort that is usually only short-term.

The referenced diagram provided by Dr. Applegate provides examples of efficient ways (on the right) and inefficient ways (on the left) to fulfill our internal psychological needs. Review each category to look at some of the inefficient decisions and the associated actions. Then, review the alternative decisions and actions that come from efficient decisions.

Next, you will need to evaluate your decisions. Have you ever noticed the relationship an inefficient decision or action has on other needs areas? Begin your personal choice by simply observing the impact of inefficient decisions. Which other needs categories are frustrated when you make an inefficient decision? Look at it the other way as well. Which needs categories are frustrated in your life? Are there inefficient decisions you've made that have created frustration? Remember, you are 100% accountable for your life. If there is an area of frustration, there are decisions you have made that created the frustration. When you identify the relationships between frustrated need categories and the associated inefficient decisions, you then have the choice of changing your inefficient reactions into decided responses that will be efficient. You have the choice, though it might not be easy.

In the audio series "Your Wish Is Your Command," Kevin Trudeau explains the four levels of learning.[13] The four levels are:

- Unconsciously incompetent
- Consciously incompetent
- Consciously competent
- Unconsciously competent.

Before we apply these four levels of learning to our task at hand, let's examine these levels and their application to one of my passions, the game of golf. In level one, one doesn't know they don't know how to play the game of golf or that the game even exist, thus we are unconsciously incompetent. As we move to level two and we see parents, siblings, or others playing the game, yet we've never been taught the game, we are at the consciously incompetent level. When we take golf lessons and play the game reasonably well from time to time, we are at level three—the consciously competent level. At this level, we do a lot of conscious thinking about the skills we are learning and using. When we reach level four, the unconsciously competent level, we are operating on autopilot, where we address the golf ball and swing without consciously thinking about the mechanics of the game (and by the way, the ball goes where you intended it to go, too.)

Now, let's apply these levels of learning to efficient and inefficient decisions. If you've had psychological need areas that are frustrated in your life and you were unaware of the relationship between your inefficient decisions and the frustration, you were unconsciously incompetent in your decision making process. You didn't know what you didn't know about these relationships. That's okay. Nobody had informed you before, but now, if you've taken the time to understand the relationship, you move to the second level of learning and become consciously incompetent. You now know that certain decisions you make (either consciously or unconsciously through reactions) create the consequence of frustration in some of your other need areas. In order to move forward, you will need to make different, efficient decisions. These won't come naturally and may be uncomfortable at first. After you identify the decision and actions that provide your immediate need without frustrating your other needs, you will need to use the third level of learning and become consciously competent in making the efficient decisions. It might feel awkward or slow and unnatural at first. Eventually, after repetition, and especially if you can make the efficient decision more frequently, you can become unconsciously competent in making the efficient decisions.

In order to make good decisions, most people believe you simply need to have good information. However, information is just data. Obviously we need to be able to obtain good data. What we really use to base our decisions on is our knowledge. Merriam-Webster dictionary defines *knowledge* as "the body of truth, information, and principles acquired by humankind."[14] Therefore, individual knowledge is the body of truth, information, and principles acquired by an individual. From the information of the sound of thunder, coupled with truths I've learned from personal experience, I know or have knowledge there is a storm somewhere in the vicinity. (When I look outside, I also know from the sight of rain that the storm is in my immediate vicinity.)

Our accumulated knowledge is our personal knowledge capital. If, according to Paul Gustavson, "Knowledge capital for a business is the purest source of competitive advantage,"[15] then is personal knowledge capital the purest source of contributor advantage we have in achieving our dreams? Clearly, it's our knowledge that leads us to more efficient decisions to meet our psychological needs, and it's our knowledge that enables us to interpret if our dream mechanisms are contributor, contributor-enabling, life essential, compliance, or waste. So yes, personal knowledge capital is the purest source of contributing advantage.

Since knowledge is such a valuable asset, it must be organized. We organize our knowledge into one of four quadrants on the Knowledge Organization Grid.[16] The horizontal axis forms columns of Know-how and Know-that. The vertical axis forms rows of Encoded and Non-encoded. Encoded may not be the most precise term. Encoded knowledge is stored in our memories, notes, books, or audio recordings we have ready access to as needed to make decisions. Non-encoded knowledge is know-how or know-that that was once readily available to us, but has been lost, misplaced, or is otherwise no longer with us. As individuals, we care about our personal knowledge capability. Earlier it was referred to as the teach-ability index, but I want you to realize it is really a capability you can develop. Personal knowledge capability is the product of our ability to discover knowledge and our willingness to use the knowledge to move us toward our goals, aims and dreams. An individual who is able to find and discover knowledge, and then uses that knowledge to move toward his/her goals, has a high personal knowledge capability. A person who has a low discovery capability, or a person who has an unwillingness to use the knowledge, has a lower personal knowledge capability.

Zig Ziglar confirms this theory on the unwillingness side of the equation in his statement (from his book See You At the Top), "The person who won't read is no better off than the person who can't read. The person who knows, but won't use success principles is no better off than the person who doesn't know them."[17] The same is true whether it is knowledge of success principles, welding principles, money-making principles, or teaching principles. If you have knowledge of either kind, know-how or know-that, and you won't use that knowledge, your personal knowledge capability is no greater than the person that doesn't know it.

That leads us to the *discovery capability* side of the product. Discovery is the act or process of discovering. Discover is a verb meaning to "make known."[18] It almost sounds like a circle, but it's not. Discovery is the action it takes to make known. Discovery takes action. It is not passive.

The active process of getting good information to become knowledge is what I call informating. (Yes, this is an original word, or at least one I can't find in the dictionary.) Have you consciously thought about where you get your information? We receive information through all five of our senses: sight, sound, smell, touch, and taste. All of our senses provide information to us that we can convert to knowledge, but for this discussion I will focus on sight and sound. Sight and sound: What we see and what we hear. We see and hear things wherever we are, but think of the many sources of sight and sound we receive. Think of the people and things we see and hear. Some of the major sources are our family, our friends, our acquaintances, and our fellow workers. The television, radio, and Internet are sources. Hmmm. This sounds like our external influencers list, doesn't it? That's because those influencers also influence our sources of information and knowledge. There may be, and probably are, other potential sources of information and knowledge, however. It is your choice on how and where you get your information. That's why I said that knowledge discovery should not be passive. You need to choose how and where you discover or make known your knowledge.

With all the sources of information growing exponentially today in the Information Age, there is a new term called *Information Literacy*. The American Library Association defines *Information Literacy* as the set of skills needed to find, retrieve, analyze, and use information."[19] So in today's new world, personal knowledge capability might be termed *information literacy* since it includes discovering knowledge and using it. I only mention this term in case you personally wish to learn more about the concerns in today's society regarding our ability to maintain, let alone grow our personal knowledge capability.

What happens if you only choose to discover your knowledge from the same sources where you've discovered your know-how and know-that in the past? Well, that fits right into the basic belief of the SLSD Model. You are perfectly designed to get the success you've received up to now. The acceleration of goal and dream achievement and the improvement of your character might not change.

In order to be living by design, get your needs met through efficient decisions. Consider changing some or all of your sources of discovery, and willingly use your knowledge. This is especially true as you invest more of your time and your resources in contributor and contributor-enabling mechanisms. Let your personal knowledge capital, your personal knowledge capability, and efficient decision making accelerate you forward to your dreams as you live by design.

====================================

The exercise associated with this chapter is:

- Decision Making Efficiency (Day 14)
- Personal Knowledge Capital Matrix (Day 14)

====================================

Chapter Thirteen

Your Personal Relationship Processes

Between the several discussions about external influencers and having relationships as a suggested dream category, I'm sure you are already conscious and aware of the importance of your relationships. Good, supportive relationships can accelerate your goals and dreams. Bad or negative relationships not only slow you down, but they can actually keep you from achieving your goals and dreams. Your relationships are the people in your life. You need to have the right people in your life to aid in the acceleration of goals, aims, and dreams. Therefore, it is critically important you understand and create strong relationship processes and sub-processes.

Businesses obviously depend on the people in their company. Over time, businesses have created a proven approach to having the right people work for them. In the Management Theory course, this process is called the Human Resource process. The objective of the Human Resource process is to find, develop, and keep the right people for the business.[1] This is analogous to the relationship process that will help you toward the achievement of your goals and dreams.

The Human Resource process is made up of six sub-processes. Those sub-processes, according to Chuck Williams, author of the text used in the Management Theory course, are:

- Recruiting
- Selection
- Training
- Performance Appraisal
- Compensation
- Employee Separation.[2]

In Paul Gustavson's Organizational Systems Design model, the compensation sub-process is part of the Rewards System area of the model.[3] In the Successful Life Systems Design Model, the analogy to compensation will be discussed with the Recognition System area of the model in the next chapter.

Often people only think of relationship processes after the relationship has been established. How one then develops, maintains, or grows that relationship is the subject of many articles and books. Though relationship development is important, it is not the whole process. It is just one of the five sub-processes. The sub-processes for the Relationship Process are:

- Relationship Recruiting
- Relationship Selection
- Relationship Development
- Relationship Evaluation
- Relationship Separation

This chapter will define and discuss each of these sub-processes.

Before diving right into the first sub-process, there's another parallel I need to make between how businesses use the sub-processes and how you may personally choose to use the sub-processes. The concepts of each sub-process exist in business at all levels of the organization. However, the execution tools, the amount of energy spent, and the amount of time consumed changes for the different levels of the organization. In general, the higher the position in the organization, the more energy spent and time consumed. Why? Because of the level of influence the higher positions have on the overall results and the culture of the business.

Does this sound familiar? You bet! The people that have the most influence on your success and your character are most important to you. According to Jack Canfield in his book The Success Principles, "Every high achiever has a powerful team of key staff members, consultants, vendors, and helpers who do the bulk of the work while he or she is free to create new sources of income and new opportunities for success."[4] You need your powerful team, your coalition of support and influence, to accelerate the achievement of your goals. This is such an important group of people for you that the focus of discussion explaining the five sub-processes will be directed toward this group. I call these people your *Inner Circle of Influence.* After you understand each of the five sub-processes, you will then need to determine how you choose to execute each step of the relationship process for the people outside of your inner circle. My caution to you is to consciously choose how you want to execute each sub-process on each of the influencers.

You may have thought earlier as you were thinking about several key influencers in your life that many of them, including some of the big influencers, may not sound like a "coalition of support." Overlooking some of the negative influencers in your life, you may have some *missing* influencers that would accelerate your progress. You are now designing your success instead of living by default. You now get to choose if you have all the influencers you need on your side.

Finally, you already have relationships in your life. Do you put all of those through the entire process? No, not necessarily. You may just start those individuals in the appropriate sub-process. You may want to develop the relationship, evaluate the relationship or you might even need to separate from the relationship. Thoughts being shared with you can help you with existing relationships. For the missing influencers that you identify, you will want to begin at the start of the process.

Relationship Recruiting

The first step in the relationship process is relationship recruiting. Like other forms of recruiting, relationship recruiting is a deliberate act. Relationship recruiting is the act of developing a pool of qualified candidates that can provide you the influence you need. Many people never think about the relationship recruiting they do. In the past you've probably thought of attracting relationships. I've chosen to call it recruiting because attracting is sometimes viewed as too passive. It's not normally as overt. Recruiting your past relationships may not have been as planned as employers do for a new executive to join their company. Think about it though. Wouldn't an inner circle relationship have just as much impact on your success as an executive has on a business? Making conscious decisions about the type of people you want to recruit into your inner circle only makes sense. In business, a tool used in the recruiting sub-process is a job analysis. A job analysis is a systematic, purposeful process for collecting information on the important work-related aspects of a job.[5] A job analysis creates job specifications and job descriptions for each role. A job description is a description of the basic tasks, duties, and responsibilities of an employee. Job specifications summarize the qualifications needed to perform the job. From these you know the knowledge, skills, and abilities needed for the job.

What I am suggesting is that you perform the personal analogy to a job analysis by consciously designing your inner circle of influence. Create your own inner circle influencer analysis. Create descriptions of the type of roles you want and need filled to achieve your goals and chief aim. You think I'm kidding? I'm not. Do you think most successful professional golfers just show up to the course, tee the ball up, and hit it today? Heck no! They *design* the team of influencers around them. Most have a swing coach, a physical trainer, a psychology coach, a business manager, and a financial advisor. Some have a massage therapist and separate short-game coach. Each of these brings specific expertise and skills to improve the professional golfer's results—to help them achieve their goals. So design the inner circle of influencers you will need to achieve your goals and dreams. List the key expertise and skills you'll need from each advisor or coach. Don't just assume you have the right inner circle team. Benchmark with other successful people on who advises and counsels them. I recently benchmarked a bit and found that even though I had an accountant and a financial advisor, I was lacking a true Tax Expert. I'm now in the process of recruiting that inner circle member for myself. Think also about the support you need for lower value work you are doing. Lower value work includes tasks that do not leverage or utilize your uniqueness. They may also be tasks discussed in Chapter 10 as not being Contributor techniques or Contributor Enabler techniques. Then, recruit your inner circle team. How do you do that? In the recruiting sub-process, you are creating a pool of qualified candidates to enter your inner circle. You haven't let them in yet.

Your form of recruiting most of these people will be using your network to identify candidates or learning about individual's skills and qualifications as you have normal conversations with them. *Normal* conversations for you will now also include learning about the skills and qualifications of the people you meet. You're always maintaining your pool of candidates.

You say that you've never recruited before? I beg to question that. Have you ever dated? Isn't dating really a process you used to identify candidates for one of your major inner circle influencers: your spouse? You may not have completed the selection process yet, but you did recruit as you considered who to ask out or who to accept a date with. During dates you talked and learned about the other individual. Based on the information you gained, you either saw the person again or moved on to other candidates. Recruiting does and has occurred in your life's influencers. For your inner circle influencers, make the sub-process a conscious step designed for your success.

Relationship Selection

The relationship selection sub-process is the process of gathering information about the qualified candidates to decide who will be in your inner circle. The purpose of gathering the information is to project the best person who will perform for you. Before you begin gathering the information, you need to have defined for yourself the selection criterion. Selection criterion is a prioritized list of skills and attributes you have defined as ideal for the position. Not all skills and attributes are equally important, so you need to define for yourself whether each criterion is a must-have, need-to-have, or nice-to-have. Obviously a candidate would cease to be qualified if you discovered through your information gathering techniques that a must-have criteria is missing. Similarly, if several need-to-have criteria are missing, the candidate would become disqualified, but probably not if just one need-to-have criteria is missing. An example might be that you decided a need-to have criteria for your financial advisor was to have coached others successfully five to ten years. One of your candidates meets each of the must-have criteria. They also meet the other need-to-have criteria, but have only coached others for four years. You might decide their experience is close enough to the five-year criteria. Nice-to-have criteria are kind of like extra credit. Failing to meet nice-to-have criteria wouldn't disqualify an individual, but having fulfilled several of the nice-to-have criteria would give them extra consideration.

Once you've created, reviewed, and firmly decided on your criteria and the priority of each individual criterion, you are ready to gather the information you need to make your selections. Since past performance is the best predictor of future performance, you want to get as much information as possible about how each candidate has performed for each of the criterion you have defined for the role(s) for which the individual is being considered. Where do you get the information? Consider finding out from others how the individual has performed. You can get some information from the candidate as you either casually talk with them or ask them directly. Are you interviewing them and doing reference checks? That depends on how formal you want to be, but your information gathering is analogous to the information gathering that occurs by interviewing and doing reference checks.

Once you feel you have the information you need to make your selection, make it and move on to the relationship development sub-process.

Relationship Development

I love the definitions found in Webster's New Collegiate Dictionary for *develop*. They include: "to evolve the possibilities of," "to promote the growth of," and "to make available and usable."[6] So think of relationship development as the actions taken to promote the growth of the relationship, evolving the possibilities of having and using shared knowledge and resources. This definition suggests that our relationships need to become win/win relationships. Greg Anderson states in his book The 22 {Non-Negotiable} Laws of Wellness that "Win/Win is the state of mind and heart that constantly seeks to find the mutually beneficial position in all human relationships."[7] Further, he teaches that "Win/Win is a paradigm of cooperation, not competition; of allies, not adversaries."[8] Additionally: "The only way we'll change our relationships is to change ourselves."[9] Again, you are 100% accountable for your actions. To change your relationships, to grow your relationships, you have to change.

So what are some of the actions to take to promote the growth of relationships? You'll have to decide based on your current actions. A resource is the landmark book on relationships, Dale Carnegie's How to Win Friends and Influence People. There are so many terrific actions[10] provided in this great book that help create an environment for a win/win relationship. Instead of a long discussion, I will provide a series of questions for you to ask of yourself. For more in-depth understanding, I highly recommend you get a copy of the book and digest it.

- Are you genuinely interested in other people?
- Do you smile regularly and especially as you catch the attention of others?
- Do you remember people's names?
- Are you a good listener?
- Do you engage other people's interests?
- Do you sincerely make other people feel important?
- Do you avoid having arguments?
- Do you show respect of other people's opinions?
- Do you quickly and empathetically admit when you are wrong?
- Do you seek to find common ground in disagreements?
- Do you let others do a lot of the talking?
- Do you try honestly to see things from the other person's point of view?
- Are you sympathetic with other people's ideas and desires?
- Do you appeal to the nobler motives of others?
- Do you share your ideas interestingly and dramatically?
- Do you create exciting challenges for others?

- Do you begin your interactions with praise and honest appreciation?
- Do you indirectly call attention to other people's mistakes?
- Do you talk about your own mistakes before making negative observations to others?
- Do you ask questions instead of give orders?
- Do you let the other person save face?
- Do you praise every improvement?
- Do you have people follow your lead or obey your orders?
- Do you promote other people's positive reputations?
- Do you use encouragement to help make others' faults seem easy to correct?
- Do you align what people are doing for you with their personal goals or interests?

The early days of relationship development is a critical time. First impressions can last a lifetime. As you are bringing in new members to your inner circle, you want the relationship to create positive outcomes. In business, this initial period of the relationship process would be termed the assimilation period. The Webster's New Collegiate dictionary definition for assimilate is "to take into the mind and thoroughly comprehend."[11] To assimilate an individual onto a team or into your inner circle is similar. In business, I focused on doing things during the assimilation period for new individuals joining the existing team, which accelerated the new individual's understanding of the business (including cultural norms) and increased the probability for short-term and long-term success.

I had a recent discussion on assimilation issues with Brian Boling, founder and principle of Pine Valley Resources, a boutique firm that specializes in recruiting and assimilating executives into companies. Brian, through his career as a Human Resources executive for several companies, understands that the success of a new executive is highly dependent upon how well the executive assimilates during the first year with the new company. Brian identified three key questions an executive needs to be asking as he/she assimilates in that first year. The first questions are: "What's not being said?" and "What are the under currents?" The second question is: "Do I teach or do I tell?" The third question is "Do people follow me or do they obey me?"[12]

Brian's role in the assimilation process for his client companies is to coach the new executives. Therefore, Brian views the new executive as being 100% responsible for their success or failure. Brian's company is successful and growing in a tough economy. Roughly seventy-five percent of his business is repeat business from companies where he has helped coach the new executives to a successful first year.

During the assimilation period of your inner circle members, you want to ask reciprocal questions. "What are they not telling me and why? Am I being taught or being told? Am I led or being commanded to obey?"

According to Brian, "Executive derailment during the assimilation period seldom occurs due to a lack of technical skills or a lack of intelligence. It usually involves issues around these three questions that derail them."[12]

If this is true, then the success and acceleration toward your goals and dreams depends on having members that are open and candid with you, that teach you as you progress, and that help lead you. You are 100% responsible for the relationship assimilation sub-process of your inner circle. It is your success and it is your inner circle that is influencing you either toward or away from your goals, your aims, and your dreams.

Relationship Evaluation

Relationship Evaluation is the process of assessing how well your influencers, in this case specifically your inner circle, are doing their roles. People usually dislike making evaluations even though we make them with our opinions and judgments quite often.

One of the big errors that can be made is not gathering enough information or performance data. As we evaluate our inner circle members, people may evaluate the individuals based on our personal reactions. This is a very intuitive evaluation based on thoughts immediately following interactions with the inner circle members. Another basis of evaluation is on how much knowledge over a period of time we gain from the inner circle influencers. A third method is how much we actually change our behaviors and improve our habits in desired areas. The final method is to evaluate the change in results over a time period. Let's look at each of these methods for members of the golf professional's inner circle. We'll use the swing coach and the fitness trainer.

When we are using the reactions method, we'd be evaluating whether we like the instruction techniques of the swing coach and the fitness trainer. Were the instructions clear? Did I enjoy the drills or exercises provided, and did I seem to make a little improvement through the practice period? Were the objectives of the practice or exercise sections stated before the sessions, and were they achieved by the end of the sessions? These are some of the reactions we might seek answers to in this evaluation methodology.

Using the learning evaluation, you would observe your knowledge and understanding of the swing, and which exercises are affecting which muscles. Your knowledge of the faults—and fixes of the faults—in the golf swing would increase. You'd understand why each exercise was incorporated in the exercise session and how to rotate through various series of exercises to work on key strength or flexibility needs.

With the behavior method, you would be evaluating whether your swing makes long-term changes you can take to the course and whether it works for you consistently under stress. You'd observe that your exercise techniques improve and the exercises themselves becoming easier. You might also observe you stick with the program more consistently.

With the results method, you'd look for improvement in fairways hit and greens in regulation. You might track shots lost outside of forty yards and average distance from the pin on greens hit in regulation. For the fitness coach, you'd track weight increased and number of repetitions or sets in strength training. You'd measure flexibility rotation and lap times. You'd look at the analytics and track progress or regression.

All of these are valid techniques and can be used, but for me, the proof in the pudding is results. Am I making progress on my goals? Is the progress fast enough to meet my associated chief aim? Your purpose for having an inner circle is to achieve your goals and dreams, so I suggest you use results to evaluate the areas your influencers are expected to influence.

The performance appraisal system, the analogy to the relationship evaluation sub-process, uses performance results and leadership competencies as the other major sections of the evaluation. This appraisal process was one of the best evaluators I used during my career. Now hang in here with me as we go through this process step by step and transition from the business model to your personal model. The process for evaluating the performance results section actually started before the performance evaluation period when the manager (you) and the employee (the inner circle member) sit down and draft objectives to be accomplished during the evaluation period. Throughout the period, the employee (inner circle member) would update the manager (you) on progress being made, resource utilization, and if there are any issues or projected misses by the end of the evaluation period. At the end of the evaluation period, all objectives would be evaluated. First the employee would evaluate whether the objectives had been met, then separately the manager reviews the employee's evaluation and would add an evaluation of his or her own. A benefit of this process is the calibration effect. The calibration effect is where the employee and the manager are calibrated on the employee's performance and contribution. Said another way, the measurement by each participant becomes the same. (There may not be perfect agreement, but each knows where the other measures the performance, and the employee has the chance to adjust how he/she measures their own performance in alignment with how the manager measures them.) It provides an added dimension of feedback to the employee.

A similar sequence occurs for the evaluation of leadership competencies at the same time as the performance results are evaluated. The major difference was that the leadership competencies to be evaluated and the standards for evaluation are pre-determined by the business. As you evaluate your inner circle influencers, the competencies you'll evaluate are pre-determined now as well. They are the personal guiding principles you have developed for yourself as you determined your strategic choices. If integrity is a guiding principle for your life and success, then can you tolerate inner circle influencers not meeting your standards for integrity? It would create a doubt on your part and lack of trust that would erode the right influence and potentially worse, negatively influence you.

Don't overreact with the evaluation. Part of the relationship evaluation is jointly deciding on developmental improvements that can be made if areas of performance need to improve. Even if all areas are at the selected targets, you and your inner circle influencer can discuss how to improve. Life is about continuous improvement. Ed Foreman has a saying that I've quoted for years about life improvement: "Life is like a tomato. You're either green and growing, or ripe and rotting. There's no such thing as staying the same."[13] Let your relationship evaluation process create growth for you from your influencers.

My youngest daughter did an excellent job of evaluating her inner circle when she changed high schools. Although challenging for her, I changed companies during the middle of her sophomore year. She was very slow to bring new friends into our new home. Her mom and I were at first a bit worried, but after a short conversation with her, we realized she was carefully evaluating through observation which circle of individuals she wanted to befriend. She took the time to get to know each of the individuals and their values before accepting them into her circle of new friends. Interestingly enough, she did a very, very good job, and one of those first new friends is now a graduate of Annapolis (the U.S Naval Academy) and is also now her husband. I'd say she did a great job!

I strongly encourage you to evaluate your inner circle influencers regularly on performance and congruence with your personal guiding principles. Don't forget that evaluation has to occur in some form with all of your influencers! This is absolutely critical for your on-going success. Jack Canfield stated it perfectly in his book <u>The Success Principles</u>:

> *"You're better off spending time alone than spending time with people who will hold you back with their victim mentality and their mediocre standards.*

Make a conscious effort to surround yourself with positive, nourishing, and uplifting people—people who believe in you, encourage you to go after your dreams and applaud your victories."[14]

Relationship Separation

As in business, separation should not be the first option. You should try, through the development and evaluation sub-processes, to give people a chance to change their behavior. If problems continue after multiple opportunities for them to improve, the influencer may need to be separated from you.

In all of the companies I worked for, we used a progressive disciplinary process. If a person was struggling with results or absenteeism, the individual was counseled several times before separation (termination) occurred. Most of the time, the individual resolved the issue through counseling before separation was required.

Sometimes, when you reach this sub-process on a personal basis, separation means simply creating distance or reducing contact frequency. There is a powerful word that can help you with this. The word is no. "No, I don't have time to talk right now." "No, I don't want to join you tonight." "No thank you, I'm busy." No is a very powerful way to avoid situations and create distance, but some people are hesitant to use it for fear of hurting others' feelings. If you have evaluated the need to create the separation, but don't follow through, then who's really being hurt? You are.

In the book The 7 Habits of Highly Effective People, a fourth option of engagement is pointed out. We all want to be in Win/Win relationships. We've also experienced situations that create Win/Lose and Lose/Win relationships where one person is gaining and the other is always compromising or losing. The book points out another option: Win/Win or No Deal[15]. It's a perfectly acceptable solution and should be used when you get into the situation where you are always compromising, especially if your guiding principles are being compromised. In a negotiation, Win/Win or No Deal means you walk away from the deal. If both parties don't gain acceptably from the deal, it's obviously not a good deal for at least one of the parties. Win/Win or No Deal for you means you respectfully separate from the situation.

In business, I once experienced an excellent example of this. The company I was with provided a product to a major customer. At the price the product was initially sold to the customer, both my company and the major customer were happy and making an equitable profit. It was a Win-Win because both parties profited. Over time, through inflation, the cost of the materials used to make the product increased quite dramatically. The customer during the same period wanted to maintain the initial price of the product because it was growing so well for them. It grew so well my company needed to spend more money to increase capacity to produce the product. Unfortunately, this cost increase to create the capacity occurred during a major inflationary period. My company needed a major price increase. The major customer strongly opposed the price increase for fear of slowing down the profitable growth for them. The situation had become a Win/Lose situation. From one perspective of the situation, the major customer won and wouldn't need to increase the cost they paid my company for the product while maintaining their growth and profit margin. With this perspective of the scenario, my company lost. The company's profits would continue to seriously deteriorate. Looking from the other perspective of the situation, my company could win and mandate a significant cost increase to the major customer. This solution worked for my company, but hurt the major customer's growth potential. The final solution: No deal. My company understood the major customer's needs, but couldn't provide them, so they worked with the major customer to find and qualify new providers of the same product, and slowly withdrew from that segment of the market. The customer won by still having the product at the price they desired. My company won because they freed up capacity for higher margin product segments and maintained a great relationship with the major customer in other market segments. Win/win or No Deal!

Notice two words in the sentence in the previous paragraph: situation and respectfully. Sometimes you don't have to completely sever a relationship as much as you have to separate from the situations with that individual that promote the unacceptable behaviors.

Always, however, separate respectfully. Always respect your personal guiding principles as you create the separation. As a leader in business, there were too many times when I had to create employment separation from individuals in my organization. After the evaluation was complete and the decision to separate was made, my first objective was to execute the separation in a fashion where the separated individual was able to leave with their head held high. The separation is tough enough. Why add to the situation by acting without respect for the individual? When I could bring the other individual to realize the need for separation prior to me having to tell them, the separation for the individual was much better accepted. One time, after several attempts to find the right position for him and after lots of coaching, an eighteen-year employee came into my office and said: "Okay, I understand. Let's say the 'marriage' is over. Can we talk about an amicable divorce?" After he left our company, he was happy and successful in a new position at another near-by employer.

I don't want to paint an unreal picture. If, after your evaluation, you decide to create separation, recognize there are going to be consequences for you. You may need to find another inner circle influencer. You may, no matter how respectfully you handle the separation, create some ill will. You may set back your progress toward a goal for a short time. However, there are also consequences to you for not making the decision and not creating the separation. The worst situation is to not make the separation and live a unsuccessful life of mediocrity because you didn't create the separation. Yes, there are consequences, but you also have positive consequences that occur as well. Most importantly, the acceleration of success toward your dreams.

From experience, the last sub-process of relationship separation can occur in your life even when you haven't made that choice. Sometimes, it's a much larger power that makes the decision. I separated from two of my inner circle influencers, and it wasn't my choice at all. Each of these individuals died: one from the side effects of leukemia treatment and one from a rare lung disease. I share this with you because in looking back, the loss of each of these terrific people had a tremendous impact on me. Yes, I went through the natural shock, denial, anger, and acceptance process and moved on fairly quickly with my life, but I didn't move on with my success. You see, in the relationship process, there's an arrow that goes from the relationship separation step to the relationship recruiting step. I failed to add individuals into my inner circle after each of these great people passed away. What I thought was that I could never replace the special relationships each of these individuals played in my life. That was true. I could not replace them personally, but I could find (and needed to find) others to fill the roles they played in my life. I learned I now needed to find others to provide the support, encouragement, and coaching they had provided in order to get me back on track. I encourage you to make sure you don't make my mistake and think you don't need the support. That support provides you strength you don't know you have. Great inner circle members make a difference for you in ways you might not even notice until it's gone.

Design the relationships in your life. Recruit people who will encourage you and celebrate your victories. Select Inner Circle influencers who accelerate your success. Develop strong, supportive relationships. Evaluate consciously. Create separation from those who hold you back. Develop relationships that create wind in your sails; eliminate relationships that are like anchors, but make sure you know the difference!

==================================

The exercises associated with this chapter are:

- Inner Circle Role Definition (Day 15)
- How I Influence People Survey (Day 15)

==================================

Chapter Fourteen

Recognition Systems for You and Others

IT WAS PROBABLY THE BEST basketball game I had ever played, by far! Something had happened at half time. My inhibitions had been erased. From only scoring two points in the first half, I scored twenty-one points in the second half. In the paper the next week, the article about the game was very complimentary of my play, but my coach, after sending high praise to two other players, was only quoted as saying, "and Ward played well." I never played that well again. I was so disappointed in the comment from the coach that the inhibitions returned. It was my issue. I'm 100% accountable, but one never knows what impact our words have on others.

Recognition of others is a powerful tool. Mother Teresa is quoted as saying, "There is more hunger for love and appreciation in this world than for bread."[1] We provide that love and appreciation as we recognize others. Mary Kay Ash agrees with Mother Teresa as she shares with us, "There are two things people want more than sex and money…recognition and praise!"[2] However, before we discuss providing recognition to others, there's another opinion that I want to share first and dig into.

"It is up to us to give ourselves recognition. If we wait for it to come from others, we feel resentful when it doesn't, and when it does, we may well reject it."[3]

-Spencer Tracy

It's very important we provide recognition. We can make a positive difference in others' performance and others' lives, but it's at least, and probably more important, that we provide recognition to ourselves. Look again at the story I told about my best basketball performance. It wasn't that my coach didn't recognize me, he did. I rejected it because I wanted more. I wasn't confident enough at the time to value my own recognition as being more important. I didn't let that terrific half of basketball become the standard of potential performance I expected of myself from that point on. Years later in a different sport, I responded much differently. In a round of golf, I shot two under par on the back nine to shoot even par for the round. At the time, my golf handicap was a 6. I enjoyed the two under par and recognized it as my best ever nine holes of golf. The big difference was that I recognized I had the potential to shoot a four under par round when I put the two under par performances together on both the front and the back nine. My handicap for the next ten years reached a level equal to or better than the year before. Have I ever shot four under par? Yes and no. I've had several three under par rounds on eighteen holes, but haven't shot four under par on eighteen holes yet. I have, however, shot four under par on nine holes, so now my target and personal potential is eight under par!

Notice the difference in the way that same person (me) reacted. When I relied on my own recognition, I created more potential, not disappointment. I was inspired to improve instead of creating a lower ceiling on my performance.

Positive self-recognition is an important part of developing your own self-esteem and self-image. According to Dr. Joyce Brothers, "An individual's self-concept is the core of his personality. It affects every aspect of human behavior: the ability to learn, the capacity to grow and change, the choice of friends, mates and careers. It's no exaggeration to say that a strong positive self-image is the best possible preparation for success in life."[4]

In the Management Theory course, I teach about two different types of recognition: intrinsic and extrinsic rewards. Rewards that employees receive in business are the analogy to the recognition we receive in life. Intrinsic recognition is the recognition that originates from the inside. It's the positive self-recognition that we've been discussing. It's self-satisfaction. It comes as a part of developing and then maintaining a positive self-image.

In Zig Ziglar's best selling book See You At the Top, he identifies self-image as the first step on the stairway to success.[5] In the chapters on self-image, Zig lists fifteen steps to a positive self-image. Two of the fifteen steps are techniques that help you recognize yourself. Step nine is to "make a list of your positive qualities on a card and keep it handy for your reference."[6] In this step, you are providing yourself self-recognition that you have several positive qualities. You do, and you should, recognize it often.

The next step of Zig's that guides you toward positive self-recognition is step ten. "Make a victory list to remind you of your past successes. This list should include those things that gave you the most satisfaction and confidence."[7] Self-recognition provides self-confidence. Early in my career, I was advised to maintain an accomplishments list. Though the purpose of creating the list was to assure these accomplishments weren't forgotten for my resume, the value of the list was much greater. It was personal recognition that I could make things happen and create results. It gave me confidence that I could create improvement. I brought value to my employers. I was a person of value.

I didn't realize it then, but I now realize that without self-esteem and self-confidence, I couldn't provide the sincere recognition and appreciation for others' qualities and accomplishments. So begin a program to recognize yourself.

This leads us back to the importance of recognizing others. That's the equivalent to the extrinsic rewards discussed in my Management Theory course. Extrinsic recognition is the recognition that comes from the outside. It's the appreciation you provide to others (from the outside of them). According to Margaret Cousins, "Appreciation can make a day—even change a life. Your willingness to put it into words is all that is necessary."[8] Steve Brunkhorst adds further, "Feeling appreciated is one of the most important needs that people have. When you share with someone your appreciation and gratitude, they will likely not forget you. Appreciation will return to you many times."[9]

Appreciation and gratitude goes so far with others. It doesn't have to be a big celebration, either. As Sally Koch says, "Great opportunities to help others seldom come, but small ones surround us everyday."[10] It doesn't take much effort to make a difference in someone else's day, and what may be surprising to you is that you actually benefit as much or more than the person receiving the recognition.

Sonya Lyubomirsky has written a terrific book entitled <u>The How of Happiness, A New Approach to Getting the Life You Want</u>. Ms. Lyubomirsky has researched and developed twelve *Happiness Activities*.[11] Two of the twelve activities involve providing recognition to others. Happiness Activity No. 1 is expressing gratitude and Happiness Activity No. 4 is practicing acts of kindness. Both are ways that involve providing recognition to others.

According to Ms. Lyubomirsky, "The expression of gratitude is kind of a mega-strategy for achieving happiness. Gratitude is many things to many people. It is wonder; it is appreciation; it is looking at the bright side of a setback; it is fathoming abundance; it is thanking someone in your life; it is thanking God; it is 'counting blessings'."[12] Expressing gratitude not only helps others as you provide them recognition, it is one of the "mega-strategies" to help yourself achieve happiness.

The second happiness activity that allows you to improve your own happiness while providing recognition and doing something for others is practicing acts of kindness. The acts don't have to be large. They don't have to cost a lot or even any money. The acts could be holding the door open for someone with their arms full; offering to take a photograph for a family so all members can be in the picture; letting someone go in front of you in a line if they are obviously in a hurry; shopping for a sick friend or simply providing those that are serving you a very sincere thank you. Each act recognizes the other person. The act provides them recognition that they are valued and appreciated. And think about it, as you are doing small things for others, you're the one who benefits most as you are doing things that increase your own happiness. The value of practicing acts of kindness, as well as the positive effect it has on you, are also documented in Happy by Ian K. Smith M.D..

Dr. Smith recommends, as a happiness booster for yourself, that you "commit five acts of kindness each week."[13] He provides several great ideas for some of these acts.[14]

- Make, purchase, or give a meal to a homeless person.
- Send flowers to an unappreciated person at your work.
- Donate clothing to a family whose children need it.
- Help plant a garden at a school or church.
- Be a Secret Santa.
- Visit a nursing home or a senior citizen's home.
- Collect and deliver things like blankets, etc. to an animal shelter.
- Run your own canned food drive for displaced families.

One of our family's best Christmases occurred when we bought clothes for a young, unwed mother and her child. We then had them delivered to the family by a friend the mother didn't know. The joy it brought to that young family brought the true spirit of Christmas to our family.

I truly suggest you consider employing small acts of kindness in your life. It's truly a win/win for you and for others along the way.

Recognition at work is important as well. There are more things employees do at work that are right than things they do that are wrong. Why not recognize more of the right things they are doing? Ella Wheeler Wilcox points out: "A pat on the back is only a few vertebrae removed from a kick in the pants, but is miles ahead in results."[15] There's a tendency to only focus on the problems in the workplace environment, but focusing on them will just bring more problems to you. Make sure you provide positive recognition more than negative criticism. According to Dave and Wendy Ulrich in their book The

Why of Work, "Leaders who are shaming, critical, and grumpy may evoke a lot of action, but not necessarily a lot of learning and productivity."[16] If you want your employees to be more productive and grow, assure you provide more positive recognition than negative feedback.

So examine your own current recognition systems. Do you regularly recognize yourself and others? Consider creating your own intrinsic recognition by appreciating your successes, talents, and total value. Consider creating extrinsic recognition for others by expressing gratitude and practicing acts of kindness…at work and throughout your life!

====================================

The exercise associated with this chapter is:

- Recognition to Self and Others Reflection (Day 15)

====================================

Chapter Fifteen

Your Personal Development Processes

AT THIS POINT IN USING the Successful Life Systems Design Model, you may have identified a few or maybe many areas of your life you can modify to improve the success in your life. An explanation of the analyses you will need to do will come in Part II. At this point, continue to focus on understanding the elements of the model and options that might exist.

The last design choice category is your personal development or renewal system. Renewal is important for several reasons. First, you must keep growing as an individual and you must design this system into your life. Additionally, you must have a way to ensure continual alignment of your design choices with the external environment as it changes.

Now, here's the question I have for you. How are you going to continue to grow and thrive? Are you going to make some modifications and then just stop there and become complacent? Or are you going to also initiate personal development processes for yourself? Think of the personal development process as a continuous self-renewal system to keep you making progress toward your goals and dreams.

Without systems set in place for renewal, we reach a plateau and our growth slows down. We get into physical and mental ruts. At times we need to create paradigm shifts in different areas of our life. We need to challenge some of our basic assumptions to identify other approaches that move us closer to the success we desire.

Remember Ed Foreman told us: "Our lives are like a tomato. We are either green and growing, or ripe and rotting. There's no such thing as staying the same."[1]

Since I buy-in and believe this little saying, what are the areas in our life that have to keep growing in order not to rot? Dr. M. T. Morter Jr., creator of the MorterHealth System, gives us some direction to think about as he describes the "Six Essentials of Life."[2] These six essential areas are:

- What you eat
- What you drink
- How you exercise
- How you rest
- What you breathe
- What you think.

Of the six, Dr. Morter says the last area, what you think, is the most important!

Let's think about this for a minute. What we really need to keep renewed is our physical, mental, and spiritual wellness. Don't the six essentials cover our physical, mental, and spiritual wellness? Do you believe food and drink provide our bodies nutrition and hydration each day? I do. Do you believe that rest and exercise provide renewal and development to our bodies? I do. Do you believe that what we breathe renews the oxygen in our bodies and is important for the development of our mind and bodies? I do. That leaves what you think. Does the knowledge and thoughts you feed your mind impact your development (or lack of it) and create renewal (or lack of it)? I absolutely believe it does, so let's pursue these six areas in terms of how to renew and develop ourselves.

What We Eat

Go to a bookstore and try to find definitive direction on what to eat. There are so many diets today that provide direction on what to eat, mostly for the purpose of losing weight. There are books on every angle one can think of for diets to lose weight. Which one are you going to believe?

I'm not a doctor or an expert on dieting (though I can't tell you how many of those books I've read), but there are some simple principles that seem to make sense to me.

If we eat food, it should be as close to nature as possible. Now this may sound easy, but it's not. Because of the Industrial Age that caused large segments of the population to move to cities where the factories were, fewer people were working on farms and a need developed to be more productive and efficient in growing food. At first the changes were more mechanical, with the improved machinery developed to plow the fields, plant the seeds, and harvest the crops. Later, however, more chemicals were used to improve the yield of the crops. Now, in addition to many of the chemicals used, the plants have been genetically modified to grow larger, tolerate heat or cold more, and grow despite the use of the harsher chemicals. I don't know what all these chemicals and genetic modification means for us in the long term. I'm not sure anyone truly does because it may take quite some time for the impacts to show up.

So here's what's right for me: I try to find foods that are organically grown. I also try to minimize the number of processed foods I eat. Further, I eat more raw foods today than I ate in the past because of the additional nutrients and enzymes gained. I gain these additional nutrients and enzymes because they are not lost or killed in the cooking process (whether prepared at home or in a factory).

Isn't this more expensive? Yes it is. It is more costly for the farmers to raise organic foods than it is to raise non-organic (conventional) foods. I have to pay more for these items, but that is a choice I make because I want to eliminate (or at least minimize) the contaminants in my body. Chemicals are contaminants. In my opinion, genetically modified plants are unknowns at this time. That makes them risky to me, so I choose to avoid them. So how do I make up the difference in cost?

I probably don't directly make up the cost, but indirectly I believe I do with improved health and fewer illnesses. I do make up some of it by eating less proteins, especially animal proteins, and eating less calories overall. By consuming 75% of my food as fruits and vegetables and only 25% of my food as proteins and grains, I reduce the overall cost of my food. I also pick up another benefit. As my foods are digested, the residual ash left in my body is alkaline instead of acidic.

Many wellness experts, including Dr. Morter, believe having a body with an alkaline-ash based nutrition intake will reduce the potential for disease.[3] I recognize that others, including Web-MD, state that the body will regulate the blood to the proper alkaline levels, and I believe many agree on the importance of blood levels within the body regulating our pH of between 7.35 – 7.45 (alkaline)[4]. My engineering background looks at it this way. The more acidity I put in my body, the more work my body has to do to maintain my blood levels to be alkaline. If my body has to do something to regulate my blood at an alkaline level, then it has to get alkalinity from other places in the body to make the adjustment to regulate. It seems more efficient to help the body by having an alkaline-ash nutrition base. I understand that the evidence to date has not convinced all medical authorities of the total value of an alkaline-based diet.[5] You will need to determine if such a diet is best for you. I'm not a doctor, nutritionist, or expert in wellness. You should consult your physician on whether a diet with increased fruits and vegetables, less animal proteins, and less total caloric intake is harmful to you.

What You Drink

In general, there's the same argument in this category. Gee, should I drink water and natural fruit juices? Or is it best if I drink sodas with artificial sweeteners, artificial flavors, carbonation, caffeine, and other ingredients in them? I think we all know that water and natural fruit juices are better for you. Filtered water is even better than tap water.[6] Some parts of the year it is more difficult and much more expensive to get the fruit you need to create your own natural fruit juices. I then choose to find and purchase organic fruit juices. Again, it's the same argument about the chemicals in non-organic fruit juices. Do I want contaminants, or the possibility of contaminants, in my body? Not if I can avoid them. (By the way, fruit juices are also alkaline-ash drinks. Coffee, alcohol, sodas, and teas are all acid-ash after digestion[7]). It's strictly your choice. I totally avoid artificial sweeteners if I'm aware of them.

There are numerous cases of severe side effects of these chemicals (that's what they are) on people[8]. My wife, Emily, is one of those cases. In 2005, she began having vision issues and got to the point where she became afraid to drive. She had all the medical tests the doctors recommended, such as an MRI and an EEG. They just couldn't identify the cause of her issues and said nothing else could be done. She would just have to live with it. A friend suggested she eliminate diet sodas. She only drank one or two a day, but within two weeks from eliminating them, the vision issues were gone and have never recurred. (She's never had another diet soda since.) We can look at these effects on people as side effects or direct effects. I now think of the so-called *side* effects, as *direct* effects. It's just that the severity of the effects for some people isn't severe enough to create noticeable symptoms. If artificial sweeteners had that effect on my wife, they are having some effect on me, so I choose to avoid them. (By the way, I view pharmaceutical side effects the same way—as direct effects. I'm not a doctor. This just is my logic and why I choose to look for more natural remedies.)

Let me provide a "recognition of reality" regarding both how I eat and how I drink. Not every place I choose to eat and drink controls the ingredients of their food as much as Emily and I do at home. There are times when we eat foods that are not organic and unfortunately have genetically modified ingredients. We choose not to embarrass our hosts and hostesses when we are invited out. We also go to restaurants at times where we just don't know whether ingredients are organic or genetically modified. Our preferred restaurants make all their food fresh and have many local, organic choices on the menu. We do not make these choices an obsession. Most of the time, however, we eat and drink according to these principles because it is our choice!

How You Exercise

I am of the generation that was introduced to the benefit of exercise very early in life. I remember the emphasis President Kennedy created when he renamed the President's Counsel on Youth Fitness to the President's Counsel on Physical Fitness[9]. I remember being among some of the first to take the fitness tests and learning the importance of staying physically fit. In school, in addition to the physical education classes that were required, I was very active in organized sports, beginning at age eight and continuing throughout high school and college. After college, I participated in organized sports for quite sometime and then began other activities to stay fit, such as jogging, aerobics, and working out on my elliptical cycling machine.

Most of us live more sedentary lives than the generations that came before us. We tend to ride in cars instead of walking or riding bicycles. We outsource as much of the physical work as we can afford. Yes, that often includes the gardening (i.e. growing the food we eat). We know we should be more active, but often the constant demands at work and at home cause us to want to "veg out" when we get home. That is the choice many people make today, and our physical bodies suffer for it.

The Center for Disease Control and Prevention provides guidelines for Americans.[10] To achieve important health benefits, adults need at least two hours and thirty minutes of moderate-intensity aerobic activity (i.e. brisk walking) every week and muscle-strengthening activities on two or more days a week that work all major muscle groups (legs, hips, back abdomen, chest, shoulders, and arms). Alternatively, you could combine the muscle-strengthening activities in two days a week with an hour and fifteen minutes per week of vigorous-intensity aerobic activity (i.e. jogging or running). For even greater health benefits, adults should increase their activity to five hours of moderate-intensity aerobic activity combined with two or more days of muscle-strengthening activities. The alternative would be exercising two and a half hours using the vigorous-intensity aerobic activities combined with the two days of muscle-strengthening exercises.

Aerobic activity gets you breathing harder and your heart beating faster. There are many ways to accomplish aerobic activity including riding a bike, pushing a lawn mower, or attending an aerobics class.

The key is getting your heart rate up and sustaining it at least ten minutes at a time. Remember, you still need the two hours and thirty minutes per week, but you can break it up in ten-minute increments of elevated heart-rate periods.

In her book The How of Happiness, Sonja Lyubomirsky provides us with another reason to take care of our bodies. It is another of the Happiness Activities that has been proven to increase our happiness.[11] How does physical activity improve our happiness? First, it improves self-esteem as you take control of your body and as you master the physical activity. Second, it provides a positive distraction from worries and ruminations. Third, physical activity can provide social contact opportunities when performed with others. Finally, physical activity can provide both an immediate emotional boost after the activity and chronic improvement over time.

What if you don't enjoy the physical activity you are doing? Try something different. There are so many choices to choose from there is no need to endure something you don't enjoy. It's your choice, but choose and keep choosing until you find your activity.

As you begin your physical activity routine, you should do so carefully. It is recommended that you consult a doctor or health care professional to guide you as you build up to the recommended levels of aerobic and muscle-strengthening activities.

How You Rest

Getting enough rest is important to restore and renew the body each day. According to Dr. Ted Morter III, you should generally get eight hours of rest each night.[12] There are several excellent tips on Helpguide.org on how to sleep better.[13] According to this site, having good sleep habits and strategies are essential to obtaining the restoration you can count on, but different techniques work differently for different people. Each of us needs to experiment to find out what works best for us, but the key is to stay persistent until you do find what works best for you.[14] Summarized below are some "How to Sleep Better" tips:

Sleep Tip #1: Keep a regular sleep schedule. Set a regular bedtime. Wake up at the same time each day. Nap to make up for lost sleep, but be smart about your napping. (If insomnia is a problem for you, consider eliminating naps.) Fight after-dinner napping by doing something mildly stimulating until your regular bedtime.

Sleep Tip # 2: Naturally regulate your sleep-wake cycle. Melatonin is a naturally occurring hormone that helps you regulate your sleep and is controlled by light exposure. Increase your light exposure during the day. Remove your sunglasses. Spend more time outside during daylight hours. Let as much light into your house as possible. Boost melatonin production at night. Turn off your television and computer in the bedroom. Don't read from a backlit device at night. Change your bedroom light bulbs to a lower wattage. When it's time to sleep, make sure the room is dark. Cover all the miscellaneous lights (like clock-lights), if need be.

Sleep Tip # 3: Create a relaxing bedtime routine. Make your bedroom more sleep friendly. Keep the noise down. Keep your room cool. Make sure your bed is comfortable. Create relaxing bedtime rituals like reading a book, taking a warm bath, listening to soft music, or making simple preparations for the next day.

Sleep Tip # 4: Eat right and get regular exercise. Stay away from big meals at night. Avoid (or eliminate) alcohol before bed. Cut down (or eliminate) caffeine at night. Avoid drinking too many liquids in the evening. Quit smoking. Exercise regularly, but time it such that your body temperature can return to normal prior to bedtime.

Sleep Tip # 5: Keep anxiety and stress in check. Manage your thoughts. Utilize relaxation techniques such as deep breathing, progressive muscle relaxation, or visualizing a peaceful, restful place. Practice mind-control relaxation by having a relaxation CD playing in the background to aid your relaxation process.

Sleep Tip # 6: Find ways to get back to sleep. Stay out of your head. Focus on the feelings and sensations in your body. Make relaxation your goal, not sleep. Do a quiet, non-stimulating activity such as reading a book, but keep the lights dim. Postpone worrying and brainstorming by making a brief note (keep a note pad by your bed) to get it off of your mind.

Sleep Tip # 7: Know when to see a sleep doctor. If you've tried all the tips above and are still struggling with sleep problems, you may have a sleep disorder that requires professional help. Consider scheduling a visit with a sleep doctor.

The key is to find out what works for you. On WebMD, according to Dalia Lorenzo, MD, instructor of neurology in the Sleep Disorders Center at the University of Miami Veterans Affairs Hospital: "Sleep is prompted by natural cycles of the brain activity and consists of two basic states: rapid eye movement (REM) sleep and non-rapid eye movement sleep, which consists of stages 1 through 4. Each cycle lasts about 90 minutes."[14] She further explains, "You do that cycle several times (each) night, you've had a good night's sleep. Anything that interrupts that pattern will cause sleepiness the next day."[15] Assure you are getting good, uninterrupted, restorative sleep.

What and How You Breathe

Our body needs oxygen to survive. If you are in environments or create environments that reduce the amount of oxygen you are obtaining with each breathe, then you are reducing the renewal each breath provides you. Clean, smoke-free air is essential to long-term good health. Should you smoke? No! There are enough studies to fill a warehouse on the evils of smoking, so why do it? People say: "It relaxes me." Ed Foreman shares with his audiences that you can suck on the tailpipe of your car and fill your lungs with carbon monoxide—that will relax you, too.[16] If you've never seen the difference between a smoker's lung and a non-smoker's lung, I encourage you to type 'picture of smoker's lung' into Google. You'll see the difference in a heartbeat. Why anyone would choose to do that to his/her lungs, I do not understand. All the evidence is overwhelming! If you smoke, find a technique that helps you eliminate the habit. If you don't smoke, don't even think about starting.

For those of you who don't smoke, thank you. Thank you for keeping my air clean as I go out to eat, or go to the mall, or attend sporting events. Thank you for helping me to breathe cleaner air. For those of you who still smoke, I'd like you to think about this: Why do you want your children and friends to develop lungs that look like the pictures on Google, and lungs that don't work as efficiently because they are clogged with tar? Would you poison your children? Then why would you have them breathe your second-hand smoke?

A general rule is if you can smell the air you're breathing, it's probably not good. I go one step further. If I can see the air I'm breathing, it's definitely not good. Choose to only breathe clean air. It's your choice!

It's important that you breathe properly, as well. You need to breathe properly using your abdomen. Many people are stuck in a 'fight or flight' mode and breathe more by raising their shoulders than by using their abdomen properly. How do you know if you're breathing properly? Look at your stomach. If your stomach is going outward as you breath in and inward as you exhale, then you are breathing properly, assuming that your shoulders are stable.

Dr. Morter teaches a relaxation technique that I find very effective. It is called Four Square Breathing.[18] First, breathe in to a count of four; hold your breath in to a count of four; breathe out to a count of four; hold your breathe out to a count of four; and then repeat the cycle three to four times. I use this technique for falling asleep at night and love it! (To see it in action, Dr. Morter recommends watching a baby's tummy expand as he/she breathes in. Try it!)

What You Think

Thinking is a natural process. What you think is your choice. There is a lot of evidence showing that negative thoughts, such as worry, anger, despair, judgment, and hatred, secrete toxins into the body that reduce health and wellness, whereas thinking positive thoughts secretes hormones that enhance health and wellness.[18]

One of the keys to controlling what you think about is controlling what you feed your mind. You do have a choice, you know. As we have previously discussed, you can choose what to watch on television. Ed Foreman frequently asks his audience this question: "If there's a hideous, negative program on the television, what's the best thing you can do? If your answer is turn the television off, then you've thought of the second best answer. If you've first thought of changing the channel, congratulations, you've selected the best answer!"[19] You might wonder why changing the channel is better than turning off the TV. Instead of having lingering thoughts of the negative programming you just viewed, replace those thoughts with something happy and positive.

We all need to consider whether we need to 'change the channel' on the information that is surrounding us, especially if we are serious about achieving our dreams and goals. Like we discussed in our dream mechanisms category, consider if the information surrounding you is contributing to your success or enabling contributors to your success. It might be, at best, wasting your time. However, it could be much worse for you by causing negative feelings and emotions.

What does 'changing the channel' look like? Instead of reading a fiction novel, change the channel and read a non-fiction book on a topic relevant to your goals. Instead of watching a sit-com on television at night, change the channel by reading that non-fiction book. Instead of listening to a negatively biased news channel (I don't care which one, they are all biased and promote negativity towards the other side, in my opinion), change the channel and watch a program that inspires your senses and moves you toward your dreams. Instead of listening to the local country-western or rock channel, put in a CD with inspiring speakers like Zig Ziglar, John Maxwell, or Ed Foreman.

Earl Nightingale, in his recording *The Strangest Secret*, stated: "You become what you think about most of the time."[20] Others have stated that your thoughts and actions (and income) are the average of your five closest friends. If you live by default, your environment controls what you're exposed to and, therefore, what you think. If you live by design, you choose the channels that influence you. You choose where to develop new knowledge. You choose what topics will move you closer to your next goal. You choose to control your responses toward others. You choose to learn from a negative experience.

Ever think about those channels? When someone does something that might upset or anger you, do you realize that you actually choose to be angry? In so doing, you are also choosing to secrete the harmful toxins in your body that damage your health. You can also choose to think differently. You can choose to "decide you wouldn't behave that way." You can look at a negative experience as a learning experience instead of worrying about it, or fussing and fuming over it.

Once, when I lost my job, I could have focused negative energy and anger at my former boss. I could have created my own pity-party. I could have blamed others, including my boss, for what they did or didn't do. Instead, I chose a more positive option. My choice was to figure out what I did to cause the performance leading my boss to make the decision to terminate me. Next, I needed to figure out what the cause of my performance might have been, and then fix it under my next employer by becoming an even better leader because of my learning.

Would angering at my former boss have gotten me another position any faster? Would pitying myself or blaming others improve my performance on the next job? No. The only thing that could move me forward toward my goals was learning from my past performance so I could improve future performance.

Doing the same things and expecting different outcomes has been said to be the definition of insanity. Thinking the same way and expecting accelerated progress toward your goals might be considered a close corollary, so think about how you think. Think about what thoughts you expose yourself to and ask if you are growing, renewing and developing in your thoughts, or are you stuck in a rut? The same television shows, the same news station, the same authors, the same radio stations, the conversations about the same topics are symptoms of being in a rut. Changing your thoughts by taking control and designing what you expose to your senses is living by design.

Let's discuss another channel you listen to, a very, very important channel. What is this channel? It's your self-talk channel. I am continually amazed at how poorly people talk to themselves. Have you heard any of the following? "I'm such an idiot!" "I always lose." "I'll never get a promotion." Many times people talk to themselves worse than they talk to others. They tell themselves they can't do this or that, or they are bad at math or science, or they aren't a good reader. They say things like: "I'm a terrible student." "I'm never good at sports." "No one likes me." "I am such a klutz." For others, people hold back their thoughts so as not to hurt their feelings. What about your own feelings? Even more important, what about your own thoughts?

If you believe Earl Nightingale's "The Strangest Secret," that you "become what you think about most of the time,"[20] then as you tell yourself what an idiot you are, you become one. As you tell yourself you're not good in math, you get worse, not better.

Do this: For one week, every time you hear people negatively talk to themselves, make a note of it to yourself. Two things will happen. First, you'll be amazed at how often it occurs. More importantly, though, you'll start catching yourself when you negatively self-talk. The key is once you start catching yourself, you can begin to change your own self-talk.

When I catch myself, I tell myself to "cancel that thought." I then replace that thought and self-talk positively. I tell myself: "That's not like me." "I love me." "I can do better." "I'm making better choices every day." "I'm learning from my mistakes and so what can I learn from this one?" Another example could be to replace "I'm so fat and out of shape" with "Cancel that thought. My body is becoming slimmer and healthier every day by the decisions I make and how I exercise." The interesting thing is that it doesn't take too long before you don't have to cancel thoughts so often. Have fun with it and make it a game.

Catch yourself talking better and more positively to yourself, and you actually start becoming better.

Think about the importance of the two little words "I am." "I am important." versus "I'm not that important." "I am capable" versus "I'm not able to figure that out." "I am going to win." versus "I'm going to lose." You feel the difference? "I am" may be the two most important words in your life. If you constantly tell yourself "I am" good or smart, you program yourself for more success. If you constantly tell yourself that "I am" bad or weak or bashful or slow, you become what you tell yourself you are. A powerful exercise is to repeat positive affirmations. Some excellent ones just to get you started might include: I am healthy; I am happy; I am a winner; I am excited to exercise.

Use self-talk to your advantage. You are 100% in control of how you talk to yourself (if you choose to be in control).

Here's another "I am" that will surprise you. What's the impact on your subconscious mind of saying: "I'm sorry" to other people? Have you every really thought about that response? Your subconscious mind is receiving a bad message. It's hearing: "I'm a sorry person. I'm not as good as you." Simply replace, "I'm sorry," with "I apologize," or "I regret," and you change the dynamics drastically in your subconscious mind. I encourage you to try this and incorporate it into your habits.

Talk to yourself as you would wish others to talk to you. Talk to yourself as you would insist others talk to your children and your loved ones. Talk to yourself as you would wish to be!

So what other channels do you change to? That's a great question. Consider studying more success literature that teaches general principles that create success. (Notice I said principles that create success, not ways or specific charismatic techniques. Stephen Covey discusses this difference[21] in his book The 7 Habits of Highly Effective People.) Consider listening to CDs that teach, not just entertain. Consider choices that leave you feeling good with belief in yourself. Consider finding other people who are achieving high goals. Next, research what they are reading and listening to that has made a difference in their lives.

Believe it or not, that's how Ed Foreman's *Successful Life Course* began. Ed and his team met off-site and each brought something that had helped them in their business career or in their life. Some brought books, some brought records (yes, records! It was way before the days of CDs.) Through sharing what had helped each of them, there started to be a more positive approach to the various businesses. Soon, spouses were invited. Later, suppliers and customers wanted to get involved because of the noticeable difference in dealing with the people in Ed's business. It all developed into the *Successful Life Course* that inspired me twenty-five years ago and continues to inspire people today.[22]

So think about and design your renewal and development systems. No one gains more from your development than you do. Design what you eat to renew your energy and nutrition. Design what you drink for hydration and nutrients. Design how you renew your body and energy through an active exercise routine. Design how you rest to create daily restoration for your body. Design what your environment provides you to breathe. Most importantly, design what you think by creating a development program for your mind. They are all your choices by design.

Additionally, your renewal system must also deal with keeping your choices aligned. This renewal system is how you review your progress, make course corrections, and avoid complacency. There are different models available. I will share three models with you.

Corkscrew Model of Learning

The first is the Corkscrew Model of Learning.[23] You might envision a corkscrew lying on its side. This model begins with developing a hypothesis of the outcomes before taking a proposed action. Next, act according to the hypothesis. Afterwards, ask: "What happened?" and determine the actual outcomes. Then, compare the actual outcomes to the hypothesized results. If there is a difference, ask why? Determine the causes of any discrepancy between actual and expected results. Follow this by asking: "What did I learn?" Finally, hypothesize again and incorporate your learning from the past into your new hypothesis.

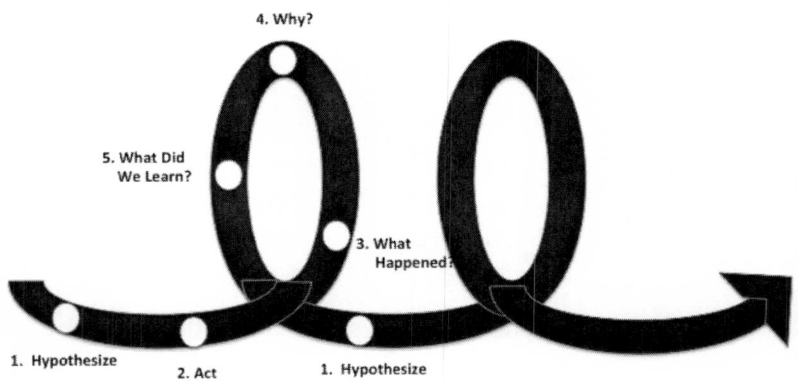

Corkscrew Model

PDCA Cycle

The second model is called the PDCA Cycle.[24] This cycle emerged out of W. Edwards Deming's work with quality. PDCA stands for Plan, Do, Check, and Adjust. So begin by planning the actions you anticipate will cause an improvement. Identify the results you are targeting and be clear about why you expect the results. Do the work. Carry out your planned actions. Check the results. Determine the actual outcomes and then compare them with your expected outcomes. Did the improvement occur as you anticipated? Adjust your reasoning about how to get a given set of results and incorporate the learning as you enter a new cycle. Plan again and repeat the cycle.

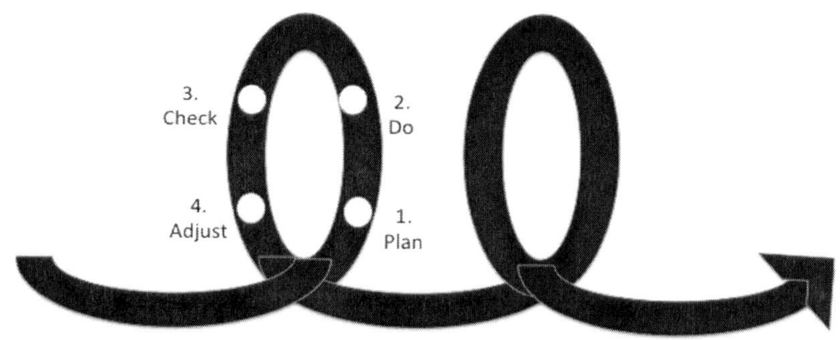

PDCA Model

7 Step Process

The third model is one used by one of my past employers. It's called the 7 Step Process.[25] The process is shown on the next page. Let me explain the process. Notice the circle at the top of the process on the left. The process begins with what you have just done: understand your current reality. Once you set your first goal that is different from your current reality, you create a tension between where you are today and where you'll be when you arrive at your first goal. I described this tension earlier.

You'll want the tension to be large enough to be attractive to you. It's almost like magnetism. Allow the attraction to have a magnetic pull toward you. In order to relieve the tension, you will need to take action. Remember that with each goal, you will develop an action plan. This is the action displayed in the process. After taking action, you need to know the impact. You do this by measuring the performance that has occurred from your action. If the action has not moved you as expected, you will modify the action and then execute it, which leads you back to the take action step. You will continue the iterative process until your measured performance has achieved the results expected.

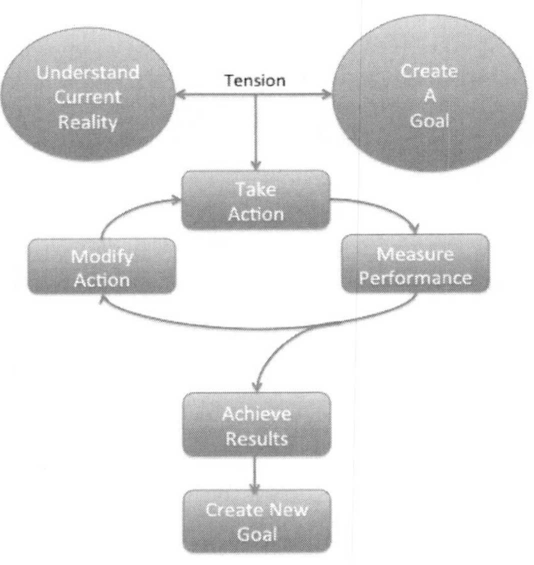

7 Step Process Model

At this point, you've achieved the first goal. It has now become your current reality, so you can now create a new goal and begin the process to relieve the tension created by the new goal. This process, like the other two, is an iterative approach toward renewal.

Design your personal development processes; determine a renewal system approach that is right for you. Then cycle after cycle, iteration after iteration, make progress toward your chief aim as you live by design.

==

The exercise associated with this chapter is:

- Six Essentials Assessment (Day 15)

==

Chapter Sixteen

Additional Tools and Thoughts

CONGRATULATIONS! YOU HAVE NOW GONE through the entire Successful Life Systems Design Model. This chapter adds some tools, thoughts, and reference materials to help you along your journey.

Before we get to those thoughts and tools, let's review quickly all the elements of the Successful Life Systems Design Model.

Personal Mission: Your primary reason for being and your distinctive competencies. Your mission should be simple, concise, easily remembered, and personally exciting.

Outcomes: Relationship, environment, spiritual, passion-time, wealth, and health results that you define as your dream.

Personal Style: Elements of your character that mediate between your personal design choices and your outcomes. These are the habits essential to get the desired outcomes you want. They include the emotions (hopes, concerns, attitudes) you need to drive to the desired outcomes. They also include the skills and knowledge required to achieve the desired outcomes.

Personal Guiding Principles: Beliefs that drive the habits, emotions, and attributes necessary to achieve your dreams. These are the principles that guide your decisions and design choices.

Strategies to Influence: A coherent set of actions aimed at responding to and influencing your external influencers. What will be your competitive strategy based on your findings through analysis? What will you do to exceed your own expectations?

Chief Aims and Goals: Long term objectives (chief aims) that are aligned with and will drive habits and behaviors towards the outcomes. Goals are aligned with the long-term objectives and should be A-S.M.A.R.T. Chief aims should include all outcome categories (relationship, environment, spiritual, passion-time, wealth, and health).

Success Mechanisms: The various activities you do and processes you use each day and week to achieve your success. Will some of the actions (or reactions) you take or activities you do today need to change given the new information you've learned? Will you need to change any techniques you use?

Personal Organization: The way you are organized to coordinate yourself. Do you need to eliminate clutter in your environment, your time, or your mind?

Decision Making/Informating: How you make decisions and how you gain your knowledge. Will your decisions be efficient? Will you need to change the sources you currently use to gain your knowledge? How will you retain access to the knowledge, and will you *use* new knowledge once discovered?

Relationships: Required competencies: recruiting (proactive attracting), selecting, developing, performance evaluating, and separation. Are the people in your life the right people with the right support to move you toward your chief aims and dreams?

Recognition: How you recognize yourself and others in your positive circle of influence.

Personal Development and Renewal: How you develop, learn, grow, review your progress, and make personal design changes. How often do you review your progress toward your chief aims? What systems are in place to assure continuous progress?

Napoleon Hill said: "The starting point of all achievement is desire."[1] How much desire do you have? Let me share a little formula I learned several years ago. The formula was documented in Richard

Beckhard and Rueben T. Harris' book Organizational Transformations: Managing Complex Change. They explain: "One of the ways of looking at readiness for change (desire), and the attitudes and motivation towards implementing change, is to think in terms of the cost of changing." They further share a simple formula shown below, developed by David Gleicher, known as the Gleicher Formula.[2]

$$C = (ABD) > X$$

where

- C = Change.
- A = The level of dissatisfaction with the status quo.
- B = A clear desired state.
- D = The practical first steps to the desired future state.
- X = The personal cost to change.

Said another way, change will occur when the product of the dissatisfaction with the status quo (the current reality) multiplied by the clarity of the desired future state (the chief aim and dream) multiplied by the practical first steps toward the desired future state (next steps) is greater than the personal cost to change. Now let's clarify this a little further. In order for you to be motivated to make personal changes you must be dissatisfied with where you are today, you must have a clear chief aim (that is aligned with your bigger dream), and you must have an action plan where you believe the first steps are practical. If you are dissatisfied with where you are today—I mean really, really dissatisfied—but you don't have your chief aim clearly defined, then change isn't likely to occur. That's why so many people stay in the rut they live in. Without a clear aim, without any goals, there's not enough desire to get out of the rut. Even if you are really, really dissatisfied with your current reality and you have a very clear chief aim, then reaching your chief aim isn't likely either if you don't believe the first step is practical. If any of the three factors (A, B, or D) are low, your motivation stays low and your progress toward your dream slows down or even stops. Who hasn't been there at one time or another?

Further, if the cost of your personal change is high, your motivation must be higher. The relationship between these factors is important throughout the voyage to your chief aims and dreams.

WARNING: If along the voyage, your dissatisfaction with your existing reality reduces to a point where the personal cost to achieve the next goal is too high, the formula would predict that your progress towards your chief aim slows down. That's one reason why your dream needs to be much larger than your chief aim and you need to be able to visualize and truly feel the satisfaction of achieving the dream.

I've said it earlier, but at one point, my desire to change—to grow and improve—slowed down. Looking at the Gleicher Formula, I would attribute my reduced desire to a reduction in the dissatisfaction with my status quo. Said another way, I became too comfortable. A harsher word would be that I became complacent. Eventually I did become dissatisfied enough to overcome the personal costs to change. I developed new chief aims and associated goals and created the practical first steps to start moving toward the new goals. Today, I am so glad I woke up from the comfort (or complacency). It has made an enormous difference in how much I enjoy every single day!

One of the tools very helpful to me is a system I designed to help me set my weekly priorities. It helps to assure I make progress in each dream category each week, and monitors if I'm staying on track over time. I felt like I needed this monitoring system because, as I mentioned above, without it, even with the terrific knowledge I had learned from Ed Foreman and others, I slowly drifted away from the new practices and techniques that were working so well.

On a later page is a form I developed to fill out each week. I choose to complete the form on Sunday evening in preparation for my upcoming week. There are two sections of the form for each day. The top section has space to list the tasks I plan to complete each day in each of the six dream categories. The bottom half of the form is twelve daily routines I have defined for myself that I need to do each day to stay on track. Your "daily dozen" will be your choice.

On Sunday evening I first complete the upper part of the form for each of the next seven days. Notice that at this point I have not assigned any appointments in my diary or calendar. I'm just identifying the important tasks to complete each day for each dream category. You may have an exception with prior scheduled appointments, such as a dentist appointment that may have been set weeks in advance, but generally, you would begin by just identifying your important tasks.

After I have decided the tasks for the week, I then go to my calendar and schedule the time. Ed Foreman recommends you first schedule the items that must be done at a specified time. Then you schedule items that must be done, but require no specified time. Next you schedule the things you'd like to do, including personal fun.[3] Using this priority system, not only will you schedule your items on the list (which are probably contributing and contributor enabling tasks), you will schedule life essential and compliance tasks that are not on the form referenced.

You now have your week scheduled with tasks you've defined for each dream category, and for life essential and compliance tasks that must be done.

On the following Sunday, you repeat the process for the next week. Additionally, you score yourself for the week you've just finished. For each of the priority categories, I give myself up to 3 points each day (6 x 3 = a potential of 18 points each day). I then give myself zero or 1 point for each of the twelve daily tasks. Therefore I have a potential of thirty points each day.

For each day and each dream category, I evaluate whether I accomplished everything that I had planned. Let's say I had three items under the relationship category on Monday and only accomplished two of the tasks. I'd give myself a score of 2. What if I only had one task planned for Monday? If I accomplished the task, I'd give myself a 3. If I didn't fully accomplish it, I'd score 0. I follow this procedure for each of the dream categories. Similarly for the daily routines, I score either a 0 or a 1. At the end of each day, I give myself a daily score by looking at the percentage of potential score I achieved. (E.g.: 25 points of a potential 30 equals 83.3%) Sometimes, I choose not to schedule a task in one or more of the dream categories for a particular day. (This is usually a day when I'm traveling and can't make progress

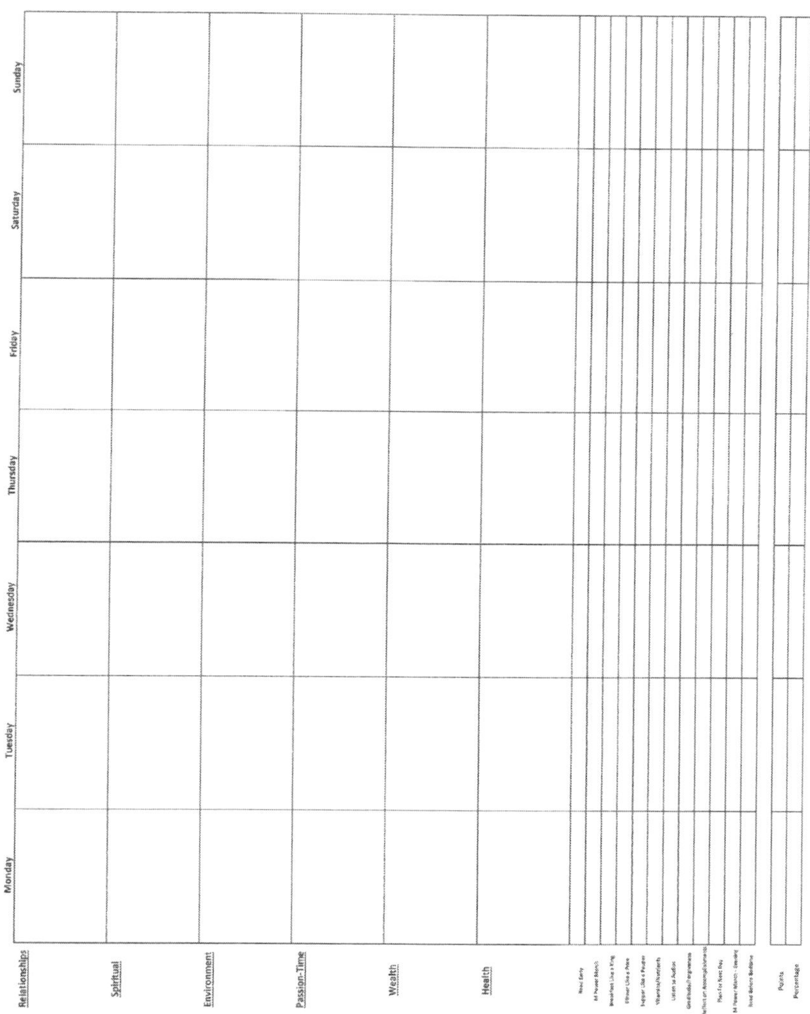

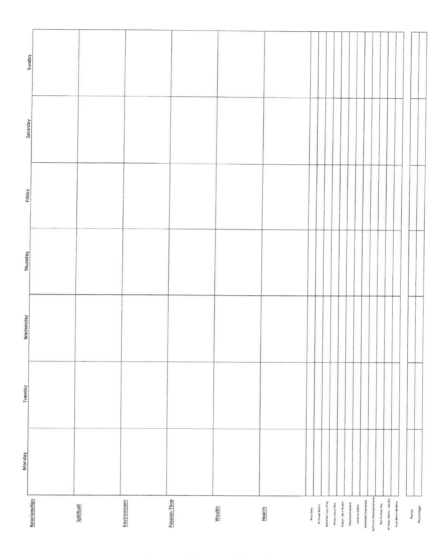

Priority Planning Template

on, for example, the environment category.) On these days, I simply reduce the denominator by the value of the category. At the end of the week, I then look at the weekly percentage achieved and keep a graph of my weekly percentage week-to-week. The value of the graph is to see when or if I start trending a reduced percentage accomplished. This is my way to catch drift before it leads to complacency.

I showed this system to an associate who now uses the system and loves it. He has modified the scoring such that two thirds of his score comes from the top section and one third from the daily routines. This way, if he has chosen not to work in a particular category one day, he still has the same potential (100%) each day.

Both systems are working effectively for each of us. The point is you need to plan your contributing and contributor-enabling work in order not to let things slide. Most of this work is important, but often not urgent, so it slips. If you consciously create a system to assure you continue working on the contributing and contributor-enabling tasks, you'll keep making progress toward your chief aim and dreams.

The second point made above is to keep track of how you are doing so you don't drift too far before taking corrective action to get yourself back on track. Nobody else will be monitoring how you are doing in your habits and in your progress toward your dream, so *it's up to you* to stay on track.

Others prefer to stay away from the analytics, but still need a reminder or daily progress tracking technique. A method for this is to find a folder with pockets on both sides when opened. You then create twelve 3"x5" cards with each of your chosen daily (dozen) tasks on them. You will use these cards each day. Next you label six 3"x5" cards with the your category topics. For me, that would be "Relationships," "Spiritual," "Environment," "Passion-Time," "Wealth," and "Health." Then, on each card list the tasks you plan to do that day for each specific category. (New category cards will need to be created each day.) You then have eighteen cards each day. Begin the day with all eighteen cards on in the left side pocket of the folder. As you complete each card, transfer the card to the right side pocket of the folder. By the end of the day, if all eighteen cards are in the right side pocket, you've completed your "next step" tasks for the day. Congratulations!

Another system I'd like to share with you is the system that got me started on the right track twenty-five years ago. It's Ed Foreman's system. He calls them Prescription No. 1, Prescription No. 2, and Prescription No. 3.

Prescription No. 1 is a daily prescription.[4] Ed recommends you take this prescription for thirty days without interruption (and as long as you desire to feel and do goood!) In this prescription, Ed describes habits and actions for you to develop. Those actions include:

- Getting up early.
- Reading something inspirational for 10 to 20 minutes immediately after awakening.
- Going outside for a walk and appreciating the beauty of nature,
- Stretching and exercising for 30 minutes or more.
- Showering and dressing professionally.
- Eating a nourishing breakfast ("Breakfast like a king!")
- Leave for work with plenty of time.
- Listen to inspiring CDs as you drive to work.
- Mid-morning, check to see if you're really working on the important things.
- Take a refresher break: walk around and stretch.
- Just before lunch, practice mind-controlled relaxation to reenergize yourself.
- Eat a reasonable lunch ("Lunch like a prince.")
- Mid-afternoon, recheck to assure you're still focused on accomplishing the important things.
- At the end of the day, reflect on your accomplishments and congratulate yourself.
- Listen to inspiring CDs on the way home.
- Eat a light dinner ("Dinner like a pauper.")
- Enjoy a moderate walk before retiring for the evening.
- Read something inspiring before going to sleep.
- Sleep 7 – 9 hours.

Prescription No. 2 is a once-a-week routine.[5] Ed prescribes that you do this weekly for ninety days (and as long as you desire to improve your performance and productivity).

Prescription No. 2 activities are:

- Find a location to be completely alone.
- Take your time and review the events of the week in a fair amount of detail.
- Dwell on what you did right and what you accomplished.
- Think only briefly about what you did wrong and only in terms of it being a learning situation.
- Think back over the accomplishments of the past weeks and months, focusing on the things that have helped you accomplish your success.
- Think about how these things can help you improve in the future.
- Think about how you can apply these things in the next week.

Prescription No. 3 is an annual, all-day event.[6] Do this as soon as possible within the next sixty days, and at least once every twelve months. Set aside and schedule a day to spend at least six hours following Ed's rules. You'll need to go somewhere you can be completely alone and outside. It needs to be somewhere that you will not see anyone (or at least speak to anyone).

For the first two hours:

- Relax and let your mind wander.
- Sit, lie on your back—just relax.
- Watch the clouds roll by. Just relax.

For the next two hours:

- Let your mind go back to your earliest recollection.
- Slowly, during the next two hours, think about the events of your life to date.
- Think about the positivity these events have brought to your life.
- Even the tough side of your life brings character, so think of the positive learnings from each event.

For the last two hours:

- Think about where you are now…the present.
- Realize how much you have to be thankful for: your spouse, your family, your friends, and your business associates.
- Think about what you really want to accomplish.

- Decide now to achieve it by going after it in a determined fashion that moves you steadily toward it.

Go home with renewed vigor and a fresh attitude.

These are powerful prescriptions. Incorporate these specific recommendations with other daily, weekly, and annual rituals that improve your success. I will also share how to use these as you develop your personal redesign.

Finally, I'd like to share one other opportunity to improve your voyage to success. It's called the B.E.S.T. technique. Over the past forty years of clinical practice and research, Dr. M.T. Morter Jr. has developed this technique. B.E.S.T. stands for Bio-Energetic Synchronization Technique. According to The Book of B.E.S.T. by Dr. M.T. Morter Jr., et al, B.E.S.T. is "a hands-only, non-forceful procedure that allows for the removal of primary interference, permitting structure and function to normalize and the body to heal."[7]

As we all deal with the day-to-day stresses of our lives and the constant need for immediate gratification, we activate our fight-or-flight reflexes often—too often. Along with these conscious thoughts and subconscious responses come psychological responses in our body. It is normal to respond to emergency stress this way, but today's lifestyles and constant demands are causing us to stay in this mode too much of the time. Sometimes we lock ourselves in this "emergency" state and our body is working overtime "fighting or flighting." Normal physical processes, such as proper digestion and blood pressure, are altered when we are in this state in order to conserve energy for the fight or flight. We need to be able to get out of this mode and return to a more natural state of calmness so our bodies can function as designed.

Over time, between the constant emergency state and other negative impacts of negative emotions, our body will override its normal functions on a full-time basis. Eventually, Dr. Morter states, exhaustion of our autonomic, our immune, or our hormonal systems can occur.[8]

B.E.S.T. is an active system that helps reduce the interference in the brain that causes the constant overrides utilizing several B.E.S.T. techniques. B.E.S.T. can also help eliminate the interferences in your brain that create "stops" to your beliefs in your success. By testing your beliefs with B.E.S.T. techniques, you can eliminate some of the roadblocks that have been holding you back from your goals and dreams. Timothy Lambright, a B.E.S.T. practitioner near Nashville, Tennessee, has helped some of his clients create some remarkable results. For more information on B.E.S.T., visit www.morter.com. There you can locate a B.E.S.T. practitioner near you who can fully explain the system to you and can help you eliminate your interference.

I leave you with one final thought or, in this case, a poem. The poem is *Invictus* by William Ernest Henley.[9] This was my father's favorite poem as I grew up. It is powerful to me and emphasizes why you want to live by design. I hope you enjoy it!

Invictus

Out of the night that covers me,
Black as the pit from pole to pole,
I thank whatever gods may be
For my unconquerable soul.

Through the fell clutch of circumstance
I have not winced nor cried aloud
But under the bludgeonings of chance
My head is bloody, but unbowed.

Beyond this place of wrath and tears
Looms but the horror of the shade,
And yet the menace of the years
Finds and shall find me unafraid.

It matters not how strait the gate,
How charged with punishments the scroll,
I am the master of my fate,
I am the captain of my soul.

PART II

Chapter Seventeen

A Design and Implementation Approach

WITH THE SLSD MODEL, YOU are in a better position to understand the relationships between your external environment, your design choices, your character, and your results. Understanding these relationships provides you an opportunity to align the elements of design to produce the optimal relationship, environment, spiritual, passion-time, wealth, and health results.

Simply understanding these relationships, however, is not enough if you are going to make informed, design choices that fit together. You will need to use some analysis tools to gather data in order to make better-informed choices. You'll need to define your personal mission and the personal guiding principles to keep authentic. You will also need to define, for yourself, dreams that excite you and create joyful desire.

The analysis tools help you gather data. The data gained will aid you to make optimal choices and improve alignment. There will be three analyses you'll need to do as you design your successful life. These analyses are an environmental scan, a mechanism analysis, and a social analysis. Each of these analyses consists of two phases: a data collection phase and an implication determination phase. Once you have collected and documented all the implications, you will make your design change decisions and lay out your success plan.

Paul Gustavson suggests you think of the analysis tools as a mop—use them to soak up information.[1] In environmental scanning, you soak up information about the external environment, including your dream categories. In the mechanism analysis, you soak up information about all the mechanisms you have now. In the social analysis, you will soak up information about your social interfaces. Once you have the information, you will then 'wring out' the information into the different buckets of the SLSD model.

Along with the SLSD model and the analysis tools, there is a design methodology that will guide you through your personal change. The Successful Life Design methodology is a *systematic* change process. It guides you through the use of the SLSD Model and tools. It shows you how to implement the choices you make. There are six steps to the design methodology: Visioning, alignment, transition, implementation, evaluation, and renewal.

Throughout this book, there have been numerous items and areas to consider. You may have already used the exercise references at the end of each chapter to work on a single choice area, or potentially several choice areas. If you haven't referenced ahead and started using some of the exercises, below is a twenty-eight day plan to navigate you through the redesign process, from start to finish. You can go slower than twenty-eight days to create your design; you can also go faster, but twenty-eight days (or four weeks) is an appropriate pace.

As you review each of the twenty-eight days, you'll notice there is a phase where you are analyzing your current reality. When I was first introduced to the seven-step renewal process described in Chapter Fifteen, I was amazed at how often people I was working with could agree on "where they wanted to go (in the business)." In other words, there was very high agreement on the "future state." The problem was that, as a group, we never slowed down to agree on where the business currently was, and we each had a different perspective of where we were. This created a negative tension in regard to what we should do because we were dealing with too many starting points.

As you begin your redesign, you will want to take enough time to clearly define your current reality. It's *your* starting point. If you create action plans from the wrong starting point, you'll be less efficient in accelerating your progress, so take whatever time is necessary to do a thorough job defining your current reality. The importance of the twenty-eight day plan is learning the sequence of actions to take in developing your personal redesign.

The outcome of your twenty-eight day redesign activity is a clearly defined action plan for the following three months. I recommend a scheduled day after ninety days to review the progress your plan has created. Remember, one of the seven steps is to monitor. If you are not making the progress desired, you will advance to the next step in the loop. That step is to modify your plan. Things change in our environment and we must make course corrections in most plans. Think of a pilot in an airplane. A plane never takes off without a flight plan. However, if a storm moves in more quickly or even stalls, the pilot will make course corrections during the flight to assure the plane gets to its destination safely. *You* are the pilot of the redesign flight. You'll want to keep checking the weather along the flight and make course corrections as necessary. Quarterly checks during the first year of the implementation create a good balance between making the desired changes and giving the changes time to create outcomes.

Finally, before I start laying out the twenty-eight days, let me say that all days are not created equally. There will be some days, like Day One and Day Twenty-Eight, that are full day events. Other days may only take an hour or so. As I said, all days do not require the same amount of time commitment to complete the task(s). You may also want to do some pre-work before you get to Day Seven, and begin gathering materials for your dream board or dream book.

One more note: This task may seem overwhelming to some due to your current commitments or current reality. Know, once again, that it is perfectly okay to move at your own pace. Also know that if you can only do part of the plan, such as Ed's Prescription No. One,[2] this can still have a tremendously positive impact on your life as it has for countless others. Be kind to yourself, use positive and encouraging self-talk, and move on to designing your life one step at a time.

So let's begin!

Day One: In the prior chapter, I provided a bullet-point version of Ed Foreman's Prescription No. Three.[3] Begin your redesign by taking this important prescription from Ed. Below, I've repeated this prescription with just a slight modification as it applies directly to the full redesign task at hand.

Prescription No. Three

Prescription No. Three is an annual, all-day event with travel to and from your get-away location and the six hours (or more) for the exercise. Be sure to plan and schedule enough time. Do this at least once every twelve months. You'll need to go somewhere that you can be completely alone and outside. It needs to be somewhere that you will not see anyone (or at least not speak to anyone). That's why I called it a "get-away" location. To get the full benefit of the prescription, you'll need to completely "get-away."

For the first two hours:

- Relax and let your mind wander.
- Sit, lie on your back—just relax.
- Watch the clouds roll by and just relax.

For the next two hours:

- Let your mind go back to your earliest recollection.
- Slowly, during the next two hours, think about the events of your life to date.
- Think about the positivity these events have brought to your life.
- Even the tough side of your life brings character, so think of the positive learning from negative events in your life.

For the last two hours:

- Think about where you are now... the present.
- Realize how much you have to be thankful for...your spouse, your family, your friends, and your business associates.
- Think about what you really want to accomplish.
- Decide now to achieve what you really want by going after it

in a determined fashion that moves you steadily toward it.

- Create the first draft of your dream statements for each of the six categories. If you need to take more time than the two hours to complete these first draft statements, then take additional time.
- Don't worry about making them perfect because you will review them again throughout this redesign month.

Go home with renewed vigor and a fresh attitude.

Day Two: Day One has been focused on a lot of positive. You even considered the positive aspects and the learning from tough challenges in your life. Now, you will begin to examine the "desire" side of the Gleisher Formula[4] discussed in the previous chapter. Below is a series of questions I call the "What Needs Changing Questionnaire." Think through and answer each of these questions. If you are satisfied with your answers, then honestly, why redesign yourself? According to the formula, you won't have enough desire to overcome the cost to change. Remember, you're embarking on a month of defining your redesign and then at least three months of implementing the changes and monitoring the results. That's a big investment on your part, so we don't want low desire to "stop" your success, do we?

Below is the questionnaire. Take your time. Check your current level of dissatisfaction in some of these areas.

"What Needs Changing" Questionnaire

1. Do I have a definition of success?
2. Do I know of things that need to change in my life?
3. What conscious choices have I made that created my desired success?
4. What unconscious choices have I made that created undesired success for me?
5. Do I have a written relationship dream?
6. Do I have a written spiritual dream?
7. Do I have a written environmental dream?
8. Do I have a written passion-time dream?
9. Do I have a written wealth dream?
10. Do I have a written health dream?

11. Do I have a written personal mission statement?
12. Do I have a written set of personal guiding principles?
13. Are there one or two dream categories that are more important to me?
14. Are my dreams what I want, or are they what someone else wants for me?
15. Are my dreams real?
    15.a Do I know and can I handle the worst-case scenario?
    15.b Are my dreams aligned with my mission and guiding principles?
    15.c Am I willing to invest the projected time to achieve the dreams?
    15.d Am I willing to invest the projected money to achieve the dreams?
16. Is my dream worthy enough of my time and effort?
17. Do others view me criticizing, condemning, or complaining?
18. Do others view me as showing genuine, honest appreciation for them and others?
19. Do others view me as thinking good thoughts about them, others, and myself?
20. Do others view that I always give others a reason to agree with me before I ask anything of them?
21. Do others view me smiling often?
22. Do others view me as someone who remembers names?
23. Do others view me as a good listener?
24. Do others view me as thinking, acting, and looking happy and successful?
25. Do others view me as one who never engages in worry conversations or gossip sessions?
26. Do others view me as responding enthusiastically and positively ("Terrific!") to the common question of "how are you?"
27. Do others view me looking for and expecting good things to happen?
28. What type of emotions would others use to describe me? Are they positive or negative emotions?

29. What skills do others recognize in me?
30. Are all my influencers supportive and positive about my dreams and goals?
31. How would I rank my willingness to learn?
32. How would I rank my willingness to change?
33. How would others rank my willingness to learn?
34. How would others rank my willingness to change?
35. Do I reflect to others that I am 100% responsible for my outcomes?
36. Do I ever blame others for my current situation?
37. Do I associate with mostly positive or mostly negative people?
38. Do I control my thoughts?
39. Do I control my emotions?
40. Do I have a strategy to influence the negative influences around me?
41. Do I have written goals for the next year?
42. Do I have wasteful activities that I routinely do?
43. Do I procrastinate?
44. Do I have any clutter in my environment?
45. Do I have any clutter in my time?
46. Do I have any clutter in my thoughts?
47. Do I efficiently or inefficiently meet my security needs?
48. Do I efficiently or inefficiently meet my faith needs?
49. Do I efficiently or inefficiently meet my worth needs?
50. Do I efficiently or inefficiently meet my freedom needs?
51. Do I efficiently or inefficiently meet my belonging/love needs?
52. Do I efficiently or inefficiently meet my fun/enjoyment needs?
53. Do I efficiently or inefficiently meet my knowledge needs?
54. Do I efficiently or inefficiently meet my health needs?
55. Do I have an inner circle of advisors that will aid me in obtaining my dreams?
56. Do I recruit positive influences into my life?
57. Do I regularly recognize my accomplishments?

58. Do I talk to myself positively or do I put myself down?
59. Do I regularly recognize the accomplishments of others with genuine praise and happiness?
60. Do I eat properly?
61. Do I drink properly?
62. Do I rest well?
63. Do I exercise regularly?
64. Do I breath properly, keeping my lungs free of smoke and other contaminates?
65. Do I think positively?
66. Do I make a conscious effort to feed my mind with positive materials?
67. Do I have a renewal process?

From your answers, you'll know whether you have a low or high dissatisfaction with your current reality. Assuming it is high (since you've finished the questionnaire and read this far in the book), proceed to Day Three and Four.

Day Three and Four: Time for some review of some of the important concepts early in this book. Your task for Day Three is to reread Chapters One and Two. On Day Four, reread Chapters Three and Four. As you reread Chapter One, consider what your personal definition of success is. Not my definition. Not Paul Gustavson's definition. Not Ed Foreman's definition. Not Newt Gingrich's definition. What does personal success mean to you? As you review the chapter, remind yourself: "If I want things to change in my life, if I want the answers from the questionnaire yesterday to change, I am going to have to make changes in my life!" Seek to really understand the core components of the Successful Life Systems Design Model and the ten choice elements of the model. After reviewing the elements, come up with a personal example of when you made a change in one element. Determine if there were effects to the other elements. You might even find an example of where you made one change, but failed to make a change in another element, and the result was not as satisfying as you had hoped. What would have happened if you made the change in the second element? Could you now project a more favorable outcome?

Rereading Chapter Two is about reviewing the importance of dreams in your life. Be sure you understand the relationship between dreams, chief aims, and goals. Review the six dream categories I have chosen to use. Notice I said, "categories I have chosen…" Can you eliminate or change a category? Sure you can. These are your dreams, not mine. I would caution you to maintain multiple categories to assure balance in your life and in your success. Many people tend to focus so much on the wealth category that they lose the balance. Often, even if they achieve the wealth goal, they still are not happy. I believe that happiness is part of success. Finally, understand how to test your dreams. These simple tests will help assure you create goals that create the magnetism you'll need and prevent the "stops" that slow you down.

During your Chapter Three reread, think about Life's Daily Menu[5] and which side of the menu you have been choosing each day. Consider each of the Habits of Winners[6] and whether the lack of any of these habits has created a block or a reduction of your success outcomes. Finally, consider your emotions and skills. Are they enabling your success, or is a skill missing?

Day Five: Today, you begin to develop your personal mission statement. There are many techniques available to help you develop your personal mission statement. Some recommend short, precise mission statements. Others recommend longer, more inclusive mission statements. One I suggest is in Jack Canfield's book The Success Principles. He describes an exercise[7] from Arnold M. Patent.

Personal Mission Statement Exercise

Mr. Patent first has you identify and list two of your most unique personal qualities. As an example, these might be passion and creativity. He then has you think of one or two ways you enjoy expressing those qualities. These might be ways like "to teach" or "to help others." Next, he has you assume the world is utopic. What do you see when you think about that? How are people relating to each other? How do you and others feel? Think of expressions like "Everyone is open with each other," or "Everyone appreciates each other's talents and shows each other gratitude through recognition," or "People accomplish great feats together." Mr. Patent then has you combine the three prior exercises into a single statement like: "My mission is to use my passion and creativity to teach and help others appreciate their talents and the talents of others by openly showing gratitude for what they have accomplished together." Now use this process or the process[8] from Jon Gordon's book The Seed, to develop the first draft of your personal mission statement.

Day Six: Now that you have developed your personal mission statement draft, you will want to test it. Take time to sort out your mission.

Personal Mission Survey

Survey three to five of your closest friends or family members. Ask them what they see as your unique personal qualities. Ask them how they see you using these qualities. Find the areas of overlap between what you think and the impressions you have left with your friends and family. Are the overlaps qualities that make you smile when you are told about them? If so, you may be on the right track! Continue to refine your mission statement until you can use it to help make decisions in your life.

Personal Mission Statement Test

Test your personal mission statement with past decisions you've been happy with. Is there alignment between the decision and your mission statement? Now test the statement with a decision that didn't work out so well. Would your mission statement have steered you toward a better decision? Your personal mission statement should help you with the decisions that move you closer to your dreams and closer to the style and character you desire.

Day Seven: You probably were happy yesterday with your personal mission statement after gathering the input from friends and family to confirm your own thoughts. Sleeping on my thoughts always helps me, so look at it again today. If you are still happy with it, then congratulate yourself and let's move on. If not, your personal mission statement is too important not to get right. Keep working on it until you are happy with it, and then you can finalize your personal mission statement.

Today you will begin to create your dream board or your dream book. A dream book is a scrapbook or notebook you fill with images of your dreams, whereas a dream board is a single collage of images of the successful completion of your dreams.

Dream Board Exercise

A nice how-to for creating a dream board[9] or book is provided on www.wikihow.com/Make-a-Dream-Board. Below is a summarization of the procedure:

1. *Gather Materials*: Find magazines or websites with pictures of the topics that interest you. There are other places to gather material. If there is a particular car you are interested in, then go to the dealer and get some brochures (or even get your picture taken with the car of your dreams!) You are searching for visual images of your dreams from each of your categories that will motivate and excite you when your look at them.
2. *Cut Out Images*: From all the material you've gathered, cut out pages with the images that appeal to you. Minimize the words you keep. Pictures are much more powerful! Try to use at least one page of images for each of the dream categories.
3. *Purchase a Board or Scrapbook*: You can use a magnetic board or a pre-strung canvas on a timber frame for the dream board. A blank scrapbook or journal works nicely for a dream book. Make the dream board a decent size. Some recommend three feet by four feet to get enough images posted. For a dream book, I recommend at least a page per category. Two pages across from each other are even better! I also put my personal mission statement in the front of the book, followed by my personal guiding principles. You'll define yours later.
4. *Paste the Pictures*: Now take the images you've selected, neatly cut out the pictures, and paste or

place them on the board or in the book.

5. *Place your Dream Board*: Position your dream board in a location where you will see it regularly and can look at it at least twice per day. One of those viewings should be just before you go to sleep. Enjoy your image dreams. Project yourself into those pictures enjoying the attainment of your dreams.

Day Eight: You've been working with your dreams and personal mission for this first week. You should now have a stronger sense of your dreams and dream categories. Review each of your six dream category statements. You may sense a need to modify them. If so, then make the modifications. Check back on your dream board or book. Does it need to be updated, too?

Personal Guiding Principles Exercise

Next you are going to develop your personal guiding principles. So how do you develop your set of guiding principles? Try this. You can do two activities and then see how they meet in the middle. First, start with a clean sheet of paper and make a list of the habits and characteristics that you value.

Next, review the list of values below:

Achievement	Harmony	Religion
Adventure	Health	Respect
Affection	Honesty	Risk Taking
Autonomy	Hope	Security
Beauty	Humor	Self-Acceptance
Belonging	Independence	Self-Control
Challenge	Inner Peace	Service
Communications	Innovation	Simplicity
Community	Integrity	Spirituality
Competence	Intelligence	Status
Competition	Intimacy	Strength
Courage	Knowledge	Success

Creativity	Love	Teamwork
Curiosity	Loyalty	Travel
Decisiveness	Material Possessions	Trust
Dependability	Open-Mindedness	Truth
Discipline	Order	Variety
Diversity	Passion	Wealth
Effectiveness	Patience	Wisdom
Empathy	Perseverance	
Enthusiasm	Peace	
Environment	Persistence	
Equality	Personal Growth	
Excellence	Physical Appearance	
Fairness	Play	
Faith	Pleasure	
Family	Power	
Flexibility	Productivity	
Freedom	Prosperity	
Friendship	Quality	
Growth	Rationality	
Happiness	Recognition	

Purchase some 3"x5" index cards. You'll need at least 90. On the top of each card, write one of the values listed above. Below the value, write out your definition of this value. Don't hesitate to use references to see how others define each value, but make sure the definition you write out is what you believe the value to mean. Do this for each of the values in the list. Develop one card for each of the values. Are there other personal values you hold that are not on the list? If so, then add that value with its definition.

Now create four additional cards, one for each of the following words: Consistently, Often, Sometimes, and Rarely.[10] Use these cards as the headers for four columns of cards you are going to create. Now take each value card and decide if you consistently, often, sometimes, or rarely act as described by the definition of the value. For instance, one of my cards is for Belonging. The definition is "being part of groups, having personal and professional affiliations, being accepted." Being honest, I'm sometimes part of groups, I sometimes have personal affiliations, I rarely have professional affiliations, and I often am accepted. So, for this value I'd put the card in the Sometimes column. Another card is Rationality. My definition is "the ability to be logical, reasonable, and unemotional." I'm very consistently logical, often reasonable, and often unemotional. So, I'd put this card in the Often column. You get the gist of it. If you know how to "muscle test" or have a friend that can "muscle test" you, this is another technique to find your values as well.

After you have sorted the cards into the four columns, take a closer look at the values you consistently and often use. Sort these again looking for the values you really feel strongest about. These are probably your core values. Now, using the most important values to you, create your personal guiding principles statement. This statement can take many forms. One approach is to create a one to three paragraph statement using all of the sorted values. Another approach might be to create a page stating how you demonstrate each of these values, followed by the value word. Reviewing my personal guiding principles, I took the words and created a "command" for myself to live by. Do what feels good to you with the values you choose. That's why they are called *personal* guiding principles...because they should be personal to you! Next, add your personal guiding principles statement to your dream book, if that was the technique you chose to create on Day Seven. If you chose to create a dream board, then find a way to display or keep your principles with you for daily review. I made a bookmark for myself with my personal mission on one side and my personal guiding principles on the other side.

Day Nine: Today, you will begin to create your list of key influencers. You may want to refer back to Chapter Four.

Key Influencer Identification Exercise

At this point, reflect and recognize the individuals and organizations that influence you in your life. Are you still not sure who or what influences you? Do this: Look at your calendar. With whom are you spending most of your time? Not just your meeting time, but your thought time, too. Scan how you spent your last week and month. How much time was at home with your spouse and family? How much time was spent at work? How much time was spent in front of the television (and what did you watch)? How much time was spent with friends or neighbors? You get the gist of my questions. Really examine where you are influenced today. What about in the past? Do your past contacts influence you today?

Create categories of influencers in your life. Using the far left column of the template provided, list all of specific individuals or other specific influences. After you've created your initial list, ask others close to you (for example, your spouse or best friend) who and/or what they believe influences you. Sometimes they bring up an influencer you've not thought of or considered.

After you feel you have the list fairly well completed, consider if the influence each of these has on you is positive, neutral, or negative. What does this mean? It's simple. Is the individual or organization helping move you toward each of the dream categories we discussed in Chapter Two? Now really think about this one. Is your best friend a positive influence on you achieving your relationship dream? Your environment dream? Your passion-time dream? Your spiritual dream? Your wealth dream? Your health dream? The answer can be different for each individual's influence on the different categories. Your best friend may be helping you achieve your passion-time dream, but may not be a positive influence on your wealth dream or your relationship dream. In another instance, your manager at work may be terrific at helping you learn, grow, and get promoted, which moves you toward your wealth dream. However, the same individual may not be helping you with your health dream if they are encouraging or requiring you to eat or drink excessively. It's not necessarily easy, but you need to be honest with yourself when doing this part of the redesign process. For now, just identify the influencers and how they impact your dreams today.

To the right of each influencer listed on the Key Influencer Template are six boxes. In each box put the number representing the intensity or level of influence for that dream category and then put the type of influence. Use a "++" for very positive influence; "+" for mostly positive influence; a "0" for neutral influence or no influence; a "-" for some negative influence; and a "--" for very negative influence.

You now need to review and consider how much influence each individual or organization has on each of your dream categories. To make it simple, just rate the impact on a scale of one to five, where one is very low influence and five is very high influence (1 = very low; 2 = low; 3 = medium; 4 = high; 5 = very high). Fill in your rating in the columns on the left half of the template designated for each dream category. Be honest with yourself. Some areas or groups that we may intellectually want to have a high influence on us may not, and vice versa.

Using the example of your best friend, put his/her name in the first column. The next column reads: Relationships. Let's assume your friend helps you with other good relationships, including an ever-improving relationship with your spouse. In the relationships column, then, you would put a ++4. Your friend has a high influence on you in the relationships dream category and is a very positive influence. The 4 rating indicates that the friend has a high influence on you achieving your relationship dream and the "++" indicates the influence is very positive in moving you towards your goal. Next, let's say your friend is not very good about cleaning up after himself/herself when they come over to visit. The friend visits at least once a week so the intensity is high, or a 4, but this time the influence isn't positive. Let's call it slightly negative, so you rate the type of influence as a "-". In the column for environment, rank the friend a -4. Proceed to rank the other four columns for that friend. Then move through the entire list of influencers you have identified, rating them in each column. At this point don't worry about the ratings, just be honest.

Enough for today! I applaud you for taking the time and energy to reflect on your influencers during this powerful exercise. This tool will be discussed again as you begin to make some strategic choices in your life.

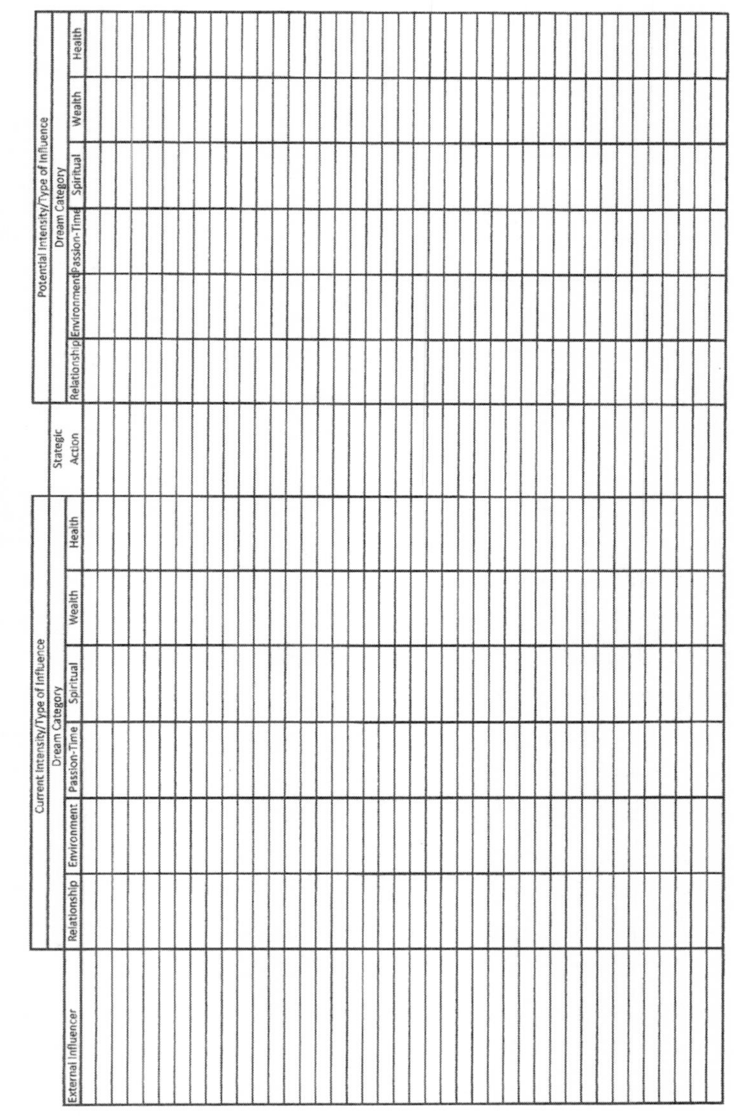

EXTERNAL INFLUENCE WORKSHEET

External Influencer	Current Intensity/Type of Influence Dream Category						Stategic Action	Potential Intensity/Type of Influence Dream Category					
	Relationship	Environment	Passion-Time	Spiritual	Wealth	Health		Relationship	Environment	Passion-Time	Spiritual	Wealth	Health

External Influencer Worksheet

Day Ten: Back to work on the Key Influencer Template. At this point you have identified the key external influencers in your life. You've also decided the intensity and the type of impact each of these key influencers has on each of your six dream categories: relationship, environment, spiritual, passion-time, wealth, and health.

Key Influencer Strategy Exercise

Before you proceed to develop the strategy you will deploy in the future, really consider the typical strategy you have been using in the past. By this I mean have you been coping with the external influence, reacting to the external influence, adapting to the external influence, or truly influencing the external influence? In pencil, so that you can later design your new strategy, put a C for coping, an R for reacting, an A for adapting, and an I for influencing, in the column on the worksheet entitled "Strategic Action."

Now, for each external influencer, consider the strategic actions you choose to take in the future. In some cases there will be no change. Where you are moving from a C, R, or A to a strategy to influence the influencer, create your own codes for proposed action. Some examples might be: EE (Eliminate Exposure); IE (Increase Exposure); ME (Minimize Exposure); CRE (Create Routine Exposure); or RFE (Reduce Frequency of Exposure). Feel free to create your own codes. Replace the past strategies in pencil with your new strategic actions.

Next, project what the action(s) will create in potential future rankings in regard to type and intensity, or amount of influence on each dream category. Your Key Influencer Template should now be complete.

Will the right-side columns of dream categories be all neutral and positive? That would be ideal, but is probably not realistic. What you should work for, especially the first time, is a dramatic shift to create more positive impact on your dream categories. Remember, it is like pushing a cart up a hill. When the hill is steep, you're pushing more force against the cart to move it up the hill. When the slope of the hill is much less, it's easier to push the cart to the top. Making a dramatic shift to create more positive force is like dramatically reducing the slope of the hill, or even getting to where the path of the cart is going down hill. As Han Solo said to Luke Skywalker in Star Wars,[11] "May the Force be with you!"

Day Eleven: Time to start setting chief aims and goals for each of the dream categories.

Chief Aim Exercise

Develop your one-to-three year chief aim for each of the dream categories. First, develop an A-SMART goal for each dream category. Remember: A-SMART goals are aligned, specific, measurable, achievable, relevant, and timely. Next, begin taking action toward each of these goals. Don't delay! You want to take an action toward an intention (a goal) within forty-eight hours of setting the intention. Have you ever noticed how some people get stuck or, as they say, suffer paralysis by analysis? Take immediate action toward these new goals! Do the goals have to be competed in the forty-eight hour time period? No, but you really should complete a next step. Remember those? We discussed them in Chapter Nine. Use the Weekly Priority Planning Template provided in the Appendix to schedule one action step for each A-SMART goal. Work hard to take an action, even if it's small for each area in the first two days, then work on completing one action for each of the categories over the next seven days.

Day Twelve: Today is the time you begin to review the mechanisms you use in your life. Before you start this work, you may want to go back and review Chapter Ten.

Dream Mechanism Identification

Some of your current mechanisms are probably working well for you. Some of them may not be. In order to identify the dream mechanisms you currently employ, you need to think about how you spend your time. In the future you should consider how you *invest* your time toward your goals. Time is a precious commodity. What activities or processes do you deploy for each dream category? Make a list of all the things you do to achieve your goals. Check your old calendars and list all the activities on the calendar. What's not on your calendar? How are your evenings and weekends invested? Don't worry about categorizing each mechanism right now. The purpose of this exercise is to get a list of all of your mechanisms—a list of all the things you do and how you spend or invest your hours every day.

Day Thirteen: Review your list from yesterday. Add to it, if needed, and categorize those items. Now begin to look at your personal organization.

Personal Clutter Identification

Identify areas of clutter in your time, your environment, and your thoughts. Look at the past four weeks in your calendar. See any clutter of your time? Walk around your home and your workplace and look for areas of clutter. Open every closet and assess it. Document them all (i.e. make a list of the areas of clutter). Today, eliminate one of these clutter areas. Don't make it a huge project, but make it large enough that you will feel the improved energy flow from the clutter-free space. It could even be just cleaning and organizing a drawer or shelf.

Day Fourteen: Finalize your personal guiding principles and update them in your dream book. Review and update your dream mechanisms list again.

Decision Making Efficiency

Now, review Dr. Applegate's eight psychological needs[12] areas for yourself. Review questions 47-54 of the "What Needs Changing Questionaire." How do you go about meeting each need? List the top three ways you go about meeting each of the needs areas. Identify your efficient and inefficient decision/response techniques. Included is Dr. Applegate's Psychological Needs Chart[13] again for your reference.

Survey your family, friends, and associates about how they perceive you getting your needs met. Are they efficient techniques or inefficient? Do any of your inefficient techniques cause your character to reduce your effectiveness to achieve your dreams? These are tough questions, but need to be considered as you redesign forward.

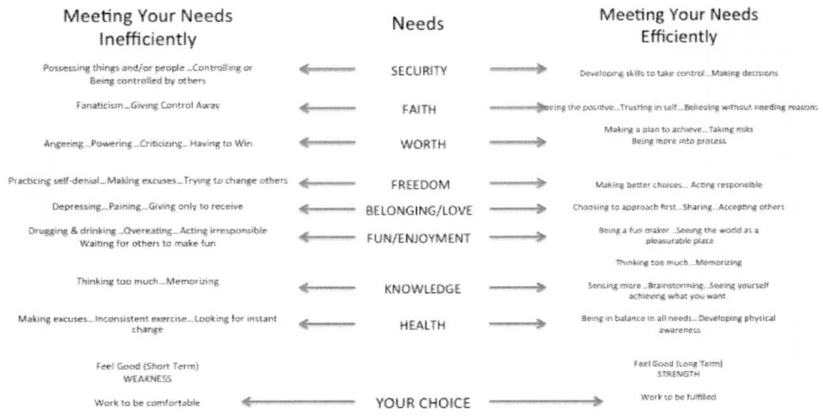

Psychological Needs Chart

Personal Knowledge Capital Matrix

Now, create a current Personal Knowledge Capital Matrix regarding your "know-how" and "know-that" information for each dream category. You will create a two by two matrix. The horizontal axis forms columns of "know-how" and "know-that." The vertical axis forms rows of "encoded" and "non-encoded." Encoded may not be the most precise term. Encoded knowledge is stored in our memories, notes, books, or audio recordings, which we have ready access to as needed to make decisions. Non-encoded knowledge is know-how or know-that that was once readily available to us, but has been lost, misplaced, or is otherwise no longer with us.

You will create six knowledge capital matrixes: one for each dream category.

Capture the implications of the know-how and know-that that you have and don't have. Some of the knowledge you never had. Some of the knowledge is "knew-how" or "knew-that," but you can't retrieve the knowledge now. There's a hidden implication in why it was not retained or retrievable. Find those hidden implications.

Day Fifteen: Finalize your dream category statements and update them in your dream book.

Inner Circle Role Definition

Consider your current inner circle. You probably have one, but was it created consciously or unconsciously? Take time to define the inner circle roles that you will need to be successful in the future.

- What roles do you need help with to achieve your relationship dreams?
- What roles do you need help with to achieve your environment dreams? Do you need a home organization consultant to get you off to a good start? Do you need to hire a housekeeper to create the weekly routines that don't allow clutter to build?
- What roles do you need to achieve your spiritual dreams? Are there leaders of your faith that you need to have a closer relationship with?
- What roles do you need to achieve your passion-time aims and goals? Is there an instructor that you need to regularly learn from? Is your frequency of instruction adequate today?
- What roles do you need to achieve your wealth objectives? As I reflected, I had an accountant, but not a good tax advisor, so I needed to add one. I also lost two of my inner circle members that I regularly bounced professional ideas off of. After their deaths, I failed to replace them and drifted into thinking I didn't need that type of professional network. I also quit getting promoted. Do you have a professional network outside of your employer that you can benefit from?
- What roles do you need to achieve your health goals? I recently added a fitness coach. I had specific "must-haves" as criteria to select my coach. I was delighted with the outcomes. Do you have a health coach to help you consider alternatives and help you develop and stay on your plan to achieve your goals?

Do you have individuals filling these roles now, or will you need to begin the relationship process to fill these voids?

How I Influence People Questionnaire

Turn all the questions on page 142-143 from "do you" and "are you" into "do I" and "am I" questions, and create an anonymous 360-degree survey of your closest associates: your spouse or significant other, your children, your siblings, your parents, your manager, your employees, your peers at work, your neighbors, and your best friend(s). There are several things you can do with the feedback you receive from the survey. You can identify areas where others answer the questions differently than you answer them. You might find some trends where a cluster of individuals answered the questions one way and others answered the questions another way. This self-analysis will provide you with insights. You can then choose to turn these insights into actions that can lead to new relationship practices and habits. Remember: "The only way to change our relationships is to change ourselves."

Recognition to Self and Others Reflection

Define how you currently provide recognition to yourself and others. Reflect on questions 57 and 58 of the "What Needs Changing Questionaire." Ask your friends how they see you recognizing them and others. Ask them about your self-talk that they hear. I had an associate at work that was terrific at finding ways to recognize people that he worked with and the people that worked for him. Even with all the strengths he had developed over the years, he never seemed to reinforce it with positive self-talk. Just the opposite. He could often be heard calling himself Dummy or worse. Let others help you assess this as an area of strength or weakness.

Six Essentials Assessment

Assess your current practices regarding the six essentials.[14] Review your responses to questions 60-66 of the "What Needs Changing Questionaire." Return to Chapter Fourteen to consider alternative strategies for each of the six essentials.

Gleicher Formula Consideration

Assess your personal cost to change, clarity of vision, planned first steps, and current reality dissatisfaction for each dream category. Consider questions 31-35 of the "What Needs Changing Questionaire." Rate each of the four components (personal cost to change, clarity of vision, planned first steps and current reality dissatisfaction) on a scale of 1-10. Multiply your personal cost to change rating by one hundred. Multiply clarity of vision, planned first steps, and current reality dissatisfaction rating. If your personal cost to change product is greater than the product of the other three areas when multiplied, consider the area or areas that need to increase to get the product of the three areas greater than the personal cost to change.

Let me give you an example. When I first retired, my weight had crept up to almost 200 pounds. I had never weighed 200 pounds and was extremely dissatisfied with being that close. I'd rate my level of dissatisfaction at a 9. I wanted to weigh 185 pounds, so my vision was very clear. I'd rate it a 10. The practical first steps were really aligned and understood. I needed to begin a simple exercise program of walking every day and alter my diet by reducing the processed foods and the amount of proteins, and eliminating my bowl of ice cream each night. I'd rate my planned first steps as an 8. How much did it cost me? I do enjoy ice cream, so that was a loss. I really enjoy the early walks, so making them more routine only cost me getting up a bit earlier. The new way cost a little bit more. So put them together, and I'd rate the cost somewhere above a small nuisance. Let's call it a small loss and rate it a 4.

So let's look at what I have:

Clarity of Vision:	10
Planned First Steps:	8
Level of Dissatisfaction:	9
Product of all three:	720
Personal Cost to Change:	4
Multiplied by 100:	400

Since 720 > 400, the Gleischer Formula predicts change will occur. It did. I got back to 185 pounds and have maintained that level within a few pounds for almost two years.

Try the Gleisher Formula Exercise for one of your goals. It will help you identify the area(s) that are stopping you, and from this you can consider new actions as you get into the redesign process.

Day Sixteen: With the exception of where you've engaged close friends and family, much of the reflection about yourself has been fairly intuitive. It is now time to begin your formal environmental scan.

The Environmental Scan Analysis

The environmental scan is an analysis looking at the impacts, forces, and requirements on the outside perspective.[15] As an individual, you are an open system—you exist in an environment that influences you.

The concept of open systems comes from biology. An organism is an open system. When its environment changes, it must adapt to survive. For example, as the weather gets colder, some aquatic organisms adapt by swimming deeper beneath the water. Some organisms put on more clothes; others may hibernate.

The same principle is true for each of us. Our environments are probably more complex than we really realize. We have many forces outside of us that are changing, and they are changing quite rapidly. For example, technology, globalization, the stock market, and the world economy. We have to recognize our dependency on our external environment. Beyond some of the macro factors mentioned above, we also have our micro-environment—our family, friends, employer, church, and other external influencers that you identified earlier. Most successful individuals do not just adapt to their environment, they influence it! They actually change what the environment requires of them in many cases.

Environmental scanning is done to identify which groups most affect you, what are the specific requirements of each group, and how the requirements might be changed. It gives you the data needed to formulate an effective strategy.

Step 1: *Identify the environmental forces.* You've probably already begun this task using the External Influencer Template. Now, if you haven't already, expand your thinking beyond your micro-environment to your macro-environment. One category you might not think about is role models. These are the individuals that have accomplished some of your chief aims and dreams. By gathering data on how they achieved their success, you may gather data and implications that affect various categories in the model. Additionally, don't forget that you have competitors. You will want to identify them as well.

Step 2: Hypothesize the environmental requirements. Up front, determine what you already believe you know about the requirements of the groups of your environment. Think not only about what they require today, but what they might require in the future. Additionally, imagine what would be ideal for them to require of you. For example, you and an associate might team up on a revenue generation project that might require you to share part of the benefits. However, their expertise would save you time and money getting the project started. The revenue can flow earlier and easier. Similarly, a project or task could be done among family members or friends, also saving time, energy, and money. My wife and two of her friends created a "Working Wednesday" routine for several months. Each Wednesday they would meet at one home to work on that person's project-of-the-day. Landscaping, mulching, pruning, weeding, painting, organizing, and lots of de-cluttering was accomplished by working together instead of just their individual efforts. They stayed on task, and much was accomplished through their group efforts while enjoying each other's friendship.

Step 3: Prepare for interviews. You will need to contact individuals and groups to interview them. To prepare for the interviews, take a few minutes to jot down the questions you want to ask the individual. Remember, you need information about their current and future requirements. You need to ask yourself two questions as you prepare: "What do I know about the influencers requirements that I just need to validate?" and "What don't I know about the requirements that I need to know to complete the design?"

Use the left side of the Environmental Scan Template on the next page to record your thoughts.

EXTERNAL SCAN TEMPLATE

External Influencer	Pre-Interview		Interview Questions	Interview Results	
	Requirements Hypothesis	Ideal Requirements		Current Requirement	Future Requirements

Environmental Scan Worksheet

Day Seventeen: Today you will continue with the environmental scan.

Step 4: Validate your hypothesis. Conduct and document the interviews, determining current and future requirements, and testing reactions to ideal requirements. It is really not enough to intuitively describe your environment. You must rigorously gather and analyze data in order to increase your knowledge about the external world.

Continue using the template from yesterday to document your perceptions of the requirements prior to the interview, your perceptions of ideal requirements, and interview questions for the external individual or group. To the far right, you can then document the requirements you discover in the interview process.

Step 5: Evaluate the accuracy of your hypothesis. Compare and contrast the actual interview data with your hypothesis. In this step you will learn how accurate your hypotheses were. With the data collected in Step 4, what differences were there in the hypotheses you made in Step 2? Record what you've learned. Over time you can track your ability to evaluate the environment. You may notice trends in your tendency to overlook or overestimate environmental factors.

Day Eighteen: Today you will again work on the completion of the environmental scan analysis.

Step 6: Determine design impact and implications. The conclusions you have reached about the requirements of your external environment will have an impact on your success and implications for your strategy and other design choices. Use the SLSD model to help you organize your thinking about design choices. This is the "wringing out" of the information you have discovered. Use the template with each of the elements down the left hand side, and record implications that might affect each of the design elements. This template is available on the website: powerofivingbydesign.com

Step 7: Document what you learn. The last step in the environmental scan is to document what you've learned. At the very least, create a list of your most important conclusions. This documentation is a way you can encode the knowledge for yourself. It can also help you for future environmental scans you may conduct.

Let me warn you that some of the implications may not be what you expected and may not be what you want. You may find that some of the requirements the external influencers have of you will take you away from your dream or are compliance or waste, as it relates to the mechanisms required to fulfill them. Some of the requirements may be too lopsided: everything in it for the other person and nothing for the achievement of your dreams. These can lead to very tough choices you may need to make.

Congratulations! You have just completed the environmental scan analysis.

Day Nineteen: So far, you have not spent much time looking inside yourself. What must you do to meet the requirements you have discovered that are expected from the outside environment?

Mechanism Analysis

The next step is your mechanism analysis. You will now soak up information about your mechanism needs and, again, "wring-out" the implications into the SLSD model buckets.

Why do you want to do a mechanism analysis? A mechanism analysis provides crucial information about your optimal design. It is in the mechanism analysis that you reengineer your processes, identifying what you do that helps you advance directly toward your contributing advantages, and what does not.

A mechanism analysis also looks at where there may be high variability in your work. Does that ring a bell with you? By reducing the variability and eliminating non-value added tasks, a mechanism analysis helps you eliminate the clutter in your environment, your time, and your thoughts.

A mechanism analysis determines who should be involved with your core work, not just what the core work mechanism should be.

This output will be a set of design recommendations. These recommendations will be combined with the recommendations from the environmental scan and, later, the social analysis recommendations.

Together, these should provide a personal advantage through a focus on what makes the difference for your success. Moreover, when you become organized in a way that taps your capacity for improvement, you can generate results that impact all dream categories.

Mechanisms in your life are value-creating activities—the activity or collection of activities that create (from one or more inputs) an output that is worthwhile to the fulfillment of your dreams, depending upon your mission. Why should you think in terms of life and success mechanisms? Speaking of different mechanisms is not the same as speaking about different roles you have in your life. When you think in terms of roles, you generally think in terms of only parts of your life. You also tend to become activity oriented, with much of the activities being compliance mechanisms such as doing what your family, friends, and co-workers want you to do. Being mechanism-oriented, on the other hand, focuses on the larger categories of your dreams and chief aims. As you take on more roles, your life becomes more fractionated. Organizing yourself around life mechanisms brings the fractionated activities back together and makes life more challenging and meaningful. The focus is turned to the needs that must be met to fulfill your dreams and chief aims.

Furthermore, recognizing the life mechanisms you have legitimizes (or not) the activities we have been doing for a long time, but that have never been adequately examined in terms of design. Sometimes we do things because its been done in the past instead of because it adds real value to achieving our dreams.

There's a story that has been told, time and time again, about a young couple just back from their honeymoon. The wife was making a ham for supper as the husband walked into the room and watched her cut off each end of the ham. When he asked why she was cutting off the ends, she replied, "I'm not sure, but it's the way my mother always made her hams." The next time she saw her mother, she asked her mother about cutting off the ends of the ham. Her mother replied that she wasn't exactly sure why, but that's the way her mother had always cooked a ham. They decided to call Grandma to find out why she started the habit. When they asked Grandma why she cut off the ends of the ham, she replied, "Because the ham wouldn't fit into my baking pan!"

Often times we pick up habits and mechanisms without knowing why. The mechanism analysis causes you to examine the whys and determine not only if they still create value, but how they add value: contributing, contributor-enabling or life essential. These were all discussed in Chapter Ten.

Now, to help bring all this into focus, what are some of the mechanisms in your life? How about developing the strategies to achieve your dreams? When you were dreaming as a child, some people teased you about "having your head in the clouds." I guarantee you that none of the top wealth generators in the United States generated so much wealth by chance. They strategized how to create the wealth. The same is true for the majority of people who truly *own* their own home (no mortgage). They figured out ways to make extra payments, or which other assets could be liquidated to pay off the mortgage, or they saved all the money up front to purchase the home. Those are strategies and they are contributing work. This is an action step potentially resulting from a design choice…not just living by default. Do you think you would pay off your mortgage without creating a plan to do it? This action becomes a life mechanism.

Another contributing work is developing your personal knowledge capital. As Paul informed us earlier, knowledge is the most fundamental competitive advantage.[16] It's true for business and it's true for your personal success. The accumulation of know-how and know-that, encoded for your use, contribute to your dreams as a contributing mechanism.

A contributing-enabling example is a personal development activity that improves your mind, body, or spirit in such a way that you are better able to use contributors to fulfill your dreams.

To help clarify this, let's begin by looking at where you currently are in three of your dream categories, and then work backwards. Which of your routine activities positively contribute or move you in your desired direction? For example, for my wealth dream (notice my dream is stated such that to move toward it, I must generate new revenue sources), I receive a small stipend for teaching, which contributes toward revenue above my current core income. Royalties from this book, future books, workbooks, and seminars will create additional income. Each of these sources of income is aligned with my mission of helping others achieve their fullest potential. They will create additional revenue, so all of the activities associated with teaching the class and writing, publishing, and marketing the book are contributors. You will need to work backwards from each of the three dreams and associated chief aims you've selected by looking at the clusters of activities you are doing to move toward them. My guess is that once these are listed, you will notice there are many other things you do each day. You'll need to list these as well, and then determine if these activities enable the contributing activities to be effective, if they are life essential, or if they are waste. For example, each morning my wife and I need to eat breakfast. This is a life essential activity. If I fix and eat a healthy, balanced breakfast salad, this moves me toward my health dream, and it becomes a contributing activity. Fixing a breakfast of bacon, eggs, and waffles versus the healthy, balanced breakfast salad is an inefficient life essential activity. I need to eat (life essential), but the bacon and waffles are not moving me toward my health dream (therefore, it is inefficient). Additionally, watching television is usually a waste activity for me. Seldom does it contribute to any of my dream categories.

From the dream mechanism exercise on Day 12, now add to your list of mechanisms. After you think through the many other things you do each day, begin to designate all of the mechanisms as contributing, contributor-enabling, life essential, compliance, or waste. As demonstrated above, you will need to determine if the activities are efficient or inefficient. Ironing clothes while watching television is inefficient. Ironing clothes listening to success CDs that give you inspiration and ideas is efficient because you accomplish a life essential task on top of another task that moves you toward your next goal or chief aim. Meeting friends for a healthy, aligned meal is efficient, too, because you are achieving both relationship building and health building tasks at once. Meeting the guys at the bar and getting intoxicated is inefficient (it's probably waste, too) because even though it may move you toward your relationship dream, it moves you away from your health goals. I suggest you look back at your many activities over a period of at least a week or two. You'll soon get the hang of the designations and the efficient/inefficient differences.

As you go through this exercise, you'll most likely notice some things you need to do, or maybe you used to do, that are contributing or contributor-enabler activities. Document those, too, and designate them. You may also think of things you need to do. Don't lose those thoughts—document them!

At the end of this exercise, you will have a long list of your activities and the groups of activities you have designated as contributing, contributor-enabling, life essential, compliance, or waste. Further, you will have determined if each of these activities is efficient or inefficient. Remember, an inefficient activity is any activity that moves you away from *any* dream category fulfillment, even if it moves you closer to *one* of your dream categories. Spending too much time playing golf with friends is inefficient. Yes, it moves me towards my passion-time dream (and maybe beyond), but it takes me away from spending time with my wife each day and therefore is inefficient. My last job contributed terrifically toward my wealth dream, but my health dream category suffered, so it was inefficient.

Once you have compiled all of this information, as in the environmental scan, you need to determine the implications for your life design. Do you need to play less golf? Do you have enough activities to achieve all three of your chief aims, not just one?

Expand the chart of implications from the environmental scan. Create columns for the implications from each analysis for each element of the SLSD model. Document the implications discovered for the three dream categories analyzed relative to the elements of the SLSD Model.

Day Twenty: Continue from the previous day by completing the above exercise for the remaining three dream categories. Document the implications discovered for these three dream categories analyzed, relative to the elements of the SLSD Model.

Day Twenty-One: Review your calendar (all activities) over the past month. Assure all activities (and mechanisms) are accounted for in the previous two-day exercise. Document the implications discovered for these additional activities.

Daily/Weekly Menu Review

Review the activities in Ed Foreman's Prescriptions No. 1 and 2.[17,18] Each of the activities are relisted below:

Prescription No. 1 activities include:

- Getting up early.
- Reading something inspirational for 10 to 20 minutes immediately after waking.
- Go outside for a walk and appreciate the beauty of nature.
- Stretch and exercise for 30 minutes or more.
- Shower and dress professionally.
- Eat a nourishing breakfast ("Breakfast like a king").
- Leave for work with plenty of time.
- Listen to inspiring CDs as you drive to work.
- Mid-morning, check to see if you're really working on the important things.
- Take a refresher break—walk around and stretch.
- Just before lunch, practice mind-controlled relaxation to reenergize yourself.
- Eat a reasonable lunch ("Lunch like a prince").
- Mid-afternoon, recheck to assure you're still focused on accomplishing the important things.
- At the end of the day, reflect on your accomplishments and congratulate yourself.
- Listen to inspiring CDs on the way home.
- Eat a light dinner ("Dinner like a pauper")
- Enjoy a moderate walk before retiring for the evening.
- Read something inspiring before you go to sleep.
- Sleep 7 – 9 hours.

Prescription No. 2 activities are weekly and include:

- Find a location to be completely alone.
- Take your time and review the events of the week in a fair amount of detail.
- Dwell on what you did right and what you accomplished.
- Think only briefly about what you did wrong, and only in terms of it being a learning situation.
- Think back over the accomplishments of the past weeks and months, thinking about the things that have helped you accomplish your success.
- Think about how these things can help you improve in the future.
- Think about how you can apply these things in the next week.

Now rate yourself on each of the Prescription No. 1 activities (A = Excellent; F = Don't do at all).

What are the implications to you of not doing some of these daily or weekly-recommended activities? Document these implications on each of the SLSD Model elements.

Day Twenty-Two: Create your own personal priority planner. Use the basic template I provided for you in Chapter Sixteen. The lower section of the "Daily Dozen" needs to be *your* "Daily Dozen," not mine. A completely blank planner document is provided in the Appendix and online: poweroflivingbydesign.com. Now begin by identifying twelve activities in Ed Foreman's Prescription No. 1[19] (or other daily routines that support the accomplishment of your dreams and chief aims) that you will commit to doing every day for the next week. Write them in the "Daily Dozen" section of the planner. Remember: it's your personal planner, not mine!

Next, in the top section of the priority planning section, plan two activities per dream category from your A-SMART goals to accomplish over the next seven days. That will make twelve activities that move you towards your A-SMART goals over the next week. You can do that! It's either one or two per day at this point. Over time, you can expand on how many dream categories you plan to work on each day. I try to do something in each category most days. I do make exceptions, like travel days. But even if the activity is small, I want to make progress each day in each area.

Interaction Needs Assessment

Next, you will conduct your interaction needs assessment. This is the first assessment of the social analysis.

Consider all types of your interactions and with whom you have these interactions. Create a diagram by jotting your interactions down on a clean piece of paper with *you* in the center and *the types of interactions you have* around you in a circle. Identify the direction of the interaction by drawing an arrow from the initiator of the interaction to the receiver of the interaction. Often you'll need arrows in both directions because sometimes you initiate the interaction and sometimes you don't. Identify the frequency of the interaction. (1 = too little; 2 = just right; 3 = too much). Remember, this frequency rating relates to supporting your dream categories. An abbreviated example is shown later.

You may feel discussions and interactions with your next-door neighbor are just right, but if your neighbor is an expert in a field that could help support one of your dream categories, then maybe it's too little. Now identify the content of the interaction—chit chat, weather, current events, value-adding topics, professional areas, etc. Write it on the line of the arrow. Next, identify the effectiveness of the interaction with an H for high satisfaction, M for medium, and L for low. Finally create a list of suggestions for improvement. You may need to divide yourself into different roles and do one interaction assessment per role. Examples of your role might be parent, co-worker, etc. An example is shown below.

What are the implications of your interactions and your thoughts on recommended actions? Do you have the right interactions with all of the roles you identified in the inner circle role definition exercise? Document these implications on each of the SLSD Model elements.

Day Twenty-Three: Complete the next of the four social analysis tools—the personal needs assessment.[19]

Personal Needs Assessment

The personal needs assessment is designed to determine the extent to which your personal needs are being met. You bring a lot of energy to your life. If your individual needs are being met, you will most likely channel your energy in a positive direction. However, if your needs are not being met, you tend to devote energy counterproductively.

Interaction Needs Assessment

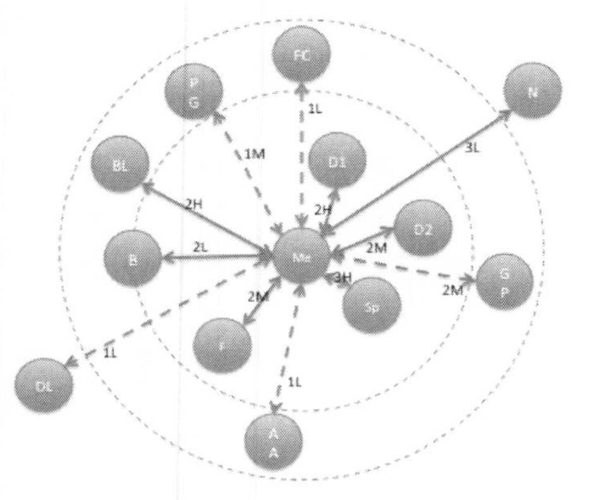

SUGGESTIONS FOR SELF IMPROVEMENT

1. Create quarterly reviews with Financial Consultant
2. Set up meeting with PG to discuss how to better network and be mentored.
3. Create bi-weekly call with Author's Agent (AA) to set goals and create timeline for publishing plan
4. Create bi-monthly lessons with Golf Pro (GP) and use statistics to determine areas to work on.
5. Create monthly network call with DL to mentor each other.

Interaction Needs Assessment

First, write down your answers to the following question:

I am most energized in what I do when:

1. ______________________________
2. ______________________________
3. ______________________________
4. ______________________________
5. ______________________________

Now think of any roles in your life that you have enjoyed in the past. Record your answer to the following question:

I am most energized in this role when:

Role 1: ______________________________

Role 2: ______________________________

Role 3: ______________________________

Role 4: ____

For example: As a dad, I am most energized when my daughters demonstrate new personal growth from a lesson or concept I taught them.

Look for individual needs that you have. Determine the satisfaction (H = High; M = Medium; L = Low) for each need that you have in the mechanisms in your life. Think of design choices where you have low need satisfaction, and consider choices that might improve the ratings in the future. Consider and document these implications for each element of the SLSD model.

Day Twenty-Four: The third of the four social analysis tools is the vision assessment.[20]

Vision Assessment

A vision assessment determines the extent to which you display the habits, emotions, and attributes required to move yourself to your desired outcomes.

Rate the following statements 1 – 5 or NA. (1 = to a very small extent; 2 = to a small extent; 3 = to a moderate extent; 4 = to a great extent; 5 = to a very great extent and NA = Not Applicable)

1. I understand my mission and vision.
2. I understand what is important to deliver the outcomes of my goals.
3. I communicate in an open and honest fashion.
4. I work toward specific and measurable goals.
5. I understand how my goals are aligned to my dream categories and my chief aims.
6. I am organized in a manner that eliminates time clutter.
7. I work to improve myself continuously.
8. I work to eliminate waste mechanisms in my life.
9. My environment is free of clutter.
10. I get the support I need to achieve my goals.
11. Information I need is available when I need it.
12. I make decisions that are efficient for

all my psychological needs.

13. I have a personal development system that improves my six essentials for life.
14. I look for and receive feedback on how I'm performing.
15. I recognize myself when I accomplish my goals.
16. I recognize others for the support they provide to me.
17. I learn from all my successes and mistakes.

Look at the areas you rated 3 or below and the areas that you ranked a 4 or 5. What are the implications for the SLSD model elements for these responses? Document these implications like you have in previous assessments.

Day Twenty-Five: The last of the four social analysis tools is the skills analysis.[21]

Skills Analysis

A skills analysis identifies what skills are needed for each contributing mechanism and contributor-enabling mechanism, and then identifies the level of expertise needed for that skill. A Skills Matrix is a useful tool development and selection initiative.

Begin by listing all the contributing mechanisms on a sheet of paper. Beside each mechanism, determine the skills and what level of skill is needed. Consider using a scale of A = Apprentice; J = Journeyman; and M = Master craftsman as a way to rate the relative skill needs. Next to each skill needed for each mechanism, rate in one column the skill needed. In the next column, rate your current skill level.

For example, I am considering the creation of DVDs to explain and coach people through the SLSD model. Presentation skills and grammar skills will be required for this mechanism, each at a Master craftsman level. My grammar and speech is currently at that level, but my presentation skills to a camera is at a Journeyman level (at best). I should entertain training in front of a camera, and enlist an inner circle member that can coach me as I get started in the production of the DVDs.

The last step in the social analysis, as in the environmental scan, the mechanism analysis, and the other assessments in the social analysis, is to determine the impact of what has been discovered on our dream success rate. We need to once again, "wring out" the mop into the SLSD model categories. Add these implications. By now, the sheet should have all the design elements going down the left hand side and a column of implications organized by element for each of the three social analysis exercises: the environmental scan, the mechanism analysis, and the social analysis.

Day Twenty-Six: Now it is time for Joint Optimization and Alignment.[22]

Joint Optimization and Alignment

At each stage of analysis, you have considered the implications for design using the elements of the SLSD Model to keep the implications organized.

Here is where the real redesign work (and fun) begins. Let me repeat: here is where you begin the real redesign work. So far, you've been gathering data and analyzing. Now it's time to quit analyzing and begin making design choices for your self.

To start, review all of the data and implications you have gathered and then free your self by asking yourself:

- What if I were to wipe the slate clean?
- What if I were to rub out all of my existing mechanisms?
- What if I were to start over?
- What if I could do any mechanism any way I wanted to?
- What if I started with a completely blank sheet of paper?

You've possibly created some new insights and potential implications by starting fresh and clean. Some of these ideas may not be at all feasible. Sometimes, however, you'll uncover an idea or thought that, with a little manipulation, can make a huge impact. Document these implications.

Designing yourself so that you meet all the needs of your environment, your mechanism system, and your social system is called *Joint Optimization*.

You must also consider the alignment of your choices. Think of the boxes in the SLSD Model as a set of compasses. When all the needles are aligned, you will drive the habits, emotions, and attributes essential to achieving your desired outcomes of success. It can be a powerful and exciting visual when you see before you everything perfectly aligned.

Day Twenty-Seven: Create an Implications Matrix Board (or wall). Use Post-It notes to document each implication for each element of the SLSD Model. Arrange the notes with the element areas of the SLSD Model going vertically, and a column for each analysis or assessment. An example of the layout of the Implications Matrix Board is provided in the Appendix or on the poweroflivingbydesign.com website. Your columns and rows may vary in height and width based on the number of implications you wring out of each analysis, but this layout will allow you to look across all of the elements and across all of the analyses to search for priorities and conflicts. The purpose of doing this today is to post all of your implications on a wall or everything on a large brown paper. (Brown paper is created by taping lengths of butcher paper together.) Next, draw the implications matrix board on the brown paper and either tape it to the wall or place it across a large table. You can then use the Post-It notes to post each implication you have found in the appropriate box.

Post every implication that you have uncovered in the appropriate box of the implications board. For instance, if during the environmental scan you learned that one of your key influencers had requirements that added clutter to your environment, post the implication "My office is being cluttered by Influencer A's expectation," in the personal organization folder. This may sound like a silly example, but I've had clutter of others stored in my office before. It was called my wife's stuff! I seldom used the home office for a couple of years. In our new home, we built two offices, so that problem has been eliminated.

Day Twenty-Eight: Today is probably an all-day assignment. Begin by reviewing all the implications first. Read the implications for each element of the SLSD Model across all of the analyses and assessments. Are they aligned? Do they compliment each other or conflict with one another? Eliminate the conflicts.

Now review the implications by analysis across all elements of the SLSD Model. Ask yourself the same questions and resolve any conflicts.

Personal Action and Influencer Plan

Now begins your action planning. You will now create your three-month action plan and your three-month influencer plan. Once you finalize your design recommendations, it is time for you to engage in transition planning. How will you move from your old self to your new self? What actions must you take to develop the new design choices for your future? Careful transition planning is also crucial because in the middle of your transition, you are likely to long for "the way you used to do it," even though you didn't like the old way. In transition planning you ask, "How will I manage this sentiment?"

There are two types of transition plans you will find useful.

- *Action plan*: To identify the transition activities and then to sequence and time the implementation of the design choices.[23]
- *Influencer commitment plan*: To determine who needs to be committed to the design, where are those people now, and where they need to be for the design to be successful.[24]

There are several techniques to develop your action plan. One of the more sophisticated methods is called a Gantt Chart, which you could research further, if you so choose. It is an excellent tool to use to create your action plan.

A simpler technique is to create a chart with action steps down the left hand side and three headings across the top: sequence, time allotted, estimated completion date. After you get all of your action steps listed, you can then go through and sequence the steps. By knowing the time you allotted for the action step and the sequence, you can then assign an estimated completion date to each task.

How do you decide on a sequence? Some the contingencies will be very obvious to you, some won't. One method of figuring out which item to do first is to rate each action item twice. First go through and rate the impact each step will have. (A = Big Impact; B = Medium Impact; C = Small Impact). Next, go back through and rate the difficulty of each action step to be completed. (1 = Easy; 2 = Medium; 3 = Difficult). Now survey the combined rating of each independent or cluster of action steps. Start with the A-1s. They are big impact and easy to complete. You get a big bang for your initial effort. Create momentum in your personal redesign implementation!

The second plan is your Influencer Commitment plan.[25] This plan helps you track who needs to be committed to your design, where the commitment of the individual is now, and where it needs to be for your future success to occur. These influencers could be in business, family members, community leaders, etc. On the next page is a chart graphically showing an example of the migration needed in a commitment plan. There are four steps to the Individual Commitment plan:

1. Decide which influencers need to be committed to your plan.
2. Determine their current level of commitment and the commitment levels required.
3. Develop a plan for moving the commitment of the individual (you might record this plan as part of the Action Plan).
4. Create a monitoring system to assess progress.

In the example Harry, Sally, and George all need to move to different support or commitment levels. The actions to move Harry and Sally will probably not be as difficult due to the distance they need to move. Consider George. You would need to move George from "Against the Change" to "Helping it Happen," so your plans should include actions to assure success since you have identified the need for the support of George to help make your design change happen.

Commitment is likely to be strengthened when people:

- Fully understand the reasons for the new design and its desired outcomes
- Understand that the design choices were arrived at by careful analysis
- Understand what the likely disruption of implementation will be
- Are familiar with the implementation time-table
- Know what training will be provided before and after implementation

- Have any and all questions answered

Influencer	Against Change	Unknown	Let Change Happen	Help Change Happen	Make Change Happen	Comments
Harry	✖ →	→	→ ▲			
Sally		✖ →	→ ▲			
George	✖ →	→	→	→ ▲		

Commitment Chart

Up to this point, you have analyzed the needs for a new personal design and your relationship with your environment. You have planned the migration from your old self to your new self-design. Use your newly created Priority Planning Tool to plan three actions for each dream category for the next week. Assure that there is at least one action step to impact each of the elements of the SLSD Model. Schedule a day for review of progress and renewal about three months out. Now, go implement your design choices!

Day Twenty-Nine: Celebrate and congratulate yourself! You've created your "power of living by design" plan. There has been a tremendous amount of thinking, reflecting, projecting, and dreaming over the past twenty-eight days in order to complete your design. In actuality, there's still a lot of work left to implement your three-month action plan, but today, celebrate and congratulate yourself on a job well done! Congratulations!

Three Months Later: You will want to evaluate the effectiveness of the new design and continue learning with your new renewal system. The more you can learn about the most effective ways of adapting to and influencing your environment, the more successful you will be.

Continue to exercise your new renewal system, whether you use the Corkscrew Method,[26] the PDCA Cycle,[27] or the 7-Step Process.[28]

In this phase you will want to ask, "To what extent did my new design converge on my chief aim? What will I do differently in the future?"

Some key questions you will want to ask after implementation are:

- Did the design do what it was intended to do?
- What design choices might I now change?
- Did I get rid of the non value-added tasks?
- Did I satisfy my individual needs?
- Are the right people supporting me?
- Did I create the right habits, emotions, and attributes?
- Is there anything else I should do differently in the future?
- What were the most important things learned through the process?

Stay energized and aligned with your vision. You've created your new design and are well on your way to your Successful Life! You are the master of your fate. You are the captain of your soul. You have designed your successful life. You are living by design!

Recommended References

There are several books that have been outstanding in helping me think and develop my thoughts and later my habits. Many of the books have been referenced in the text of this book, but below is a more complete reference of some great books you may want to read. I hope they mean as much to you as they've meant to me.

- *Think and Grow Rich*
  Napoleon Hill
- *The Magic of Thinking Big*
  David J. Schwartz
- *How to Win Friends and Influence People*
  Dale Carnegie
- *The Power of Positive Thinking*
  Norman Vincent Peale
- *The How of Happiness*
  Sonja Lyubomirsky
- *A Whole New Mind*
  Daniel Pink
- *Drive*
  Daniel Pink
- *True North*
  Bill George
- *Wooden*

John Wooden

- *The Magic of Believing*
  Claude M. Bristol
- *The Happiness Project*
  Gretchen Rubin
- *The Why of Work*
  Dave Ulrich and Wendy Ulrich
- *The Power of Full Engagement*
  Jim Loehr and Tony Schwartz
- *Running Into the Wind: Bronco Mendenhall, Five Strategies for Building a Successful Team*
  Paul Gustavson & Alyson Von Feldt
- *The 7 Habits of Highly Effective People*
  Stephen Covey
- *I Will*
  Ben Sweetland
- *See You At the Top*
  Zig Ziglar
- *The Law of Success in Sixteen Lessons*
  Napoleon Hill
- *The 22 (Non-Negotiable) Laws of Wellness*
  Greg Anderson
- The Power of Habit: Why We Do What We Do In Life and Business
  Charles Duhigg
- *Outwitting the Devil*
  Napoleon Hill
- *The Energy Bus*
- Jon Gordon
- *The Seed*
  Jon Gordon
- *The Leadership Challenge*
  James Kouzes and Barry Posner
- *The New Psycho-Cybernetics*
  Maxwell Maltz

- *Clear Your Clutter with Feng Shui*
  Karen Kingston
- *Dynamic Health*
  Dr. M. Ted Morter Jr.

There have also been numerous audio series that I have listened to and have added to my thoughts and beliefs. Below are just a few.

- *Laughing, Loving and Living Your Way to the Goood Life*
  Ed Foreman
- *See You At the Top*
  Zig Ziglar
- *Living Your B.E.S.T.*
  Dr. M. Ted Morter III
- *The Psychology of Winning*
  Denis E. Waitley
- *Your Wish Is Your Command*
  Kevin Trudeau
- *Think and Grow Rich*
  Napoleon Hill
- *The Law of Success*
  Napoleon Hill
- *How to Have a Terrific Day Every Day*
  Ed Foreman

Special Thanks

THERE ARE SEVERAL PEOPLE THAT have been of special help and support for the development of this book. I am sincerely indebted to each of them and want to provide special recognition and sincere, special thanks to each of them.

Dr. M. T. Morter Jr. has graciously allowed me to share the "Six Essentials for Life" and B.E.S.T. Dr. Morter dedicated over forty years of his life in the development of this knowledge and technique. I've had the pleasure of enjoying several of his seminars, which stimulated my thoughts and brought new awareness to me about health and wellness. To be allowed to share some of his knowledge in this book is a tremendous honor. Thank you!

I'd also like to thank Bill Brandt for permission to share the 7 Step Process in this book. Bill developed the process at a company where I worked. I've found it enormously helpful to understand the concept of tension. I've learned new goals are needed to replace achieved goals in effort to avoid complacency; complacency can stop you from achieving of your dreams. Thank you, Bill!

Several individuals have helped to edit the book. Thank you Ann Atkins and Josie Kirkham for your willingness to endure an engineer's approach to writing and for finding the multiple "thats" throughout the text. They really weren't needed, were they? Thank you! Ann read and edited the very first draft and asked a key question that, with Paul's input as well, led to the segregation of the information in Part I and Part II. Thank you, Ann, for your open, honest question.

I'd also like to thank my editor, Erinne Sevigny, and author account manager, Erin McCullough, at FreisenPress, Erinne took my "engineer's" style of writing and dramatically improved the readability of the book by eliminating countless distractions. Through her efforts, readers now are more able to focus on the content. This was always the real intent of the book. Erin has been a tremendous guide through this process displaying patience and support as I would ask my "consciously incompetent" questions. Thank you both so much!!

Another person that put an enormous effort into improving the flow of the book for the reader was my beautiful wife, Emily. Poor dear, she probably read through the text at least a half a dozen times and made a huge difference in the readability of the book. My daughters, Erin and Meg, also helped identify better ways of expressing the ideas I wanted to share. Emily has been a tremendous partner in my life and now has been equally supportive in making this book better for me and for you, the reader.

As we developed the book, friends and family provided input on the title and book cover design that led us in new directions. Thank you Dad, Mary Etta, Matt, Tom P., Susan, Mike, Ann, Ian, Tom D., Carrie, Tammy, Nellaine, Steve, Tim L., Karen, Zach, Rewa, Jim, Jeff, Ann-Marie, Nancy, Adam, Sheila, Chris, Debi, Ted, Tim S., Ben, Len, and Thom.

Finally, I want to thank Paul Gustavson and Ed Foreman. Each was unbelievably generous in openly sharing the knowledge and lessons they taught me and continue to teach others. When I first got the idea to write this book, I knew the only way it could become a reality was for Paul and Ed to grant their permission for me to share and leverage their knowledge. To each, I sent an email describing the ideas for the book and requested permission to use their ideas and lessons. Within three hours, each responded to my request with open, overwhelming support and generosity. Throughout the process, each has provided encouragement and support and has been my role model on how to serve and support the dreams and success of others. You've become more than just my mentors, each of you is a hero to me!

Appendix

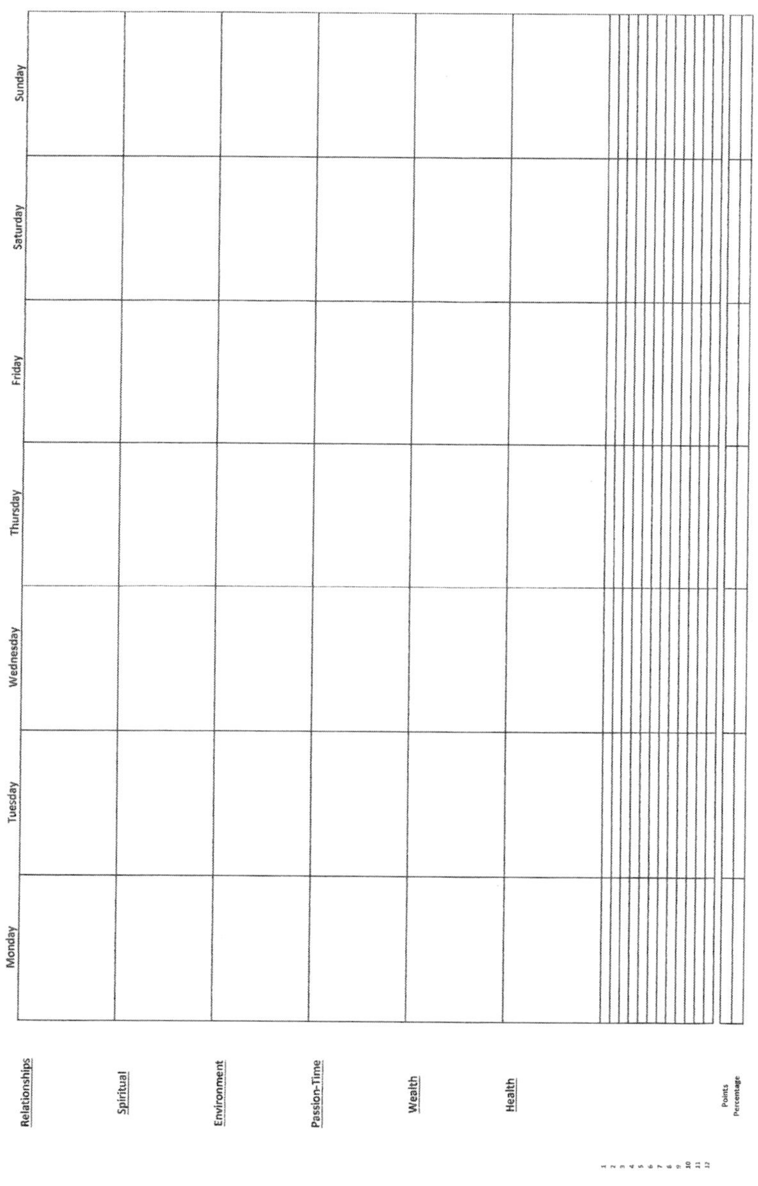

Priority Planner Template

IMPLICATIONS MATRIX BOARD

	Environmental Scan	Mechanisms Analysis	Prescription No 1 and No 2	Interaction Needs Analysis	Personal Needs Analysis	Vision Assessment	Skills Assessment	Alignment Across Analyses?
Personal Mission								
Personal Guiding Principles								
Principles/Style								
Strategies to Influence Ext. Infl.								
Goals and Chief Aims								
Dream Mechanisms								
Personal Organization								
Decision Making/Informating								
Relationship Process								
Recognition Process								
Renewal Process								
Alignment Across Elements?								

Implications Matrix Board

EXTERNAL SCAN TEMPLATE

External Influencer	Pre-Interview		Interview Questions	Interview Results	
	Requirements Hypothesis	Ideal Requirements		Current Requirement	Future Requirements

External Scan Template

About

Tom Ward

Tom Ward is a successful business executive with thirty-five years of experience in manufacturing and operations. Tom was born and raised in Tennessee. A graduate of the University of Tennessee (BSME) and Washington University, St. Louis (MBA), Tom had the great fortune of beginning his career with Procter & Gamble in the "new design" plant located in Jackson, Tennessee. On his very first assignment out of college, Tom learned that people have incredible capabilities within themselves. Those capabilities just have to be unleashed.

Tom's career led him to contribute to several of America's great companies including executive positions with Frito-Lay, Reckitt Benckiser, Campbell's Soup Company, Mead Johnson, American Woodmark, and Newell Rubbermaid. Through his career, Tom led operations and supply chain teams through successful transformations learning to create desired outcomes and winning cultures.

After 35 years of making a difference in the corporate world, in 2011 Tom began focusing on how to lead individuals through successful life transformations.

Tom lives in Loudon, Tennessee with his wife, Emily. He has two daughters, Erin and Meg, who are both elementary education teachers, and a son-in-love, Matt, who serves in the U.S. Navy.

For more information on how Tom can assist your Power of Living By Design plan, and for free downloads of the templates used in the book, go to:

www.powerofflivingbydesign.com

About
Paul Gustavson

Paul Gustavson is a leading organizational design architect specializing in strategy, the design of high performance work systems, change management, and knowledge management. For more than three decades, Paul has made an in-depth study of the strategies and design of high-performance teams and organizations.

A graduate of Brigham Young University (and former football player for BYU), Paul recently co-authored the book, Running Into the Wind: Bronco Mendenhall, 5 Strategies for Building a Successful Team, which documents the transformation of the BYU Cougars under their new head coach.

Since 1992, Paul has served as a Marriott School of Management's MOB Advisory Board Member and as its Chair for eight years. In April 1999, Paul received the prestigious BYU Marriott School of Management's William G. Dyer Alumni Award. He was also selected as a member of Work in America's National Advisory Council focusing on identifying best practices in creating and sustaining high performance work teams.

Since founding his own company, Organization Planning & Design, Inc., Paul's consulting work has included national and international projects with Fortune 500 companies as well as over fifty start-ups, greenfield sites, and joint ventures. Paul's work has been featured in more than fifty books, company magazines, and periodicals.

For more information about Paul, his company, and their services, he may be contacted at:

www.organizationdesign.com

About

Ed Foreman

ED FOREMAN, FROM A FARM boy to a self-made millionaire by the age of 26 and a former United States Congressman from two different states, Texas and New Mexico, lives his message of health, wealth, and happiness that is helping business leaders from around the world get more meaningful living out of their lives, reduce their levels of stress and anxiety, turn worry into success, and have more fun! A dynamic business entrepreneur and active civic leader, Ed has developed numerous programs and products and persuasively "sells" the success formula he lives by.

Ed was positively featured on CBS News' "Sixty Minutes." In addition to his internationally popular 3-day *Successful Life Course,* Ed tailors presentations using his client's terminology and themes to address specific areas of interest.

Ed holds the Council of Peers Award for Excellence (CPAE), the highest honor bestowed by the National Speakers Association, held by fewer than 100 people worldwide. He is also one of only eight people to receive the Distinguished Facility Award of the Institute for Management Studies. He received a standing ovation in 2008 as he was honored with a "Legends of the Speaking Profession" Lifetime Achievement Award.

Ed holds a civil engineering degree from New Mexico State University and was named one of the Ten Outstanding Young Men in America by the U.S. Jaycees in 1964. He is a board member, officer, and major stockholder of a dozen successful corporations, and is co-founder of Executive Development Systems of Dallas, Texas.

For more about Ed and his products and services, contact:

www.edforeman.com

Notes

AT THE TIME OF WRITING this manuscript, all Internet addresses were active and available. Unfortunately, I cannot guarantee their availability and content beyond this point.

Chapter 1 How do you define "Successful Life?"

[1]Newt Gingrich and Jackie Gingrich Cushman, 5 Principles for a Successful Life (New York: Random House Press, 2008), 12

[2]Yogi Berra, http://www.goodreads.com/quotes/
266663-you-ve-got-to-be-very-careful-if-you-don-t-know

[3]Bertand Russell, http://www.goodreads.com.autor.quotes/17854. Bertrand_Russell?page = 2

[4]http://www.putthewritingonthewall.com/store/WsDefault. asp?One = 205

[5]Paul Gustavson and Alyson Von Feldt, Running Into the Wind: Bronco Mendenhall: 5 strategies for building a successful team (ShadowMountain, 2012)

[6]*The Successful Life Course*, http://www.edforeman.com/live-events. successful-life-course/

[7]Ed Foreman, Laughing Loving & Living Your Way to the Goood Life Success Guide Handout, October 1985

Chapter 2 Connect with Your Dream

[1]Ed Foreman, Laughing Loving & Living Your Way to the Goood Life Success Guide Handout, October 1985

[2]Napoleon Hill, Think and Grow Rich (New York, Jeremy P. Tarcher/Penguin Group, 1937)

[3]Earl Nightingale, *The Strangest Secret*, www.vimeo.com/11731116

[4]Napoleon Hill, Think and Grow Rich, (New York, Jeremy P. Tarcher/Penguin Group, 1937)

[5]Adrian Lyne, Director, *Flashdance,* 1983

[6]Dr. M.T. Morter III, *Living Your B.E.S.T. Seminar,* March 2011

[7]Napoleon Hill, The Law of Success in Sixteen Lessons (BN Publishing, 2007), 55.

[8]Ed Foreman, *Laughing, Loving & Living Your Way to the Goood Life* (Executive Development Systems, 1982)

[9,10]Napoleon Hill, Think and Grow Rich, (New York, Jeremy P. Tarcher/Penguin Group, 1937)

[11,12]Sharon L. Lechter and Greg S. Reid Three Feet From Gold: Turn your Obstacles into Opportunities! (Sterling Publishing, 2009), 170.

Chapter 3 Style and Character: The Way You Get There

[1]Ed Foreman, *Laughing, Loving & Living Your Way to the Goood Life* (Executive Development Systems, 1982)

[2]Maxwell Maltz, Psycho-Cybernetics (New York, Pocket Books, 1960)

[3]Paul Gustavson and Alyson Von Feldt, Organization Systems Design Workbook (Organization Planning & Design, 1996), 9.

[4]Ed Foreman, *Habit Patterns of Winners* (Executive Development Systems, 2002)

5Curt Sampson, Hogan, (New York, Broadway Books, 1996), xi.

[6]James Lincoln Ray, http://www.sabr.org/bioproj/person/2242d2ed

[7]Ed Foreman, Laughing Loving & Living Your Way to the Goood Life Success Guide, (Executive Development Systems, 1982), 2-2.

[8]Ed Foreman, Laughing Loving & Living Your Way to the Goood Life Success Guide, (Executive Development Systems, 1982), 10-1.

[9]Ed Foreman, *Habit Patterns of Winners* (Executive Development Systems, 2002), Tk 6.

[10]Ed Foreman, Laughing Loving & Living Your Way to the Goood Life Success Guide, (Executive Development Systems, 1982), 10-1.

[11]Ed Foreman, Laughing Loving & Living Your Way to the Goood Life Success Guide, (Executive Development Systems, 1982), 10-1.

[12]Ed Foreman, Laughing Loving & Living Your Way to the Goood Life Success Guide, (Executive Development Systems, 1982), 10-1.

[13]Ed Foreman, Laughing Loving & Living Your Way to the Goood Life Success Guide, (Executive Development Systems, 1982), 10-5.

[14]Ed Foreman, Laughing Loving & Living Your Way to the Goood Life Success Guide, (Executive Development Systems, 1982), 10-1.

[15]Ed Foreman, Laughing Loving & Living Your Way to the Goood Life Success Guide, (Executive Development Systems, 1982), 10-1.

[16]Ed Foreman, Laughing Loving & Living Your Way to the Goood Life Success Guide, (Executive Development Systems, 1982), 10-1.

[17]Ed Foreman, *Habit Patterns of Winners: Performance Techniques That Make A Difference,* Executive Development Systems, 2002) Track 12.

[18,19]Ed Foreman, Laughing Loving & Living Your Way to the Goood Life Success Guide, (Executive Development Systems, 1982), 10-1.

[20]Ed Foreman, Laughing Loving & Living Your Way to the Goood Life Success Guide, (Executive Development Systems, 1982), 10-1.

[21]Ed Foreman, Laughing Loving & Living Your Way to the Goood Life Success Guide, (Executive Development Systems, 1982), 10-1.

[22]Ed Foreman, Laughing Loving & Living Your Way to the Goood Life Success Guide, (Executive Development Systems, 1982), 10-1.

[23]Zig Ziglar, See You At The Top, (Gretna, Pelican Publishing Company, 2011), 229.

[24]Ed Foreman, Laughing Loving & Living Your Way to the Goood Life Success Guide, (Executive Development Systems, 1982), 10-1.

[25]Ed Foreman, Laughing Loving & Living Your Way to the Goood Life Success Guide, (Executive Development Systems, 1982), 10-1.

Chapter 5 Choices: You Are Empowered!

[1]Kevin Trudeau, *Your Wish Is Your Command,* (Global Information Network, 2009) Disk 1

[2]David J. Schwartz, PhD., The Magic of Thinking Big, (New York, Prentice-Hill, 1965), 23.

[3]Andy Andrews, The Traveler's Gift, (Nashville, Thomas Nelson, 2002), 32-34.

[4]http://putthewritingonthewall.com/store/WsDefault.asp?one = 205

Chapter 6 Your Personal Mission Statement

[1]2003 Annual Report, Bristol-Myers Squibb Company, 2.

[2]Jim Loehr and Tony Schwartz, The Power of Full Engagement, Managing Energy, Not Time, Is the Key to High Performance and Personal Renewal, (New York, Free Press, 2003), 131.

[3,4]Jack Canfield with Janet Switzer, The Success Principles: How to Get From Where You Are to Where You Want To Be, (New York, HarperCollins, 2005), 19.

[5]Jim Loehr and Tony Schwartz, The Power of Full Engagement, Managing Energy, Not Time, Is the Key to High Performance and Personal Renewal, (New York, Free Press, 2003), 135.

[6]Joanne Ciulla, The Working Life: The Promise and Betrayal of Modern Work, (New York, Three Rivers Press, 2000)

[7]Sonja Lyubomirsky, PhD. The How of Happiness: A Scientific Approach to Getting the Life You Want (New York, The Penguin Press, 2007), 125.

[8]http://www.nightingale.com/tmission_examplestatement.aspx

[9]Jon Gordon, The Seed, (Hoboken, NJ, J.W. Wiley & Sons, 2011)

[10]Robert Frost, *The Road Not Taken*, http://www.poemhunter.com/ poem/the-road-not-taken

Chapter 7 Your Personal Guiding Principles

[1]http://www.businessdictionary.com/definition/guiding-principles. Html

[2]James M. Kouzes and Barry Z. Posner, The Leadership Challenge, (San Francisco, Josey-Bass, 2002), 49.

[3]James M. Kouzes and Barry Z. Posner, The Leadership Challenge, (San Francisco, Josey-Bass, 2002), 48.

[4]Jim Loehr and Tony Schwartz, The Power of Full Engagement, Managing Energy, Not Time, Is the Key to High Performance and Personal Renewal, (New York, Free Press, 2003), 141.

[5]James M. Kouzes and Barry Z. Posner, The Leadership Challenge, (San Francisco, Josey-Bass, 2002), 49.

[6]Jim Loehr and Tony Schwartz, The Power of Full Engagement, Managing Energy, Not Time, Is the Key to High Performance and Personal Renewal, (New York, Free Press, 2003), 142.

[7]Ben Franklin, http://www.living-smartlycom/2010/07/moral-perfection-virtues-benjamin-franklin/

[8]Karl Marino, *Personal Mission Statement*, http//www.paradox1x.org/personal-mission-statement/

Chapter 8 Strategies to Influence the Influencers

[1]Michael E. Porter, "What is Strategy?" *Harvard Business Review* (November, December 1996), 64.

[2]Michael E. Porter, "What is Strategy?" *Harvard Business Review* (November, December 1996), 64.

[3]Paul Gustavson and Alyson Von Feldt, Organization Systems Design Workbook (Organization Planning & Design, 1996), 15.

Chapter 9 Personal Chief Aims and Goals

[1]Andrew Carnegie, http://www.goodreads.com/quotes/122624-if-you-want-to-be-happy-set-a-goal-that

[2]Zig Ziglar, See You At The Top, (Gretna, Pelican Publishing Company, 2011), 150.

[3]"Why Set Goals?", http://www.goalmaker.com/whyset.html

[4]Chuck Williams, MGMT4, (Mason, OH, Cengage Learning, 2012), 83.

[5]Stephen R. Covey, The Seven Habits of Highly Effective People: Restoring the Character Ethic (New York, Simon and Schuster, 1989), 162-167.

[6]Chuck Williams, MGMT4, (Mason, OH, Cengage Learning, 2012), 84.

[7]Napoleon Hill, Think and Grow Rich, (New York, Jeremy P. Tarcher/Penguin Group, 1937)

Chapter 10 Your Personal Dream Mechanisms

[1]Webster's Seventh New Collegiate Dictionary, (Springfield, MA, G.&C. Merriam Company, 1969), 525.

[2]Chuck Williams, MGMT4, (Mason, OH, Cengage Learning, 2012), 3.

[3]Chuck Williams, MGMT4, (Mason, OH, Cengage Learning, 2012), 4.

Chapter 11 Your Personal Organization Processes

[1]Karen Kingston, Clear Your Clutter with Feng Shui, (New York, Three Rivers Press, 1999), 7.

[2]Karen Kingston, Clear Your Clutter with Feng Shui, (New York, Three Rivers Press, 1999), 7.

[3]Karen Kingston, Clear Your Clutter with Feng Shui, (New York, Three Rivers Press, 1999), 8.

[4]Karen Kingston, Clear Your Clutter with Feng Shui, (New York, Three Rivers Press, 1999), 13.

[5]Katrina Meyer, discussion in Nassau Airport, Nassau, the Bahamas, November 2011.

[6]Stephen R. Covey, The Seven Habits of Highly Effective People: Restoring the Character Ethic (New York, Simon and Schuster, 1989), 151.

[7]Stephen R. Covey, The Seven Habits of Highly Effective People: Restoring the Character Ethic (New York, Simon and Schuster, 1989), 153.

[8]Stephen R. Covey, The Seven Habits of Highly Effective People: Restoring the Character Ethic (New York, Simon and Schuster, 1989), 158.

[9]Stephen R. Covey, The Seven Habits of Highly Effective People: Restoring the Character Ethic (New York, Simon and Schuster, 1989), 156.

[10]Zig Ziglar, See You At The Top, (Gretna, Pelican Publishing Company, 2011), 229.

[11]Ed Foreman, Laughing Loving & Living Your Way to the Goood Life Success Guide, (Executive Development Systems, 1982), 3-1.

[12]Charles Duhigg, The Power of Habit: Why We Do What We Do In Life and Business (New York, Random House, 2012), 276.

[13]Charles Duhigg, The Power of Habit: Why We Do What We Do In Life and Business (New York, Random House, 2012), 276, 278, 280, 284.

[14]Webster's Seventh New Collegiate Dictionary, (Springfield, MA, G.&C. Merriam Company, 1969), 197.

[15]Ed Foreman, *Habit Patterns of Winners* (Executive Development Systems, 2002), Tk 6.

Chapter 12 Decision Making and Informating Processes

[1]Gary Applegate Ph.D. Happiness, It's Your Choice (Sherman Oaks, CA, Berringer Publishing, 1985), 6.

[2]Gary Applegate Ph.D. Happiness, It's Your Choice (Sherman Oaks, CA, Berringer Publishing, 1985), 29-31.

[3]Gary Applegate Ph.D. Happiness, It's Your Choice (Sherman Oaks, CA, Berringer Publishing, 1985), 29, 81-96.

[4]Gary Applegate Ph.D. Happiness, It's Your Choice (Sherman Oaks, CA, Berringer Publishing, 1985), 29, 97-114.

[5]Gary Applegate Ph.D. Happiness, It's Your Choice (Sherman Oaks, CA, Berringer Publishing, 1985), 30, 115-132.

[6]Gary Applegate Ph.D. Happiness, It's Your Choice (Sherman Oaks, CA, Berringer Publishing, 1985), 30, 133-148.

[7]Gary Applegate Ph.D. Happiness, It's Your Choice (Sherman Oaks, CA, Berringer Publishing, 1985), 30, 149-186.

[8]Gary Applegate Ph.D. Happiness, It's Your Choice (Sherman Oaks, CA, Berringer Publishing, 1985), 31, 187-204.

[9]Gary Applegate Ph.D. Happiness, It's Your Choice (Sherman Oaks, CA, Berringer Publishing, 1985), 31, 205-216.

[10]Gary Applegate Ph.D. Happiness, It's Your Choice (Sherman Oaks, CA, Berringer Publishing, 1985), 31, 217-233.

[11, 12]Gary Applegate Ph.D. Happiness, It's Your Choice (Sherman Oaks, CA, Berringer Publishing, 1985), 40.

[13]Kevin Trudeau, *Your Wish Is Your Command,* (Global Information Network, 2009) Disk 2.

[14]Webster's Seventh New Collegiate Dictionary, (Springfield, MA, G.&C. Merriam Company, 1969), 469.

[15]Shawn P. Spendlove, "Picking Up Leadership's Five Smooth Stones", *The BYU Management Society*, December 2009

[16]Paul Gustavson and Alyson Von Feldt, Running Into the Wind: Bronco Mendenhall: 5 strategies for building a successful team (ShadowMountain, 2012), 319.

[17]Zig Ziglar, See You At The Top, (Gretna, Pelican Publishing Company, 2011), 43.

[18]Webster's Seventh New Collegiate Dictionary, (Springfield, MA, G.&C. Merriam Company, 1969), 238.

[19]"What is Information Literacy?", http://www.ala.org/acrl/issues /infolit/overview/intro

Chapter 13 Your Personal Relationship Processes

[1,2]Chuck Williams, MGMT4, (Mason, OH, Cengage Learning, 2012), 197.

[3]Paul Gustavson and Alyson Von Feldt, Organization Systems Design Workbook (Organization Planning & Design, 1996), 30.

[4]Jack Canfield with Janet Switzer, The Success Principles: How to Get From Where You Are to Where You Want To Be, (New York, HarperCollins, 2005), 287.

[5]Chuck Williams, MGMT4, (Mason, OH, Cengage Learning, 2012), 201.

[6]Webster's Seventh New Collegiate Dictionary, (Springfield, MA, G.&C. Merriam Company, 1969), 227.

[7]Greg Anderson, The 22 {Non-Negotiable} Laws of Wellness: Feel, Think, and Live Better Than You Ever Thought Possible (San Francisco, HarperSanFrancisco, 1995), 105.

[8]Greg Anderson, The 22 {Non-Negotiable} Laws of Wellness: Feel, Think, and Live Better Than You Ever Thought Possible (San Francisco, HarperSanFrancisco, 1995), 106.

[9]Greg Anderson, The 22 {Non-Negotiable} Laws of Wellness: Feel, Think, and Live Better Than You Ever Thought Possible (San Francisco, HarperSanFrancisco, 1995), 108.

[10]Dale Carnegie, How to Win Friends and Influence People, (New York, Pocket Books, 1936)

[11]Webster's Seventh New Collegiate Dictionary, (Springfield, MA, G.&C. Merriam Company, 1969), 53.

[12]Brian Bohling, interview held over telephone, Loudon, Tennessee, June, 2012.

[13]Ed Foreman, *The Successful Life Course*, Kerrville, Texas, 1984.

[14]Jack Canfield with Janet Switzer, The Success Principles: How to Get From Where You Are to Where You Want To Be, (New York, HarperCollins, 2005), 193.

[15]Stephen R. Covey, The Seven Habits of Highly Effective People: Restoring the Character Ethic (New York, Simon and Schuster, 1989), 213.

Chapter 14 Recognition Systems for You and Others

[1]Mother Teresa of Calcutta, http://www.thinkexist.com/quotation/there_is_more_hunger_for_love_and_appreciation_in/149767.html

[2]Mary Kay Ash, http://www.brainyquote.com/quotes/quotes/m/marykayash148279.html

[3]Spencer Tracy, "Spencer Tracy Quotes", http://www.brainyquote.com/quotes/authors/s/spencer_tracy.html

[4]Dr. Joyce Brothers, "Dr. Joyce Brothers quotes", http://www.thinkexist.come/quotation/an_individual-s_self-concept_is_the_core_of_his/147493.html

[5]Zig Ziglar, See You At The Top, (Gretna, Pelican Publishing Company, 2011), 47.

[6,7]Zig Ziglar, See You At The Top, (Gretna, Pelican Publishing Company, 2011), 87.

[8]Margaret Cousins, "Margaret Cousins>Quotes", http://www.goodreads.com/author/quotes/32996/Margaret_Cousins

[9]Steve Brunkhorst, "Steve Brunkhorst Quotes", http://www.searchquotes.com/quotation/Feeling_appreciated_is_one_of_the_most_important_needs_that_people_have._When_you_share_with_someone/279595/

[10]Sally Koch, "Sally Koch Quotes", http://www.searchquotes.com/author/Sally_Koch/

[11]Sonja Lyubomirsky, PhD. The How of Happiness: A Scientific Approach to Getting the Life You Want (New York, The Penguin Press, 2007), 69.

[12]Sonja Lyubomirsky, PhD. The How of Happiness: A Scientific Approach to Getting the Life You Want (New York, The Penguin Press, 2007), 89.

[13]Ian K. Smith, M.D., Happy, (New York, St. Martin's Griffin, 2010), 180.

[14]Ian K. Smith, M.D., Happy, (New York, St. Martin's Griffin, 2010), 182.

[15]Ella Wheeler Wilcox, http://www.brainyquote.com/quotes/quotes/e/ellawheele146983

[16]Dave Ulrich and Wendy Ulrich, (New York, McGraw Hill, 2010), 119.

Chapter 15 Your Personal Development Processes

[1]Ed Foreman, *The Successful Life Course*, Kerrville, Texas, 1984.

[2]Dr. M.T. Morter Jr., Dr. Ted Morter III, Dr. Tom Morter, and Dr. Sue Morter, The Book of Nutrition: Understanding How Diet Choices Affect the Human Body (Rogers, AR., B.E.S.T. Research, 2002), 2.

[3]Dr. M.T. Morter Jr., Dr. Ted Morter III, Dr. Tom Morter, and Dr. Sue Morter, The Book of Nutrition: Understanding How Diet Choices Affect the Human Body (Rogers, AR., B.E.S.T. Research, 2002), 13.

[4]http://www.webmd.com/diet/features/alkaline-diets-what-to-know

[5]http://www.webmd.com/diet/features/alkaline-diets-what-to-know?page = 2.

[6]"Read, Learn, and Know about Water" http://www.allaboutwater.org/water-filters.html

[7]"Which Foods Are Highly Alkaline", http://www.acidalkalinediet.com/alkaline-foods-made-easy#.UMkDBWt5mSM

[8]"Side Effects of Artificial Sweeteners", http://www.livestrong.com/side-effects-of-artificial-sweeteners/

[9]"The Federal Government Takes on Physical Fitness", http://www.jfklibrary.org/JFK/JFK-i-History/Physical-Fitness.aspx?p = 2.

[10]"How much physical activity do adults need?", http://www.cdc.gov/physicalactivity/everyone/guidelines/adults.html.

[11]Sonja Lyubomirsky, PhD. The How of Happiness: A Scientific Approach to Getting the Life You Want (New York, The Penguin Press, 2007), 244.

[12]Dr. M. Ted Morter, Jr., The Soul Purpose: Unlocking the secret to health, happiness and success (Rogers, AK, Dynamic Life LLC, 2001),182.

[13,14]"How to Sleep Better", http://www.helpguide.org/life/sleep_tips.htm.

[15]Jeanie Lerche Davis, "Good Sleep: Can It Still Be Simple?", http://www.webmd.com/sleep-disorders/features/good-sleep-can-it-still-be-simple

[16]Ed Foreman, *How to Have a GOOOD DAY, EVERY DAY!* (Executive Development Systems, 2002), Track 5.

[17]Dr. Ted Morter III, *B.E.S.T. Living with Dr. Ted Morter*, Disk 6.

[18]Dr. Ted Morter III, *B.E.S.T. Living with Dr. Ted Morter*, Disk 7.

[19]Ed Foreman, *How to Have a GOOOD DAY, EVERY DAY!* (Executive Development Systems, 2002), Track 5.

[20]Earl Nightingale, *The Strangest Secr*et, www.vimeo.com/11731116

[21]Stephen R. Covey, The Seven Habits of Highly Effective People: Restoring the Character Ethic (New York, Simon and Schuster, 1989), 18.

[22]Ed Foreman, *Laughing, Loving &Living Your Way to the Goood Life* (Executive Development Systems, 1982)

[23,24]Paul Gustavson and Alyson Von Feldt, Organization Systems Design Workbook (Organization Planning & Design, 1996), 31.

[25]William F. Brandt, Jr., Compass---Creating Exceptional Organizations: A Leader's Guide. Winchester, Virginia: Winter Vale Press, 2013.

Chapter 16 Additional Tools and Thoughts

[1]Napoleon Hill, Think and Grow Rich (New York, Jeremy P. Tarcher/Penguin Group, 1937), 22.

[2]Richard Beckhard and Reuben T. Harris, Organizational Transformations: Managing Complex Change (Reading, Massachusetts, Addison-Wesley Publishing, 1977), 25.

[3]Ed Foreman, Laughing Loving & Living Your Way to the Goood Life Success Guide, (Executive Development Systems, 1982), 17.

[4]Ed Foreman, Laughing Loving & Living Your Way to the Goood Life Success Guide, (Executive Development Systems, 1982), 24-25.

[5]Ed Foreman, Laughing Loving & Living Your Way to the Goood Life Success Guide, (Executive Development Systems, 1982), 22.

[6]Ed Foreman, Laughing Loving & Living Your Way to the Goood Life Success Guide, (Executive Development Systems, 1982), 52.

[7]Dr. M.T. Morter, Jr., Dr. Ted Morter III, Dr. Tom Morter, Dr. Sue Morter, The Book of B.E.S.T.: Allowing the Body to Recreate the Perfection Which Was Created From The First Cell (Rogers, Arkansas, B.E.S.T. Research, Inc., 1980), 7.

[8]Dr. Don Williams, "Professional B.E.S.T. Training" (Atlanta, Georgia, March 2012)

[9]William Ernest Henley, *Invictus*, http://www.poemhunter.com/poem/invictus/

Part II: Approach to Design and Implementation

[1]Paul Gustavson and Alyson Von Feldt, Organization Systems Design Workbook (Organization Planning & Design, 1996), 36.

[2]Ed Foreman, Laughing Loving & Living Your Way to the Goood Life Success Guide, (Executive Development Systems, 1982), 24-25.

[3]Ed Foreman, Laughing Loving & Living Your Way to the Goood Life Success Guide, (Executive Development Systems, 1982), 52.

[4]Richard Beckhard and Reuben T. Harris, Organizational Transformations: Managing Complex Change (Reading, Massachusetts, Addison-Wesley Publishing, 1977), 25.

[5]Ed Foreman, Laughing Loving & Living Your Way to the Goood Life Success Guide, (Executive Development Systems, 1982), 8.

[6]Ed Foreman, Laughing Loving & Living Your Way to the Goood Life Success Guide, (Executive Development Systems, 1982), 40.

[7]Jack Canfield with Janet Switzer, The Success Principles: How to Get From Where You Are to Where You Want To Be, (New York, HarperCollins, 2005), 23.

[8]Jon Gordon, The Seed, (Hoboken, NJ, J.W. Wiley & Sons, 2011)

[9]http://www.wikihow.com/Make-a-Dream-Board

[10]David Jacobson, M.A., Goal Success, Inc., *Quest Leadership Program, Module II, Leading and Developing Others Globally*, August 2010.

[11]George Lucas, director, *Star Wars*, 1977

[12]Gary Applegate Ph.D. Happiness, It's Your Choice (Sherman Oaks, CA, Berringer Publishing, 1985), 29-32.

[13]Gary Applegate Ph.D. (Center for Skill Development, Sherman Oaks, CA, 1985)

[14]Dr. M. Ted Morter, Jr., The Soul Purpose: Unlocking the secret to health, happiness and success (Rogers, AK, Dynamic Life LLC, 2001), 21.

[15]Paul Gustavson and Alyson Von Feldt, Organization Systems Design Workbook (Organization Planning & Design, 1996), 40.

[16]Shawn P. Spendlove, "Picking Up Leadership's Five Smooth Stones", *The BYU Management Society*, December 2009.

[17]Ed Foreman, Laughing Loving & Living Your Way to the Goood Life Success Guide, (Executive Development Systems, 1982), 24-25.

[18]Ed Foreman, Laughing Loving & Living Your Way to the Goood Life Success Guide, (Executive Development Systems, 1982), 22.

[19]Paul Gustavson and Alyson Von Feldt, Organization Systems Design Workbook (Organization Planning & Design, 1996), 84.

[20]Paul Gustavson and Alyson Von Feldt, Organization Systems Design Workbook (Organization Planning & Design, 1996), 86.

[21]Paul Gustavson and Alyson Von Feldt, Organization Systems Design Workbook (Organization Planning & Design, 1996), 87.

[22]Paul Gustavson and Alyson Von Feldt, Organization Systems Design Workbook (Organization Planning & Design, 1996), 89.

[23]Richard Beckhard and Reuben T. Harris, Organizational Transformations: Managing Complex Change (Reading, Massachusetts, Addison-Wesley Publishing, 1977), 51.

[24,25]Richard Beckhard and Reuben T. Harris, Organizational Transformations: Managing Complex Change (Reading, Massachusetts, Addison-Wesley Publishing, 1977), 52.

[26,27]Paul Gustavson and Alyson Von Feldt, Organization Systems Design Workbook (Organization Planning & Design, 1996), 31.

[28]William F. Brandt, Jr., Compass---Creating Exceptional Organizations: A Leader's Guide. Winchester, Virginia: Winter Vale Press, 2013.